PRA...

WHY I AM ST...

THE POWER OF THE SPIRIT

When my friend Jack Deere asked me in 1992 to read and critique the manuscript of *Surprised by the Power of the Spirit*, I was at first honored and later overwhelmed by its persuasive and, in my opinion, irrefutable argumentation. I remain convinced it was the most important evangelical book of the 1990s. Now, much to my delight, Jack has extensively rewritten that book, although his convictions about what the Bible says concerning the Holy Spirit remain the same. With new stories of verified healings and testimonies of the life-changing power of the prophetic, Jack has "surprised" me once again. More than twenty-five years have passed since his book released, and a new generation of Christians stands in great need of the profound biblical and practical insights that Jack brings to bear on this subject. Get it, read it, and discover why Jack is "still" surprised by the person and power of the Spirit.

SAM STORMS, pastor, Bridgeway Church, Oklahoma City

This marvelous, game-changing work about the power of the Spirit is transformative and challenging. Jack Deere offers mature insights learned from Scripture, from enduring testing, and from a wider range of experience with spiritual gifts than most others, and we have much to learn from him. It's a great privilege to endorse this book.

CRAIG S. KEENER, F. M. and Ada Thompson professor of biblical studies, Asbury Theological Seminary

This book is like its author—bright, accessible, full of practical wisdom, and bursting with inspiring stories of God's love and power.

ANDREW WILSON, teaching pastor, King's Church London

Since its publication in 1993, *Surprised by the Power of the Spirit* has been a brilliant introduction to the power and presence of the Holy Spirit at work in our world today. If you're longing for a fresh baptism in the Holy Spirit—for the first time or the thousandth time—this new edition is for you. Jack Deere is a statesman in the body of Christ, and this is a wonderful update to what is arguably his classic work.

PETE GREIG, author of *How to Pray*

More than twenty-five years ago, the story of Jack Deere's encounter with the Holy Spirit rocked the evangelical world, as this cessationist seminary professor discovered to his great surprise that the Spirit was still speaking and healing today. Now, in the year 2020, Jack has shared his story anew with refreshing candor and wonderful biblical insight. I can't wait to see how this new "Surprised" book rocks a new generation of readers!

DR. MICHAEL L. BROWN, host, *The Line of Fire* broadcast

This book is the perfect example of why I am still surprised by Jack Deere. With humility, winsomeness, and competence, he is able to bring biblical clarity to some of the fuzziest and most heavily debated topics in the church. A mix of easy-to-follow theology, church history, and personal experience, this book will kindly answer the skeptic, pastorally lead the student, and safely disciple the seeker.

DAVID BOWDEN, author of *Rewire Your Heart* and founder, Spoken Gospel

Why I Am Still

SURPRISED

by the

POWER

of the

SPIRIT

Why I Am Still

SURPRISED

by the

POWER

of the

SPIRIT

Discovering How God
Speaks and Heals Today

JACK DEERE

 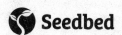

ZONDERVAN REFLECTIVE

Why I Am Still Surprised by the Spirit
Copyright © 2020 by Jack S. Deere

Portions of this book were previously published as
Surprised by the Power of the Spirit © 1993

ISBN 978-0-310-10811-5 (softcover)

ISBN 978-0-310-10814-6 (audio)

ISBN 978-0-310-10813-9 (ebook)

Requests for information should be addressed to:
Zondervan, *3900 Sparks Dr. SE, Grand Rapids, Michigan 49546*

All Scripture quotations, unless otherwise indicated, are taken from The Holy
Bible, New International Version®, NIV®. Copyright © 1973, 1978, 1984, 2011
by Biblica, Inc.® Used by permission of Zondervan. All rights reserved worldwide.
www.Zondervan.com. The "NIV" and "New International Version" are trademarks
registered in the United States Patent and Trademark Office by Biblica, Inc.®

Scripture quotations marked ESV are taken from the ESV® Bible (The Holy Bible,
English Standard Version®). Copyright © 2001 by Crossway, a publishing ministry
of Good News Publishers. Used by permission. All rights reserved.

Scripture quotations marked KJV are taken from the King James Version. Public
domain.

Scripture quotations marked NASB are taken from the New American Standard
Bible®. Copyright © 1960, 1962, 1963, 1968, 1971, 1972, 1973, 1975, 1977, 1995 by
The Lockman Foundation. Used by permission. (www.Lockman.org).

Scripture quotations marked NKJV are taken from the New King James Version®.
Copyright © 1982 by Thomas Nelson. Used by permission. All rights reserved.

Scripture quotations marked NRSV are taken from the New Revised Standard
Version Bible. Copyright © 1989, Division of Christian Education of the National
Council of the Churches of Christ in the United States of America. Used by
permission. All rights reserved.

Any internet addresses (websites, blogs, etc.) and telephone numbers in this book are
offered as a resource. They are not intended in any way to be or imply an endorsement
by Zondervan, nor does Zondervan vouch for the content of these sites and numbers
for the life of this book.

No part of this publication may be reproduced, stored in a retrieval system, or
transmitted in any form or by any means—electronic, mechanical, photocopy,
recording, or any other—except for brief quotations in printed reviews, without the
prior permission of the publisher.

Cover design: Brian Bobel
Cover photo: iStockphoto
Interior design: Kait Lamphere

Printed in the United States of America

20 21 22 23 24 25 26 27 28 /LSC/ 15 14 13 12 11 10 9 8 7 6 5 4 3 2

For Leesa—

For a half of a century,
Leesa and I have walked side by side
as brother and sister in Christ,
as friends and lovers,
as father and mother.

———————

She is still as radiant as the dawn,
as beautiful as the full moon,
as pure as the sun,
as awesome as an army with banners.

—Based on Song of Solomon 6:10 NASB

CONTENTS

one

FROM PROFESSOR
TO HEALER

They had seen water turned into wine. A boy at the abyss of death rescued by a word sent from afar. A paralytic who hadn't walked for thirty-eight years picked up his mat and walked away. Five thousand men fed from a boy's sack lunch. A storm threatening to take them under until he walked over the water and got into the boat. The eyes of a man born blind opened. A body dead and rotting in a tomb resurrected by the power buried in a single command—"Come out!" For three and a half years, it seemed there was nothing he couldn't do. He even taught this to his little band of followers when he told them, "With God all things are possible." Then on April 3, AD 33, the cross shredded their faith.[1]

The followers of Jesus lost their confidence in him to do what he said he would do.

---

1. For the date of the crucifixion, see Harold Hoehner, *Chronological Aspects of the Life of Jesus* (Grand Rapids: Zondervan, 1977), 65–93.

The people of God have always been slow to believe him. They still are, it seems.

I was slow to come to him. So he came to me. He found me in the dark on December 18, 1965, and he slipped into my heart through the crack of an open wound. I believed in him that night.

I am old now. I have walked and stumbled with Jesus for more than fifty years. The main thing I have learned in our journey together is to keep the main thing the main thing.

The only person who never needed any help chose twelve helpers.

Why?

He chose them for the pleasure it gave him to love them and to teach them to love what he loved.

This then is the main thing: loving God, loving others, and teaching others to love what Jesus loves.

Discipleship is not about passing on some skills. That's a mentoring relationship. Discipleship is not an accountability relationship. People stress accountability when they don't know how to relate.

Discipleship is loving someone, enjoying a person with whom we have a special chemistry, and teaching them to love the things that Jesus loves. Discipling someone is not an obligation; it is a pleasure.

Why did Jesus heal the sick? For the same reason he taught us to pray for our daily bread: we need to be well. Jesus loved to heal. Jesus loved to pray. He taught his disciples to heal and to pray. This is all so simple, unless you have the misfortune of being a theologian and living in the Western world.

After I had believed in Jesus, I led people to Jesus and taught them to love what I loved. I loved doing evangelism, praying, reading the Bible, studying the Bible, memorizing the Bible, reading Christian authors (especially C. S. Lewis), and making disciples. I did this because Scott Manley, a Young Life leader, eight years older than me, loved me and taught me to do these things. I became a Young Life leader like Scott.

I prayed for the sick, but not effectively. Not because I was against praying for the sick, but because I had so little practice in doing so. Almost everyone in my young world was healthy. No one becomes good at anything without a lot of practice. Then I went to seminary, where I learned that the most important thing is knowing the Bible. Our motto was not to love God, love people, and teach people to love what Jesus loved; it was to "preach the word" (2 Timothy 4:2). How can you preach the Word if you don't know the Word? I'm sure any faculty member would have said that loving God is the most important thing, but the thing I heard emphasized was studying the Bible. Eventually, I learned to equate studying the Bible with "spending time with God." And from there it was just a step to equate studying the Bible with "loving God," for we spend time with those we love.

As a seminary student, I learned early on that God no longer loves healing. Not all professors would say that God does not heal today. Some would say, "I believe in healing. I just don't believe in healers." We students were not quick enough to test this assertion by analogy with the other gifts. For example, no one would say, "I believe in teaching. I just don't believe in teachers."

I can't remember a professor telling a story of someone healed by prayer. But I did hear professors say that contemporary faith healers were fakes. One professor quoted a story written in *McCall's Magazine* about a woman allegedly healed in a Kathryn Kuhlman meeting. The woman got out of a wheelchair

13

and touched her toes onstage in front of thousands. She told the audience that it had been forever since she had been able to do that. The audience cheered. The next day, back at home, the article alleged the woman was bedridden because of injuries she had sustained on Kuhlman's stage. She died three months later. When the article was read to us, we all got the message: faith healers are fakes.

Our professors told us that God healed and did miracles in the New Testament period to show that the apostles were trustworthy teachers of doctrine. We have their doctrine now in the completed Bible, so there is no longer a need for miracles. And they maintained that subsequent history has no miracles like those in the New Testament, only alleged miracles in fringe groups with impure theology.

At seminary, the one supernatural arena we were allowed to believe in was the demonic. One missions professor told the story of witnessing a demonic ritual from a secure hiding place. He watched a man killed—stone-cold dead—and then brought back to life by the witch doctor. None of us questioned that demons were raising the dead in our lifetime. After all, demons were on every page of the Gospels. Where'd they all go anyway? Presumably they went to Africa and China, and probably Haiti as well, places where people were ignorant, poor, and superstitious.

So I came of age in a theological culture where God had hung up his guns, but the demons still blazed away.

When I turned seventeen, I didn't know a single verse of Scripture. At twenty-seven, I became a professor of Old Testament Exegesis and Semitic Languages. If I had wanted to conceal my pride in this achievement, I would have said that the Old Testament department was going through a crisis, and that technically I was not a "professor" but only a lowly "instructor" whom seminary etiquette required students to address as "prof." But the truth is that I knew I was exceptional in Greek, Hebrew, and theology. My professors told me so—many times.

Becoming a young professor in the seminary was probably the worst thing that could have happened to my spiritual life. Much later I would learn, "For though the LORD is high, he regards the lowly, but the haughty he knows from afar" (Psalm 138:6 ESV).

I served a Savior who healed, who taught his followers to heal, and whose followers taught their followers to heal. But I didn't teach my students to heal. I taught my students that faith healers were fakes. I ridiculed Kathryn Kuhlman for having heart problems. Then I ridiculed her for dying.

Then I changed.

I didn't have a crisis of faith like the apostles. One day, I just asked the Lord a simple question. "Lord, why did you heal all those people?"

This book is the story of how he answered that question and the story of how he turned me into a healer. Not a good healer. Nothing like Jesus or Paul. Just a broken person with a healing gift. So far, most people I pray for don't get healed. But I've been in the room when blind eyes have opened, crooked bones have straightened, deaf ears have opened, a wheelchair has been emptied, and maybe even someone has come back from the dead.

Someone asked me, "Why do you keep praying for people to be healed when so many people you pray for don't get healed?" The short answer is because some do get healed. The majority of people I tell my story to don't respond with faith in Jesus, but some do. I'm still holding out for the day when I will become a better evangelist and a better healer.

In the meantime, I have learned some valuable lessons about healing that I want to pass on before I finish my race. I began to pray for the sick when I learned from Scripture that Jesus loved healing and wanted his church to have a healing ministry. I learned how to help people when God doesn't heal, and although healing is not predictable, I know some of the things that hinder healing and some of the things that promote healing. I know how to tell when a person is demonized, what brings a person under demonic power, and how to set them free, if they want to be free. I know how God gives spiritual gifts, how to help people find their spiritual gift, and why it's important for us to walk in our spiritual gift. I know what it means to be filled with the Spirit and why this ministry of the Spirit is so misunderstood in the church today. I have a greater understanding of the theology and practice of the Spirit's ministry than I did a quarter of century ago when I wrote this book. So I thought it would be helpful to rewrite it.

two

THE POWER OF A
CREDIBLE WITNESS

I had an unusually rough beginning before I came to faith, but God surprised me in my seventeenth year and gave this godless, fatherless boy a new life and spiritual fathers to look after me. Twenty years later, in the fall of 1985, I was a seminary professor who could do research in multiple languages and a pastor who could hold the attention of a sophisticated congregation. I was married to a beautiful woman who loved God. We had three mesmerizing children. I was thirty-six years old, and my life was on cruise control. I thought I would finish my life on earth teaching at the seminary and pastoring the church, having written a few good critical commentaries on books of the Bible along the way.

Then my phone rang in the afternoon of a cold, bleak winter day. It was one of my heroes—a man I never thought I would meet—Dr. John White, a former professor of psychiatry and the bestselling author of numerous books on the Christian life.

We had asked him to do a conference at our church in the spring of 1986. Initially, he turned us down.

Until that phone call, I had never met an intelligent and biblically literate person who believed that God was still healing people and still giving all the spiritual gifts.

He said, "Hello, Jack, this is John White. I want to thank you for inviting me to speak at your spring Bible conference. I think I may be able to work it in. What would you like me to speak on?"

His publisher had told us that if Dr. White accepted our invitation, he would only speak on the subject that he was currently researching.

I replied, "Oh, I don't know. How about something you are writing or researching now?"

"Well, I'm working on a book on the kingdom of God. How does that sound?"

"That's wonderful! We love the kingdom of God around here. We would like four lectures for the weekend. How would you like to divide them up?"

"When I think of the kingdom of God," he replied, "I think of Christ's authority. If you want me to give four lectures, I think they would go something like this. The first one would be Christ's authority over temptation."

"Right," I said.

"The second one would be Christ's authority over sin."

"Good."

"The third one would be Christ's authority over demons."

Hmm, I thought to myself, *demons? There certainly were a lot of them in the first century. And I am sure that if demons are still around, Christ must have authority over them. This is going to be an interesting lecture, even if it won't have much practical relevance.*

I said, "Well . . . sure . . . okay."

"The fourth lecture would be Christ's authority over disease."

"Disease!" I exclaimed. Certainly I had misheard him.

"You didn't say *disease*, did you?"

"Yes, I did."

"You are not talking about *healing*, are you?" I almost spit out the word *healing*.

"Well, yes, I am."

I could not believe my ears. Until just a moment ago, I was sure Dr. White was a sane person, a biblically literate person, and an intelligent person, and now he was talking about healing.

He's a psychiatrist, I reasoned. *Perhaps he's just using "healing" to refer to some kind of new psychotherapy.* I asked, "You're not talking about *physical* healing, are you?"

"Well, I wouldn't limit it to physical healing," he calmly replied, "but I would certainly include physical healing."

"You're kidding! Surely you know that God's not healing anymore and that all the miraculous gifts of the Spirit passed away when the last of the apostles died. Surely you know that, don't you?"

Dr. White didn't reply.

I thought, *Well, perhaps he is a little weak in this area. After all, he is not a theologian; he's only a psychiatrist.* I took his silence to mean he was waiting for me to prove from the Bible that these things didn't exist anymore.

I said to him, "We know that the gift of healing has passed away because when we look at the healing ministry of the apostles, we see that they healed instantaneously, completely, irreversibly, and that everyone they prayed for was healed. We don't see this kind of healing going on today in any movements

19

or groups that claim to have healing powers. Instead, what we see in these groups are gradual healings, partial healings, healings that sometimes reverse themselves—and many people who don't get healed at all. We know, therefore, that the kind of healing that is happening today is not the same kind of healing that took place in the Bible."

"Do you think every instance where the apostles prayed for someone is recorded in Scripture?" Dr. White asked.

"Of course not," I said. "We only have a small fraction of their ministry recorded in the pages of the New Testament."

"Then might there not be a case where they prayed for someone, and they didn't get well, and it is simply not recorded in the Scriptures?"

I had to concede that he was right because the Bible doesn't record every instance of the apostles praying for people. There might have been times when they prayed for people and they didn't get healed.

Dr. White had just caught me in an interpretive error. I had used an argument from silence. That was something I taught my students not to do. When the subject of the gifts of the Spirit came up, for example, a student might say, "You don't have to speak in tongues to be spiritual because Christ never spoke in tongues." I would ask, "How do you know Christ never spoke in tongues?" The student would reply, "Because the Scriptures never tell us he spoke in tongues." I would correct that student, reminding him that you cannot use what the Scriptures *don't say* as proof of your view. For example, the Bible does not tell us that Peter had children, but we're not justified in concluding from the Bible's silence on this point that Peter was childless. That is what is meant by an argument from silence.

Yet I had just used an argument from silence with Dr. White, and I was embarrassed. I was still sure I was right. I had four more biblical arguments lined up and ready to go, but I thought I should be more careful this time. I didn't want to get caught in another mistake.

My next argument was going to be that at the end of Paul's life, he couldn't heal Epaphroditus (Philippians 2:25–27), Trophimus (2 Timothy 4:20), or Timothy's frequent ailments (1 Timothy 5:23). I thought this proved that the gift of healing had left the apostle Paul, or that it was in the process of leaving. But now I thought, *What would I say to this argument if I were taking Dr. White's position? I would just say that these three incidents prove that not everyone the apostles prayed for were healed!* My second proof was no proof at all!

As I examined the next three arguments I was about to use, I found something wrong with each one of them. In most theological debates, I had taken my opponent's side and examined all of my arguments from my adversary's perspective to find loopholes or weak points. But my belief that miraculous gifts had ceased had never seriously been challenged before. I had never needed to examine these arguments that closely because everyone in my circle accepted them as true.

I was still sure I was right, but I was exasperated to find something wrong with each of my arguments. I blurted out to Dr. White, "Well, have you ever seen anyone healed?"

"Oh, yes," he replied in that calm, courteous British voice. He wouldn't argue with me. He had nothing to sell me. In fact, I was the one who was trying to get him to speak at our church.

I said, "Tell me the most recent spectacular healing you've seen."

"I'm not sure what you mean by *spectacular*, Jack, but I will tell you two recent healings that have impressed me."

He then told me about a young child in Malaysia who was covered from head to toe in eczema. The eczema was raw in some places and oozing. The child was in such discomfort that he had kept his parents up for the previous thirty-six hours. The child was behaving so wildly that they had to catch him in order to pray for him.

As soon as Dr. White and his wife, Lorrie, laid their hands on the child, he fell asleep. Within twenty minutes or so of their prayer, the oozing stopped and the redness began to fade. By the next morning, the child's skin had returned to normal and was completely healed. Dr. White told me a second spectacular story of bone actually changing under his hands while he prayed for someone with a deformity.

After I heard these things, I thought, *There are only two options. Either Dr. White is telling me the truth, or he is lying to me.*

What did he have to gain by lying to me? He wasn't asking to come to my church; I was asking him to come. Furthermore, everything about his manner reflected the Spirit of the Lord Jesus. I was convinced he was telling me the truth. I was convinced God had healed the two people he talked about. But I was also still convinced God was not giving the miraculous gifts of the Spirit any longer and that there must be another explanation for the healings.

So I said, "Well, Dr. White, I believe what you are telling me is the truth, and I would like you to come to my church and give those four lectures, even the one on healing."

"There is one more thing we need to discuss, Jack. If I come to your church, I wouldn't just want to talk about healing, I would want to pray for the sick."

"Pray for the sick! You mean in the church?" I was flabbergasted. "Couldn't we just take a couple of board members and go downtown to one of those missions that care for the homeless and find some lame or blind person and pray for them there?" I was sure that if we prayed for some sick people in front of the church, they wouldn't get healed, and it would destroy everyone's faith.

"Well, we can work out the details when I come," he replied, "but I wouldn't want to just talk about healing without being able to pray for sick people." He said this gently, but I knew that if we would not let him pray for the sick in our church, he wouldn't come.

"Well, Dr. White, I want you to come and give those four lectures, and you can even pray for sick people, but it's not only up to me. The other board members have to agree to this before we can make this invitation official. I don't know how they are going to respond to this suggestion."

"No problem, Jack. I understand your fears. If the board decides to withdraw the invitation, I won't be offended. I will just take that as the Lord's will, and we will meet another time."

We said good-bye, and I went immediately from that conversation into an elders meeting.

At the beginning of the meeting I announced to the elders and other pastors that I had some good news and some bad news. "The good news is that we have Dr. John White for our spring Bible conference." Everyone was happy at that news.

"What's the bad news?" they asked.

"The bad news is that he wants to give a lecture on healing and pray for the sick in our church."

"You're kidding!"

"That's what I said to him."

For the next two hours we talked back and forth about the advisability of Dr. White doing this conference in our church. At the end of our discussion, as each of us gave our final opinions, one of the men said, "This conference could split our church."

My last word on the subject was, "I think we ought to have the conference, even though it could split our church. Look at it this way. We started this church with a handful of people. If our church splits, we could start another church with a handful of people if we needed to." We decided unanimously to invite Dr. White and hold the conference in April, even though we thought the miraculous gifts of the Holy Spirit had ceased.

The conversation with Dr. White had shaken me on two levels. First, he was a credible witness that miracles were happening in response to prayer. Second, that conversation had shown me some errors in my biblical arguments.

Praying for healing miracles didn't sound so stupid anymore.

From January to April, I studied every healing story in the New Testament, as well as every reference to the gifts of the Spirit. This time, I studied with an open mind. I asked the same question of every healing story: "God, why did you do it?" I knew the answer to that question would reveal whether the healing gifts came with a shelf life of sixty years, or whether they were acts of empowered love meant to shepherd the church into the last days. I also knew I could tell no one that I had acquired an open mind regarding the healing gifts because in my community that would have been a sure sign I was losing my mind.

By the time our conference took place in April, I was convinced God still healed and that healing ought to be a significant part of the church's ministry. I had also begun to believe that

God could speak apart from the Scriptures, though never in contradiction to the Scriptures.

My thinking had not changed because I had *seen* a miracle or *heard* God speak to me in some sort of supernatural way. I had no dreams, visions, trances, or anything I could identify as supernatural beyond my conversion experience. This shift in my thinking was the result of a patient, exhaustive, intense study of the healings and miracles recorded in the Scriptures.

Although my newfound belief transgressed the seminary party line, I was still relatively safe, for my belief in healing was only theoretical. I had not yet prayed for anyone to be healed.

three

A DEMON COMES
TO CHURCH

He was short, balding, thin, and wore glasses. John White looked like a frail grandfather. He was sixty-two when I met him, but he could have passed for seventy. Like every British person I'd ever met, he was articulate and courteous. He'd been a missionary in Bolivia and was fluent in Spanish. He introduced himself as "John," not "Dr. White."

His first three lectures raised no eyebrows. Then came the healing lecture on Saturday afternoon. I could have given that lecture at my seminary without raising an eyebrow, but John had brought someone to help him pray for people. "Bud" was the kind of flamboyant, narcissistic braggart whose specialty was bringing a dark shadow over any ministry. It turned out that John was new to the healing ministry and thought Bud, whom he had just met, would supply the healing power he lacked. John believed Bud's self-aggrandizing stories of his healing exploits. I was even newer to the healing ministry and working hard to be open-minded.

I made the mistake that is common to people who reverse their position in a controversy and who want to love what they once hated. I accepted what I should have opposed. Only after he left did I discover that Bud had damaged and fleeced people in our church. Bud was the perfect example of the kind of person the apostle Paul had warned the church against, a religious person "having a form of godliness but denying its power" (2 Timothy 3:5).

After the fourth lecture, Dr. White led a tense question and answer time. The tension was due to Bud's antics during the conference. Our people wondered why we would have given someone like Bud access to our church.

There were approximately three hundred people in the audience that day. After thirty minutes of questions, John said, "We promised to pray for people today, so if you want prayer for physical or spiritual needs, come down to the front and we will pray for you."

I thought, *We? Who's this "we"?* None of us leaders had ever prayed for the sick in front of the church. I thought a few brave souls might come down to the front of the sanctuary. I didn't think God would heal anyone. It didn't seem right to let John suffer this humiliation alone. I said to an elder next to me, "Come on. Let's go help him." We walked down to the front and stood beside John White.

Almost one-third of the people in the room rushed down to the front of the church. My sport coat blew open in the breeze.

Most of the people lined up in front of John White. Eight people lined up in front of the elder and me. I looked over at John. He had his hand on the shoulder of a woman who was crying. So I put my hand on the shoulder of the woman in front of me. I nodded at the elder. Then he put his hand on her other shoulder. We had her covered. We prayed. Nothing happened. We repeated this scene eight times. Then our line was empty. The people we prayed for now stood in John's line. I thought, *I'd better go stand beside John and learn how to do this.*

I stood beside John and could not believe what I was seeing. People I knew well, who seemed so in control of their lives, were on their knees weeping, falling apart. One wealthy woman who always looked like someone in the pages of a Neiman Marcus catalog said, "I don't feel loved by anyone except my husband." I thought, *Why haven't you ever told me that? I'm your pastor. Our kids play together. We vacation together.*

A strong man fell on his knees and wailed. "I'm eaten up by jealousy. All of my friends are more successful than me." I thought, *I see you all the time. Why didn't you ever tell me you were hurting?*

An unseen hand had reached down and pulled the cork out of all the bottled-up pain in our church. At first, I was perplexed and repulsed. This seemed like emotionalism. But emotionalism means that someone has whipped up our emotions through some form of manipulation. In this case, we had just heard a very unemotional lecture on healing, followed by a tense question and answer session during which John White never lost his temper or gave an unkind reply. And after that session, he had given a simple invitation, with no promised healing and with no music or emotional pleas, to anyone who wanted prayer.

Had I been a better student of revival history at the time, I would have understood that this very thing had happened on numerous occasions during periods of revival when the Holy Spirit had fallen on a church or a city. The honesty and courage it took for people to confess their sins and their pain was actually an indication of the Spirit's presence among us that day. But I wasn't sure I wanted this kind of thing in my church.

Then an articulate woman who had suffered from long-term depression asked Dr. White to pray for her. She said to him, "I finally figured out the root of my depression. I lust after the approval of man."

"Okay, let's pray for you then," he said to the woman. She hung her head in shame. Like a gentle father, John White put his hand under her chin and lifted her head. "Look up," he said, "you don't have to do that anymore. You are a child of the King."

I was mesmerized by this. I thought, *That's a nice touch. I have to remember that line—"Look up, you are a child of the King."* Maybe my prayers would have been more powerful if I had a pocketful of lines like that. I was brand-new to the healing ministry and did not understand that God's power is released through his friends' faith in his Son, not through the eloquence of their prayers.

Then he put his hand on her shoulder and said, "Lord, I bring your servant into your presence now in the name of Jesus Christ. She doesn't feel the affection that Jesus has for her. Let her feel in her heart how much you love her and like her."

When I heard Dr. White say this, a light went on inside me. I thought, *Of course that is why she has lusted after the approval of others. If she really felt loved by God, the approval of others wouldn't be nearly so important to her.*

Then Dr. White prayed, "And, Lord, if there be any darkness here manipulating her pain, I pray that you would make it leave now."

When he said those words, her head bobbed up and down, and she wailed. She could not stop her head or the wailing. I had never seen anything like that before. Almost everyone in the auditorium was shocked by what was happening. I had never seen a demon before, but I was convinced I was looking at the work of a demon at that very minute.

"In the name of Jesus, I command you to be at peace now," Dr. White said. And when he said that, everything stopped. He would not allow her to be humiliated by an evil spirit before all those people. Later we prayed for the woman in private, and she seemed to improve.

Why did I think an evil spirit was at work? Because this woman would never act like that in public. She had no charismatic background. There was no possibility for any of this to be learned behavior. Later she told me that a force had "come up" and gripped her, and that she was powerless to stop it. Only the name of the Lord Jesus brought it under control.

As I watched her torment, I thought of all of the wasted years she had spent in Christian counseling without having any significant improvement. Even though she prayed and read her Bible, she had not shown improvement. There had been a demonic power behind much of her depression and fear.

Tears ran down my cheeks as I thought of all the years of professional and pastoral counseling she had endured. You don't "counsel" demons out of people. Demons only come out by the power of the blood of Christ. Until John White came along, none of her pastors or counselors had had the discernment to realize what the root cause of her afflictions was.

At that very moment, for the first time that I can be certain, the Lord spoke to me. I heard these words, not audibly, but they formed in my brain as clearly as any audible words I'd ever heard. His voice said, "You're a deceiver and a manipulator, and you're just playing at church."

Those words sound harsh, but I didn't hear a condemnation. I heard an invitation offered in love. I said, "Yes, Lord." That's all, just "Yes, Lord."

I did not know my agreement with that voice had given the Lord permission to take away everything that had fueled my self-esteem for the last twenty years.

four

JOHN WIMBER

Before Dr. White left, he told me to meet John Wimber. I had never heard of Wimber, though I had danced to his music in high school. He had helped to write and perform "Little Latin Lupe Lu" with the Righteous Brothers before they were called the Righteous Brothers.

Wimber's road to Jesus had run through drugs and rock and roll. John White told me that Wimber was the most gifted healer he had ever seen, the most down-to-earth, the most practical, the most averse to all forms of hype. He kept no entourage to protect him from the people, and he took no offerings at the meetings where he prayed for the sick. Dr. White said that Wimber would stay for hours after church services to pray for the sick. "Jack, Wimber can teach you more about healing and hearing God's voice than anyone I know," said White.

Two weeks after our conference with White, John Wimber came to Fort Worth to speak at Lake Country Baptist Church. I planned to hear him on Thursday night. At noon that Thursday, on my way to the seminary library, I heard a group of students mention Wimber's name. I hung back, but still within earshot.

"One of our graduates was in a Wimber meeting in Sydney, Australia," said a student. "He told me that Wimber yelled, 'Come, Holy Spirit,' and that people fell down on the floor, vomited, and barked like dogs. And Wimber said, 'There, that's the Holy Spirit.'" The student swore that this was God's honest truth. *Uh-oh,* I thought, *what have I gotten myself into? I don't want to fall down on the floor, vomit, and bark like a dog. I used to do that before I became a Christian.*

That night, I took ten people from my church with me. We arrived late and sat in the back row, next to the door. People had already begun to worship. Some of them raised their hands, but nothing strange was going on yet. After thirty minutes of singing, the pastor introduced John Wimber. Wimber spoke on the kingdom of God.

Twenty minutes into his message, I found myself agreeing with him and enjoying his humor and his honesty about his flaws. He finished his lecture and announced it was "clinic time."

I thought, *Clinic time? Oh, this is where it gets weird.*

Wimber prayed, "Come, Holy Spirit," and then went silent for two minutes. "I think the Lord will heal back pain," he said. Many people came down to the front of the church to be prayed for by teams of church members.

After a few minutes he said, "There is a woman here who has severe back pain, but you haven't come forward yet. Come forward. I think the Lord will heal you." But no woman came forward.

I thought, *Poor John Wimber. He was doing so well when he was just talking about the kingdom. If he hadn't tried this clinic stuff, this meeting would have been a success tonight.* I felt embarrassed for him and also disappointed.

Wimber did not share my embarrassment or my disappointment. He announced a second fact about this woman. He said, "You went to the doctor several days ago. You have had this pain for years. Please come forward."

Still no woman got up and came forward.

Wimber was quiet for a moment. Then with a grandfatherly smile he said, "Your name is Margaret. Now, Margaret, you get up and come down here right now." About halfway down the center section, next to the aisle, Margaret got up and began to walk sheepishly toward the front.

I thought this was the most amazing thing I had ever seen. This was like those Old Testament prophets who could see what was going on in the bedroom of the enemy commanders. The room was filled with awe and conviction.

But before Margaret made it down to the front of the church, a wave of skepticism and disgust came over me. I said to myself, *This is too good to be true. What if he paid her to do this? What if she's Margaret on Thursday night here in Fort Worth, Texas, and then on Saturday night in some other city she is Mabel, walking down to the front of the church carrying an envelope with two malignant tumors she coughed up?*

Then the church member sitting next to me, whom I had known for fifteen years, shouted, "That's Margaret, my sister-in-law!"

Mike Pinkston's sister-in-law, Margaret Pinkston, went down to the front of the church that evening after being called out by John Wimber. Someone prayed for her, and she was healed of a condition she had had for years.

Leesa and I were the first ones in line to talk to John Wimber after the meeting was over. John answered our questions and gave us on-the-spot instruction as we watched him and others pray for people that evening.

Praying for the sick became a permanent part of my life. A couple of months after I had met John White and John Wimber, a woman in our church named Ruth Gay asked me to pray for her. She had an aneurysm—a swelling in a blood vessel so that the walls of the blood vessel become stretched and thin. The danger is that the walls of the blood vessel may burst and kill the person.

On Monday night, Leesa, another woman, and I went to Ruth's house. Ruth was divorced, lived by herself, and had been estranged from the rest of her family. We laid our hands on her head and for only a few minutes quietly asked the Lord to take away her aneurysm. And then we left. That Wednesday, she went into the hospital for a second angiogram. On Thursday, they planned to operate to repair the aneurysm.

On Wednesday morning, after the second angiogram, Ruth called. Her voice was so weak I could barely hear her. She said, "Jack, I have been healed!"

"What?"

"I have been healed!"

"You're kidding!"

"No, it's true. The aneurysm is gone."

"What did your doctor say?"

"He said I have been healed. A nurse just came in this morning and told me it was a miracle."

"Did you ask your doctor how he could explain this?"

"He can't explain it. He told me that aneurysms never go

away. They have to be corrected by surgery. He said he had never seen this before and had no explanation for it."

This was the first medically documented healing that happened in our church.

During the remainder of 1986 and 1987, John Wimber and I became close friends. Leesa and I went to several Vineyard conferences during that time. There were more than three thousand people at a conference at John's Anaheim church in the summer of 1987. After the plenary session, the prayer team was praying for a hundred or more people at the front of the auditorium. Wimber stood on the stage and said, "There is a woman here who has cancer, and you have not come forward. Please come down to the front so we can pray for you." No response. "You flew in on Tuesday. You came here to be prayed for. Let us pray for you." No response. "You're sitting in the back, and you're wearing a pink dress." A woman wearing a pink dress got up from the back row and walked up to the prayer team.

Afterward, I said to John, "That was amazing. That must have gone off like a foghorn in your mind."

"No, Jack. It was just the opposite. It was so faint I almost missed it. I was ready to walk off the stage, and I had the slightest impression that we were supposed to pray for a woman with cancer."

"What about the flying in on Tuesday?"

"When no woman came forward, I thought I should wait a moment longer. 'Tuesday' just floated through my mind. A lot of people come in a couple of days before the conference to enjoy Southern California. I thought that's what 'Tuesday' meant."

"Pink dress sitting in the back?"

"Well, when she didn't come forward, I saw pink floating over the back of the auditorium for a couple of seconds."

"John, you called out a woman in front of three thousand people because of those flimsy impressions?"

"Jack, that's the way God speaks to me when I'm praying for people. I've had better luck adjusting to his way of speaking than trying to get him to adjust to my way of hearing."

In those early conferences, every time I was around John, he taught me something new about hearing God's voice and about the healing ministry of the Holy Spirit.

In 1988, we left Texas and joined the staff of the Anaheim Vineyard. John gave me a priceless education in the power of the Holy Spirit. He took me around the world with him, put me on a stage in front of thousands, and introduced me to leaders of different denominations and movements. He taught me to love the whole church.

five

MODERN MIRACLES

When I was a cessationist, I never saw God heal anyone because I never prayed for healing.[1] How can you pray regularly for something that you believe God no longer does or that he does rarely? When someone told me they believed in healing and miracles, I shot back, "Oh, you've seen blind eyes and deaf ears opened? You've seen someone walk on water or someone multiply food with prayer?" Cessationists always go to the biggest miracles, especially to the nature miracles, to prove that God is not doing these things anymore. All this proves is that people who don't believe in miracles and don't pray for miracles are the people who don't see miracles. They are confirming what James wrote almost two thousand years ago: "You do not have because you do not ask God" (James 4:2).

When I was a student at seminary, there were some students a few years ahead of me who specialized in apologetics,

---

1. *Cessationist* is the theological term for someone who believes that God stopped giving the supernatural gifts of the Holy Spirit after the death of the New Testament apostles.

defending the existence of God and the reliability of the Christian Scriptures. Agnostic university professors who mocked God made the mistake of debating these students in front of their classes. Ken Boa was one of those apologists only a couple of years ahead of me, but I never got to know his story until recently.

In the summer of 1978, he was on a three-week tour of Israel. One afternoon, Ken went for a swim in the water that Jesus had walked on during a storm, where Jesus saved his disciples from drowning. When Jesus got into the boat, it was instantly on the shore (John 6:16–21). Ken swam out to a raft about a tenth of a mile from the shore on the Sea of Galilee. Then he turned around and headed back.

On my way back, a storm came out of nowhere. The winds began to move the sea, and like water on a shaking saucer, it was instantaneously tumultuous. I found myself embroiled in the violent movements of the water and couldn't make any progress back to shore. It was difficult just to stay afloat. I kept trying to make progress in the right direction, but the wind and the waves kept pushing me back . . .

This lasted for what seemed a really long time, and my energy was spent . . . I wasn't going to make it. I knew I was on the verge of drowning, and my life flashed before my eyes, like in a movie . . . I became aware of something bigger than the storm . . . God told me that my work for him on earth was not complete.

And then I was at the shore. I have no idea how I got there. There was no way I had the strength to swim that distance against those waves. I was just at the edge of the water. But there were rocks on the shore, and they were extremely slippery. I was unable to get a purchase on the rocks so that I could get out of the water. And then it happened again. Suddenly I found myself laid out on a grassy area above the rocks. I have no idea how I got above the rocks. I couldn't have pulled myself out of the water, and there was no one around who could've helped me.[2]

While Ken was drowning, he heard the voice of God and was supernaturally transported over the water and the rocks. This happened to one of our graduates held in high esteem by our faculty. It happened two years after I had become a professor at a seminary where I was telling students that God no longer did these kinds of miracles.

The story just before Jesus walked on water showed him feeding the five thousand from a boy's sack lunch (John 6:5–15). I told my Sunday crowd that this showed that no matter how insignificant we or our gifts were, if we put ourselves and our gifts in the hands of Jesus, he could do great things. I believed in the original miracle, but I never thought Jesus would repeat it. What purpose would that serve?

Heidi was a pretty blonde teenager raised in an affluent beach community in Southern California and destined for a country club life. On March 13, 1976, sixteen-year-old Heidi gave her heart to Jesus, and he gave her his heart for the downtrodden faltering on the fringes. From the moment of meeting Jesus, all Heidi wanted to do was to be a missionary to the poorest of the poor. She married Rolland Baker, who had the same vision for his life. By 1996, Heidi had exhausted herself caring for orphans

---

2. Ken Boa, *Rewriting Your Broken Story: The Power of an Eternal Perspective* (Downers Grove, IL: InterVarsity, 2016), 28.

in Mozambique. Two months of antibiotics could not stop various infections. She had dysentery and pneumonia. She flew back to the United States and checked into a hospital. Before she came back to Mozambique, she went to the Toronto Airport Vineyard Church, which was in the midst of a revival. She had the following vision while she was in Toronto:

> One night I was groaning in intercession for the children of Mozambique. There were thousands coming toward me, and I was crying, "No, Lord. There are too many!" Then I had a dramatic, clear vision of Jesus. I was with Him, and thousands and thousands of children surrounded us. I saw His shining face and His intense, burning eyes of love. I also saw His body. It was bruised and broken, and His side was pierced. He said, "Look into My eyes. You give them something to eat." Then He took a piece of his broken body and handed it to me. It became bread in my hands, and I began to give it to the children. It multiplied in my hands. Then again the Lord said, "Look into My eyes. You give them something to drink." He gave me a cup of blood and water, which flowed from His side. I knew it was a cup of bitterness and joy. I drank it and then began to give it to the children to drink. The cup did not go dry. By this point I was crying uncontrollably. I was completely undone by His fiery eyes of love. I realized what it had cost Him to provide such spiritual and physical food for us all. The Lord spoke to my heart and said, "There will always be enough, because I died."[3]

---

3. Rolland and Heidi Baker, *Always Enough: God's Miraculous Provision among the Poorest Children on Earth* (Grand Rapids: Chosen, 2003), 49–50.

Heidi's vision was a practical application of Jesus' teaching after he fed the five thousand when he said, "For my flesh is real food and my blood is real drink" (John 6:55).

Heidi came back to Mozambique healed and refreshed, expecting miracles to break out in the orphanage of 350 street orphans they had rescued from the most horrendous conditions imaginable. Instead, all hell broke out. The government gave them forty-eight hours to vacate their orphanage. A contract was put out on Heidi's life. The only place they had to go was their small office flat in the city of Maputo. Here's what happened when the Bakers went to Maputo:

> We were inundated by our very most needy children, the youngest street orphans with absolutely no relatives or friends to whom they could go. They had walked barefoot fifteen miles into the city and streamed into our flat. They told us they had been beaten with large sticks for singing. They said they would go where we go because they were going to worship the Lord. When I told them we had no place for them, their simple reply was, "But, Mama, you said there would always be enough!"
>
> What could I say? They kept piling in, maybe a hundred of them. We stuffed bunk beds in our dilapidated little garage full of grease and cobwebs. Loaned army cots were all over our yard and driveway. Urine ran in our hallway. We hosed the kids down to try to wash them. All our doors and windows were full of faces!
>
> We didn't know how to cope. We had nowhere near the food or the cooking and sanitation facilities we needed. Boxes, clothes, and suitcases were piled high everywhere.

Everyone was totally exhausted; everything was in complete chaos. And more children kept gravitating to our gate. We ran out of strength, crying as we watched our sea of faces gather. I wondered seriously, even after Toronto, "Does God really care? What is He like anyway?" I never thought He would leave us in a situation like this.

Our daughter, Crystalyn, began to cry because she was so hungry. I thought I was going to snap . . . A precious woman from the U.S. embassy came over with food. "I brought you chili and rice for your family!" she announced sweetly, with just enough for the four of us. We hadn't eaten in days. I opened a door and showed her all our children. "I have a big family" . . . My friend got serious. "There's not enough! I need to go home and cook some more!" But I just asked her to pray over the food. Now she was upset. "Don't do this!" she begged. But she prayed, quickly. I got out the plastic plates we used for street outreaches, and also a small pot of cornmeal I had. We began serving, and right from the start I gave everyone a full bowl. I was dazed and overwhelmed. I barely understood at the time what a wonderful thing was happening. But all our children ate, the staff ate, my friend ate, and even our family of four ate. Everyone had enough.

Since then we have never said no to an orphaned, abandoned, or dying child. Now we feed and take care of more than one thousand children. They eat and drink all they want of the Lord's goodness. Because he died, there is always enough.[4]

4. Baker, *Always Enough*, 51–52.

I've shared a conference stage with Heidi Baker. Leesa and I talked with her offstage for several nights in a row. We were staggered to hear some of the things she and her family have suffered for Jesus, things that have not been put in print. In the New Testament, the ones given the greatest miracles are also the ones given the greatest suffering. I've not seen the quantity and quality of miracles that Rolland and Heidi Baker have seen. But I have never been close enough to Jesus to groan in intercession for the orphans of Mozambique. Maybe that's why I've never seen the miracle of multiplying food. I've never needed it.[5]

When I was a cessationist, I never heard stories of God multiplying food or pulling drowning swimmers out of the water and depositing them on a grassy beach, even though that last one happened in my own backyard. I wouldn't have even known where to look for these stories. Now, thanks to a brilliant New Testament professor, these kinds of credible stories are accessible in a single work. Craig S. Keener is the F. M. and Ada Thompson professor of biblical studies at Asbury Theological Seminary. He wrote *Miracles*, a two-volume, 1,172-page work cataloging credible reports of miracles from around the world for the last twenty centuries.[6] The bibliography is 165 pages of fine print.

For the last thirty years, I have read extensively in the literature of healing and miracles from all over the world and from the present all the way back to the first century AD. Then I read

---

5. Today, Heidi and Rolland watch God provide miraculously every day for more than ten thousand children. Through their network (Iris Global) of more than ten thousand churches, Bible schools, primary schools, and remote outreaches, countless numbers of orphans and poor people are coming to Jesus and being supernaturally cared for.

6. Craig S. Keener, *Miracles: The Credibility of the New Testament Accounts*, 2 vols. (Grand Rapids: Baker, 2011).

both volumes of Dr. Keener's work and was astounded by the number of miracle claims he cites and the sagacity he employs to sift each eyewitness report.

He traces the modern Western skepticism regarding miracles to David Hume, the eighteenth-century Scottish Enlightenment philosopher and historian. And then he notes:

> In contrast to the environment assumed by Hume, today hundreds of millions of people claim to have witnessed miracles. Moreover, eyewitnesses claim what they believe are miracles even in the West, and this has been the case through most of history, even when Hume framed his argument within the theological framework of academic circles often reticent to acknowledge miraculous claims. Some of these eyewitness claims involve even the healing of blindness, the raising of the dead, and nature miracles.[7]

For more than thirty years, I have traveled around the world praying for the sick, but until I read Keener's two volumes, I never knew that *today hundreds of millions of people claim to have witnessed miracles*. These volumes demonstrate that the majority of the church all over the world believes that God is still performing miracles today.

---

7. Keener, *Miracles*, 209–10.

six

THE REAL REASON CHRISTIANS DO NOT BELIEVE IN MIRACLES

Jesus healed and did miracles—a lot of them. He sent the Twelve out to preach the kingdom and to illustrate the preaching of the kingdom with miracles. Then he sent the seventy-two out to preach the kingdom and to illustrate the preaching of the kingdom with miracles. Then the church of Jesus was birthed in the fire of prophecy. The Holy Spirit promised that we Christians would prophesy and that God would show signs and wonders on earth (Acts 2:17–21). This was exactly what the church prayed for:

> "Now, Lord, consider their threats and enable your servants to speak your word with great boldness. Stretch out your hand to heal and perform signs and wonders through the name of your holy servant Jesus."

> After they prayed, the place where they were meeting
> was shaken. And they were all filled with the Holy Spirit
> and spoke the word of God boldly.
>
> *Acts 4:29–31*

And God answered that prayer beyond anything the first Christians could have imagined. There is a supernatural event or a supernatural revelation or the report of such in every chapter of Acts, even in Acts 17 where Paul is talking to the intellectuals in Athens, for though most were hostile, some were converted by the Spirit of God on that day.[1] God gave the gifts of the Spirit to ordinary Christians so they could prophesy, heal, and do miracles. And he empowered the elders in the local church to have a healing ministry. The last book of the New Testament prophesies that this present age will end in a catastrophic outpouring of evil that will be answered by a greater outpouring of God's miracles and the return of the Lord Jesus Christ.

No one can become a cessationist by reading the New Testament. The Bible teaches that gifts like miracles and prophecy will be here until Jesus comes back to set up the kingdom where his will is done on earth as it is in heaven (1 Corinthians 13:8–12). Theologians developed the doctrine of cessationism to justify the absence of New Testament miracles in their ministries. They taught their followers that God had withdrawn the supernatural gifts of the Spirit, and the culture of cessationism was born. I will explain later where this happened in history and who the major players were.

For now, I only want to emphasize one thing. There is one basic reason why otherwise Bible-believing Christians do not

---

1. Conversion is one of the most supernatural works of God (2 Corinthians 4:6).

believe in the miraculous gifts of the Spirit today. It is this: *they have not seen them.*

MY CESSATIONIST CULTURE

When I was in the cessationist family, all my friends were cessationists, and we never prayed together for a healing or a miracle. Why pray for something you know God is not doing? So we never saw a miracle or a healing. We assumed our experience was normative for the whole church because we believed our knowledge of the Bible and our theology were superior to those of the rest of the church. We did not investigate contemporary reports of God healing someone through prayer, nor did we research historical reports of miracles.

After I had begun to believe in healing and miracles, and while I was still a seminary professor, I tried to get one of my colleagues to investigate a miracle that had taken place through the ministry of a seminary professor from Fuller Seminary. The seminary professor who had been used to do the miracle was a conservative evangelical, was the author of many books, was held in high esteem across the body of Christ, and had begun to believe in the spiritual gifts.

He prayed for the eyes and ears of a little boy, and the boy was healed. The family physician called it a miracle. I called the boy's father (they lived in California) in order to verify the miracle. The father said it was true and that he had medical documentation. The boy was the grandson of the chairman of the department of missions of Fuller Seminary.

When I told the story to my friend, the cessationist professor, I urged him to call and investigate. He did not even want the phone number. When I questioned his reluctance to investigate, he told me that he did not doubt that the miracle had occurred, but he doubted that God had done it. He never investigated the healing that a physician had called an astounding miracle.

The facts of the case were:

1. A seminary professor, who held historic orthodox theology,
2. asked God in Jesus' name
3. to do a miracle on a little child
4. from a Christian family,
5. and the miracle was performed immediately.

Even with these facts, which my friend would not dispute, it was easier for him to believe that Satan had done the miracle rather than Jesus. Thirty years ago, the cessationist, fundamentalist mind-set usually precluded any sincere investigation.

When I was a cessationist, I not only did not investigate contemporary reports of miracles, but I also did not research reports of miracles in the history of the church. The historical research had already been done by the great Princeton scholar Benjamin Breckinridge Warfield in his *Counterfeit Miracles.*[2] Warfield allowed for some miracles done in the second century by those on whom the apostles had laid their hands. But after those disciples died off, he maintained that there was no credible example of a miracle done through the miraculous gifts of the Spirit. So there was no need for further historical research.

---

2. B. B. Warfield, *Counterfeit Miracles* (1918; repr., Edinburgh: Banner of Truth, 1972). Chapter 11 is devoted to Warfield's polemic against miracles; see www.bible studytools.com/classics/warfield-counterfeit-miracles.

I was insulated intellectually, emotionally, and socially against miracles.

The recent cessationist literature I have read also lacks rigorous investigation into contemporary claims of miracles and lacks research into the many historical claims of miracles in the past twenty centuries.

Current cessationist writers do appeal to history because they can't make their case against miracles using only the Bible. They don't research history. They point to a few fringe groups with bad practices or bad theology and maintain that these are the only kind of people who have believed in contemporary miracles since the death of the apostles. It often goes unnoticed that this appeal to history, either past or present, is actually an argument from *experience*, or better, an argument from the *lack of experience*. It is common for charismatics to be accused of building their theology on experience. However, all cessationists ultimately build their theology of the miraculous gifts on their lack of experience, not on Scripture.

THE PEOPLE OF GOD FREQUENTLY LOSE THE BLESSINGS OF GOD

For the sake of argument, assume there have been no miracles since the death of the last apostle. That would not prove that God is not willing to do miracles and heal today. We would have to know why there were no miracles. It could be because God had withdrawn the gift of miracles and the gift of healing, or it could be due to unbelief that led the church to disobey God's command to pursue the gifts of the Spirit (1 Corinthians 14:1).

Throughout history the people of God have found it easy to throw away his blessings.

After Joshua and his elders died, "another generation grew up who knew neither the LORD nor what he had done for Israel" (Judges 2:10).

Sometime after the death of Moses, either the entire Pentateuch or the book of Deuteronomy was lost. It wasn't discovered again until around 622 BC during the reign of Josiah (2 Kings 22:8). Think of that—the people of God lost their Scriptures.

For all practical purposes, this occurred a second time in church history when people could no longer read the original Hebrew Old Testament, the Greek New Testament, or their Latin translation of the Bible. It wasn't until the time of the Reformation that the Scriptures became accessible to people again in their own language. God did not withdraw the Scriptures from the people; the church neglected Scripture until they lost it.

One of the most important teachings ever given to the church is the doctrine of justification by faith alone in Christ. Shortly after the death of the apostles, however, the writings of some of the apostolic fathers show that the doctrine of justification by faith was already being perverted.[3] Eventually this doctrine was lost and not widely recovered until the Reformation in the fifteenth and sixteenth centuries. Should we explain this absence by assuming that for approximately fifteen hundred years, God had withdrawn the teaching ministry of the Holy Spirit or justification by faith was no longer important to him?

---

3. *The Shepherd of Hermas* was written in the early second century and was one of the most popular books of early Christianity. The author wrote that a Christian could be forgiven for only one sin after baptism (see fourth mandate, chapter 3).

How could the church lose something that was intended to be permanent? The church seems to have no difficulty at all in misplacing the Holy Scriptures and foundational doctrines. The people of God have always been slow to believe him and careless with his gifts.

If the gifts were lost in history, the most important question is not *whether* they were lost, but *why* they were lost. It could be due to a divinely planned obsolescence. On the other hand, it is possible that God never intended that these gifts should cease, but rather it is *the church* that has neglected and then rejected the gifts.[4]

Ultimately it is only Scripture, not historical research, that will settle this question.

There is ample evidence throughout church history for the use of the gifts in the church. After studying the historical documentation for the miraculous gifts of the Spirit, D. A. Carson, a highly respected New Testament scholar, concluded, "There is enough evidence that some form of 'charismatic' gifts continued sporadically across the centuries of church history that it is futile to insist on doctrinaire grounds that every report is spurious or the fruit of demonic activity or psychological aberration."[5]

I wrote the bulk of this chapter twenty-five years ago. Even then, there was significant historical evidence to show that

---

4. At the time of the first edition of this book (1993), two widely read scholarly studies of New Testament prophecy—David Hill (*New Testament Prophecy* [Louisville: Westminster John Knox, 1979], 191) and David Aune (*Prophecy in Early Christianity and the Ancient Mediterranean World* [Grand Rapids: Eerdmans, 1983], 338)—concluded that it was the bureaucratic leadership of the church that abandoned the gift of prophecy rather than God withdrawing the gift.

5. D. A. Carson, *Showing the Spirit: A Theological Exposition of 1 Corinthians 12–14* (Grand Rapids: Baker Academic, 1996), 166.

miracles in the church had never ceased.[6] Today (2019), that evidence is overwhelming.[7]

For the last thirty years, I have seen healings everywhere I go in the world, in all kinds of settings. In August 1996, I preached the Sunday morning worship service at St. Andrews, an Anglican church in the little town of Collumpton in Devon, England. The vicar, David, is a friend of mine. The service was more formal than what I was used to, with prayers from a prayer book and special times when everyone kneeled. The church building is a historical monument dating back to the fifteenth century. The inside of the church is decorated with hand-carved woodwork. It is one of the most beautiful churches I've ever seen. The vicar escorted me to a spiral staircase leading up to the pulpit, which perched like a crow's nest above the people. I paused at the foot of the staircase.

"How long should I speak, David?"

"As long you want."

"No, really. How long do you speak?"

"Fifteen to seventeen minutes."

---

6. For example, see Ronald Kydd, *Charismatic Gifts in the Early Church* (Peabody, MA: Hendrickson, 1984); Cecil M. Robeck Jr., "Origen's Treatment of the Charismata in 1 Corinthians 12:8–10," in *Charismatic Experiences in History*, ed. Cecil M. Robeck Jr. (Peabody, MA.: Hendrickson, 1985), 111–25; Donald Bridge, *Signs and Wonders Today* (Leicester, UK: Inter-Varsity, 1985), 174ff.; Paul Thigpen, "Did the Power of the Spirit Ever Leave the Church?" *Charisma* 18, no. 2 (1992): 20–29; Morton T. Kelsey, *Healing and Christianity* (New York: Harper and Row, 1973), 129–99; James Edwin Davison, "Spiritual Gifts in the Roman Church: 1 Clement, Hermas, and Justin Martyr" (PhD diss., University of Iowa, 1981); Cecil Robeck Jr., "The Role and Function of Prophetic Gifts for the Church at Carthage, AD 202–258" (PhD diss., Fuller Theological Seminary, 1985). This was some of the most accessible historical research I could recommend to readers in 1993.

7. See Craig S. Keener, *Miracles: The Credibility of the New Testament Accounts*, 2 vols. (Grand Rapids: Baker, 2011). The whole body of historical evidence supporting miracles throughout church history generally goes unmentioned in modern cessationist literature.

"Okay, that's what I will do."

I didn't enjoy speaking from the crow's nest. I looked down on my hearers while I talked about the love of Jesus.

After the service, my kids, who were sixteen, eighteen, and twenty, said, "Dad, let's get out of here and go to London and have some fun tonight?"

"Sounds good to me. I'll ask David to let me out of the evening service."

But when I told David of our plan, he said, "No, Jack. You have to speak tonight. We've advertised a healing service all over the little towns of Devon. We promised the people that a healing evangelist from America would be speaking tonight. It will be standing room only. Half the people coming tonight will be unbelievers who only go to church for funerals and weddings. You have to be here, and you have to speak on healing."

"David, are you serious? Half the people coming to a healing meeting tonight will be unbelievers?"

"I guarantee it, Jack."

"Okay. I'll do it."

Speaking about healing to unbelievers who never go to church could be fun. No one has ever told them that God no longer heals. You have to go to church to hear that God is no longer healing.

That night the church was packed. Dressed in casual clothes, I stood on the stage and told healing stories for forty minutes. At the conclusion, I said, "If you have something you want the Lord to heal, let's pray silently for a few minutes and ask him to heal those things."

I asked the Lord to give me impressions of what he would heal that night. I waited silently with my eyes closed, tuning out distractions. A picture of a knee came into my mind. I kept my eyes closed, looking at the knee and trying to figure out if it was a right knee or a left knee, a man's knee or a woman's knee. I couldn't tell. With my eyes still closed, I said, "I think the Lord will heal knees tonight."

What I meant to say next was, "Just lift up your spirits to the Lord, and we will pray for knees." What came out of my mouth was, "Just lift up your knees to the Lord, and we will pray for knees." I kept my eyes closed because the vision of the knee would not go away. For the next few minutes, I asked the Lord to heal specific knee problems, never opening my eyes. Then I had some other impressions, and we prayed for those things as well.

I prayed the closing prayer and told people that a number of us would stay to continue praying for people. People did not want to leave. Little groups huddled around the sanctuary, praying for one another. Some said they could feel the presence of the Lord the whole evening.

I stood halfway down the center aisle and put my hand over a blind man's eyes to pray for him. A man behind me shouted, "That was the most amazing thing I've ever seen." I turned and saw him holding up his right knee, pumping it up and down.

"What happened?" I asked.

"When I came in tonight, I could not bend my knee. Now look at it. It's healed," he said.

"Who prayed for you?" I asked.

"No one. When you said, 'Lift up your knees to the Lord,' I just lifted it up, and it was instantly healed."

"I did not say, 'Lift up your knees to the Lord.'"

The blind man said, "Oh yes you did."

Then I heard a scream from the front of the sanctuary.

I saw a woman about four feet away from an empty wheelchair. She turned and walked back to her wheelchair and sat down.

Her name was Ann Roberts. A friend had persuaded Ann to go to the service. She didn't want to go and didn't expect anything to happen. She sat in the back row. I didn't see her before or after the service until I heard the scream. At the end of the service, a voice inside her head said, "Go down to the front of the sanctuary."

Two older men who had never seen a healing prayed for her to walk. Ann heard the voice a second time. It said, "You can get up if you want to."

She said to the men praying for her, "I want to get up." Both of the men said, "No! Don't do that!" Even though they were praying for Ann to get up, they expected she would crash if she tried to walk.

Ann said, "I think God is telling me to get up." The men said, "Okay." And they prepared to catch her. Instead, she took her first steps in eight years.

The next day, Ann was walking around her village with a walker. The local newspaper wanted to do a story on her.

I went back to Collumpton in the late fall for a driven pheasant hunt. On Sunday morning, I spoke at St. Andrews again. Ann stood up before the church and told the story of her healing. Her legs had filled out. You would never have known she had been paralyzed.

As of this writing (March 2019), Ann is still healed and still with us.

None of us had a lot of faith that night—not the reluctant preacher, not the men praying for Ann—but the power of the Lord was present to heal.

seven

THE MIRACLES
OF THE LORD

Here is a typical gospel summary of Jesus' healing ministry:

> Jesus left there and went along the Sea of Galilee. Then he went up on a mountainside and sat down. Great crowds came to him, bringing the lame, the blind, the crippled, the mute and many others, and laid them at his feet; and he healed them. The people were amazed when they saw the mute speaking, the crippled made well, the lame walking and the blind seeing. And they praised the God of Israel.
>
> *Matthew 15:29–31*

In the list above, the Greek word *kullos* should be translated "maimed," not "crippled." The Greek text does not say "the crippled made well," but rather "the maimed were made whole." This is the way Matthew uses the word. "If your hand or your foot causes you to stumble, cut it off and throw it away.

It is better for you to enter life maimed [*kullos*] or crippled than to have two hands or two feet and be thrown into eternal fire" (Matthew 18:8). The NIV's rendering of this same saying in Mark 9:43 is accurate: "If your hand causes you to stumble, cut it off. It is better for you to enter life maimed [*kullos*] than with two hands to go into hell, where the fire never goes out."

Just before Jesus fed the four thousand, he healed them. This is a literal translation of the crowd's reaction to the healings: "The people were amazed when they saw the mute speaking, the *maimed made whole*, the lame walking, and the blind seeing. And they glorified the God of Israel" (Matthew 15:31, my emphasis).[1]

If we had been on the mountainside with Jesus that day, we would have seen fingers, hands, and limbs growing out of the places where they had been amputated. It is impossible to overestimate the spectacular power displayed in the healing ministry of Jesus. The constant refrain of the crowd for three and a half years was, "No one has ever heard of miracles like these."

THE POWER IN JESUS' MINISTRY WAS UNIQUE

Instead of using Jesus' healing ministry to motivate us to pray for the sick, my tribe used the spectacular healing ministry of

---

1. The reason *kullos* is mistranslated at Matthew 15:29–31 in the NIV and ESV is that the standard Greek-English New Testament lexicon (*BDAG*)—Walter Bauer, *A Greek-English Lexicon of the New Testament and Other Early Christian Literature*, ed. Frederick W. Danker, 3rd ed. (Chicago: University of Chicago Press, 2000)—cites only two references from classical Greek for *kullos* where it is claimed to mean "crippled" or "deformed" (575). This meaning is assigned to its three uses in the New Testament with no discussion of any of the texts. This lexicon is a wonderful tool written by superb scholars who were not interested in healing. These scholars were careless here, and using "crippled" or "deformed" would cause us to lose one of the most beautiful portraits of Jesus' healing ministry in the New Testament. I pray regularly for amputations to grow out because of these texts.

Jesus as an argument against contemporary healing. When I was a seminary professor, we argued that none of the contemporary "faith healers" healed like Jesus healed (if they were healing at all). This proved to us that God no longer gave the gift of healing.[2]

Our reasoning was faulty. Nowhere else in life would we take the stellar example in any category and use it as the qualification for membership in that category. No one has ever loved like Jesus or taught like Jesus. Should we conclude that God is no longer giving the gift of teaching or that our experience of love is an illusion? Jesus was the only person who was given the Holy Spirit without limit (John 3:34). He was the only person who had or ever will have the character to bear that kind of power without being corrupted by it. Even though none of us will ever do anything as well as he did, Jesus is to be our model in all things. He said to his disciples, "As I have loved you, so you must love one another" (John 13:34). Paul said, "Follow my example, as I follow the example of Christ" (1 Corinthians 11:1).

JESUS' HEALING MINISTRY WAS NOT AUTOMATIC

My colleagues and I assumed that the gift of healing was automatic. Anyone who had that gift could heal anyone, anywhere,

---

2. We argued that the healings of Jesus and the apostles were always instantaneous, irreversible, and complete. Strictly speaking, we do not know that all the New Testament healings were irreversible for the simple reason that we have no follow-up studies of the people who were healed. If sin or demons were the cause of an illness and the healed person did not repent, the illness could return (Matthew 12:43–45; John 5:14). Likewise, if the illness was brought on by anxiety or stress, that illness could return if the anxiety and stress were not dealt with.

anytime, at will. We viewed the healing gift as a permanent possession to be exercised at the discretion of the gifted one.

If this is your view of the gift of healing, I can guarantee you will never find *anyone* who has the gift of healing. And when you examine the Scriptures, you will have to conclude that neither Jesus nor the apostles had the gift of healing, for even they could not heal at will—if by "at will" we mean anywhere, anytime, under any conditions.

Three incidents in the life of Jesus demonstrate that he was not free to heal at will under any conditions. At the beginning of the story of the healing of the paralytic at Capernaum, Luke writes, "One day as [Jesus] was teaching, and Pharisees and teachers of the law, who had come from every village of Galilee and from Judea and Jerusalem, were sitting there. And the power of the Lord was present for him to heal the sick" (Luke 5:17 NIV, 1984 ed.).[3]

Why would Luke say that the power of the Lord was present for Jesus to heal if Jesus could heal at any time, under any condition, and solely at his own discretion? This statement only makes sense if we view healing as the sovereign prerogative of God the Father, who sometimes dispenses his power to heal and at other times withholds it.

A second incident is found in John 5, the story of the healing

---

3. The 2011 edition of the NIV renders the sentence, "And the power of the Lord was *with* Jesus to heal the sick" (italics added). This translation could be construed to mean that Jesus could heal at will, but it is a mistranslation of the Greek text. There is no preposition or grammatical case, like the dative, in the sentence that could legitimately be translated "with." The phrase "for him to heal" is a typical purpose clause using the *eis* preposition with an infinitive construction. Furthermore, in Luke's writings, "the power of the Lord" and "the Spirit of the Lord" are used interchangeably (e.g., Luke 1:35; 4:14; 24:49: Acts 1:8; 10:38). Both "the power of the Lord" and "the Spirit of the Lord" temporarily empower believers for specific tasks.

of the man who had been paralyzed for thirty-eight years. He was lying at the edge of the pool of Bethesda when Jesus met him. There were many other sick people lying around the pool. Jesus healed the paralytic instantly and completely.

After healing the paralytic, we would assume Jesus would heal the other people there at the pool. For huge crowds frequently came to him, and the Gospels say he healed them all (Matthew 8:16; 12:15; Luke 6:19). Yet on this day, he healed only one person at the pool.

Why did he ignore all the other sick people? Immediately after the healing we find Jesus involved in a theological dispute with religious leaders. In the dispute Jesus answered this question and gave us the principle that governed his whole ministry.

Jesus said, "Very truly I tell you, the Son can do nothing by himself; he can do only what he sees his Father doing, because whatever the Father does the Son also does" (John 5:19). Jesus only healed one person at the pool that day because his Father was only healing one person. If his Father was not healing, then Jesus could not heal. Jesus was completely obedient to the sovereign will of his heavenly Father for his entire ministry.

This is not an isolated teaching in the gospel of John, but a major theme. Numerous times Jesus says he only does what his Father does and only speaks the words his Father gives him to speak, and that his teaching is not his but comes from the One who sent him (John 3:34; 5:30; 7:16; 8:28; 12:49–50; 14:10, 24, 31).

This principle answers a question I am asked all the time: "If you believe in healing and you think you have a gift of healing, why don't you go empty out the hospitals, or why don't you go into the slums of places like Calcutta where you can really do some good?" The answer to that question is that the gift of healing can't be exercised at our own discretion. The Lord Jesus was at an ancient "hospital" where the sick gathered or were carried to. Everyone there needed healing, but Jesus only healed one person there. Need by itself never determines ministry. The Lord of all the ministries directs those ministries. The only way anyone with a healing gift could have an effective ministry in a hospital or in the slums of Calcutta would be if the Lord actually sent that gifted person there to heal.

This principle is also a valid answer to the same question when it is asked in a different form. Occasionally people ask why at some healing meetings the most serious ailments are not healed while some of the "trivial" ones are. Why do healers pray for people with migraine headaches but not for people in wheelchairs? Skeptics of divine healing call this a tragedy and express "concern" for all those in wheelchairs who were not healed. They mock the healing of "trivial" illnesses as psychosomatic.

If the people who conduct the meeting are not frauds but sincere servants trying to follow the leading of the Lord, they do not actually have a say in what kind of healings take place. According to the principle of John 5:19, *God decides* who gets healed and directs his servants accordingly. It is our responsibility to listen for those directions and follow them rather than to determine who gets healed.[4]

---

4. Spiritual gifts vary in their strength. Some evangelists have a more powerful gift than other evangelists. Our faith to use our gifts also varies in strength. When I first began to pray for the sick in conferences around the world, a group of guys brought their friend to me for prayer. He was completely blind. His face and hands were covered in eczema, and the scales of his dead skin spread out over his shirt. There were other repulsive features. I freaked out on the inside. Not only did I not have the faith to pray for his healing, but I did not want to even touch him. I don't react like that today because my faith has grown, and it's still growing.

If "healers" promise that God will bring people out of wheelchairs, heal blindness, and do other miracles in their particular meetings and it does not happen, then there is room for criticism. It is right to question the discernment, if not the integrity, of those leaders.

A third incident is found in Mark 6, when Jesus returned to his home in Nazareth. The people of his hometown were offended at him with the result that "he could not do any miracles there, except lay his hands on a few sick people and heal them. He was amazed at their lack of faith" (Mark 6:5–6). Matthew writes of this same incident that Jesus "did not do many miracles there because of their lack of faith" (Matthew 13:58). God allowed the healing ministry of his Son to be limited, at least on some occasions, by the unbelief of the people. Thus, Jesus himself could not heal independently of the Father, at his own will, and under any conditions.[5]

_____

5. Mark and Matthew believe in the deity of Jesus and, therefore, in his omnipotence. Their stories of the inability of Jesus to heal at Nazareth are told with the knowledge that he voluntarily and continually surrendered the use of his omnipotence to the glory of God (see Philippians 2:5–11).

eight

THE HEALING MINISTRY
OF THE APOSTLES

The apostles could not heal automatically. Jesus told them in John 15:5, "Apart from me you can do nothing." Jesus had said the same thing of himself: "By myself I can do nothing; I judge only as I hear, and my judgment is just, for I seek not to please myself but him who sent me" (John 5:30). In the same way, the apostles could do nothing divinely powerful apart from the sovereign will of the Lord Jesus and his heavenly Father.

GOD DIRECTED THE APOSTLES'
SUPERNATURAL MINISTRY

God showed Peter the duplicity of Ananias and Sapphira when they lied to the Holy Spirit about their offering to God. Ananias fell down dead when Peter confronted him. Three hours later, Peter told Sapphira she would die, and she fell down dead at that moment

(Acts 5:1–11). When Paul was filled with the Spirit, he pronounced the false prophet Elymas blind, and immediately he was blinded (Acts 13:9–11). Peter and Paul could not do these things at will.

This same principle is illustrated by a miracle in the life of Paul. While Paul was preaching at Lystra, a man who had been crippled from birth listened to him. Luke said that Paul "looked directly at him, saw that he had faith to be healed and called out, 'Stand up on your feet!'" (Acts 14:9–10). Paul did not initiate the healing. He followed the impression that God had given him.

PAUL CANNOT HEAL HIS PARTNERS

Next to Jesus, the New Testament pictures Paul as the greatest healer in the early church. Handkerchiefs that touched his body when laid on sick people healed them and drove demons out of their bodies (Acts 19:11). But when Paul needed his three friends to help him in ministry, he could not heal them. Epaphroditus almost died (Philippians 2:25–27); he had to leave Trophimus sick at Miletus (2 Timothy 4:20); and he had to exhort his spiritual son, Timothy, to take a little wine for his stomach's sake and his frequent illnesses (1 Timothy 5:23).[1]

---

1. Some people assume that Paul could not get these three people healed because he was not free to use his healing gift on Christians. They assume that the gift of healing was only to be used on unbelievers or in the presence of unbelievers to convince them of the truth of the gospel. If this were the case, why did Paul heal Eutychus, a believer, by raising him from the dead in the presence of only believers (Acts 20:7–12)? Furthermore, the gift of healing mentioned in 1 Corinthians 12:9 is said to be for the edification of those in the church (1 Corinthians 12:7). Others have claimed that Paul's failure to heal Epaphroditus, Trophimus, and Timothy was due to God's withdrawal of Paul's healing gift at the end of his life. This is an incredible explanation. Here we would have to admit that miracles had ceased even before the death of the apostles. There is no biblical argument to back up such an interpretation.

THE MINISTRY OF SIGNS AND WONDERS IS GREATER THAN THE GIFT OF HEALING

The signs and wonders ministry of the apostles is not the same as the spiritual gift of healing. The ministry of signs and wonders is given to a small circle of people, while the miraculous gifts of the Spirit are given to the whole body of Christ (1 Corinthians 12:8–10).[2] This wide distribution of gifts across the body of Christ is what Joel prophesied when he saw the Holy Spirit come on all people in the last days (Joel 2:28–29). Peter used Joel's prophecy to argue that the gift of tongues given on the day of Pentecost was one of the signs of the fulfillment of Joel's prophecy (Acts 2:16). With the outpouring of the Holy Spirit at Pentecost, there came gifts to the *whole* body of Christ. Peter said that each Christian has received a spiritual gift (1 Peter 4:10). The Greek word for spiritual gift is *charisma*, from which our word *charismatic* comes.[3] This is the word Paul used in 1 Corinthians 12 (verses 4, 9, 28, 30–31) for spiritual gifts, and Paul maintained that all the gifts were operative in the church at Corinth (1 Corinthians 1:7).[4]

---

2. Prophecy is found in the church at Thessalonica (1 Thessalonians 5:20), in Rome (Romans 12:6), in Ephesus (Ephesians 4:11), and in other locations throughout the book of Acts (11:27; 13:1; 15:32; 19:6; 21:9). Likewise, the gift of tongues is found in Jerusalem (Acts 2), Samaria (Acts 8:9–19), Caesarea (Acts 10:46), Ephesus (Acts 19:6), and Corinth (1 Corinthians 12–14). Miracles were being done in the churches of Galatia (Galatians 3:5).

3. I don't like to think of *charisma* as "a natural ability empowered by the Holy Spirit." A Christian may be a wonderful professor of English at the university but not have the spiritual gift of teaching. A spiritual gift is an endowment of power from the Holy Spirit to be used by the gifted person to bring people closer to the Lord. It doesn't make any difference whether the spiritual gift is teaching, helps, administration, or any other spiritual gift. All gifts are given for the building up of the body of Christ (1 Corinthians 12:7; 14:26). See chapter 24 for an extensive discussion of the spiritual gifts.

4. Spiritual gifts vary in their intensity and strength. Paul admits this in regard to the gift of prophecy. In Romans 12:6, he wrote, "We have different gifts, according to the grace given to each of us. If your gift is prophesying, then prophesy in accordance

The miraculous ministry of the apostles is designated by the phrase "signs and wonders."

In the Old Testament, "signs and wonders" describe the great plagues that God sent on Egypt and the subsequent deliverance of his people from that nation (Deuteronomy 4:34; 6:22; 7:19; 23:9; 26:8; 34:11; Nehemiah 9:10; Psalm 135:9). In the New Testament, "signs and wonders" describe the ministries of Jesus (Acts 2:22), the apostles (Acts 2:43; 5:12; 14:3; 15:12; Romans 15:18–19; 2 Corinthians 12:12), Stephen (Acts 6:8), and Philip (Acts 8:6).

The phrase "signs and wonders" described an unusual out-pouring of the Holy Spirit to produce an abundance of miracles (Acts 5:12; 8:7).[5] Signs and wonders always astonished those who

---

with your faith." Different measures of grace and faith are given with which to exercise the various gifts. Paul himself had a greater gift of tongues than anyone in Corinth (1 Corinthians 14:18). Timothy had let one of his spiritual gifts decline in its strength so that Paul had to encourage him "to fan into flame the gift [*charisma*] of God, which is in you through the laying on of my hands" (2 Timothy 1:6). All of these texts demonstrate that spiritual gifts occur with varying degrees of intensity or strength. Luke draws a portrait of Apollos as a preacher and teacher who was "mighty in the Scriptures" (Acts 18:24 NASB). Some evangelists have a greater gift than other evangelists. By analogy, we should expect the same thing with healing, prophecy, and all the gifts of the Spirit.

5. Wayne Grudem defines a miracle as follows: "A miracle is a less common kind of God's activity in which he arouses people's awe and wonder and bears witness to himself." He justifies this definition by pointing out the deficiencies in other commonly proposed definitions:

For example, one definition of miracles is "a direct intervention of God in the world." But this definition assumes a deistic view of God's relationship to the world, in which the world continues on its own and God only intervenes in it occasionally. This is certainly not the biblical view, according to which God makes the rain to fall (Matt. 5:45), causes the grass to grow (Ps. 104:14), and continually carries along all things by his word and power (Heb. 1:3). Another definition of miracles is "a more direct activity of God in the world." But to talk about a "more direct" working of God suggests that his ordinary providential activity is somehow not "direct" and again hints at a sort of deistic removal of God from the world.

Another definition is "God working in the world without using means to bring about the results he wishes." Yet to speak of God working "without means" leaves us with very few if any miracles in the Bible, for it is hard to think of a miracle that came about with no means at all: in the healing of people, for example, some of the physical

saw them. Signs and wonders occurred in the midst of revival, confirming the proclamation of the gospel, and the only people who are said to do signs and wonders, outside of the Lord Jesus and the apostles, are Stephen and Philip.

Although Luke does not describe the ministry of the seventy-two sent out by Jesus as "signs and wonders," their ministry meets the criteria for signs and wonders. Jesus sent them out to proclaim the gospel with power. He gave them authority to heal all the sick people in each town they visited (Luke 10:9), as well as authority to overcome all the power of Satan so that all the demons submitted to them in the name of Jesus (Luke 10:17–20).

Thus, the Bible makes a distinction between the ministry of signs and wonders and the gift of healing. Signs and wonders

---

properties of the sick person's body were doubtless involved as part of the healing. When Jesus multiplied the loaves and fishes, he at least used the original five loaves and two fishes that were there. When he changed water to wine, he used water and made it become wine. This definition seems to be inadequate.

Yet another definition of miracle is "an exception to a natural law" or "God acting contrary to the laws of nature." But the phrase "laws of nature" in popular understanding implies that there are certain qualities inherent in the things that exist, "laws of nature" that operate independently of God, and that God must intervene or "break" these laws for a miracle to occur. Once again this definition does not adequately account for the biblical teaching on providence.

Another definition of miracle is "an event impossible to explain by natural causes." This definition is inadequate because (1) it does not include God as the one who brings about the miracle; (2) it assumes that God does not use some natural causes when he works in an unusual or amazing way, and thus it assumes again that God only occasionally intervenes in the world; and (3) it will result in a significant minimizing of actual miracles, and an increase in skepticism, since many times when God works in answer to prayer the result is amazing to those who prayed but it is not absolutely impossible to explain by natural causes, especially for a skeptic who simply refuses to see God's hand at work.

Therefore, the original definition given above, where a miracle is simply a *less common* way of God's working in the world, seems to be preferable and more consistent with the biblical doctrine of God's providence. This definition does not say that a miracle is a different kind of working by God, but only that it is a less common way of God's working and that it is done so as to arouse people's surprise, awe, or amazement in such a way that God bears witness to himself (*Systematic Theology: An Introduction to Biblical Doctrine* [Grand Rapids: Zondervan, 1994], 355–56).

are an outpouring of miracles specifically connected with revival and the proclamation of the gospel. The gift of healing is given to the church for its edification (1 Corinthians 12:7) and is not necessarily connected with revival or an abundance of miracles.

We should expect the healing ministry of the apostles to be greater than that of others in the body of Christ. The Lord chose them to be the first leaders of his church, and he gave them authority and power over all demons and over all disease (Matthew 10:1; Mark 3:13–15; Luke 9:1). After his resurrection, Jesus promised them greater power. They would be "clothed with power from on high" (Luke 24:49, cf. Acts 1:8). They possessed an authority that no one else in the body of Christ possessed.

The apostle Paul was not one of the Twelve, but he stunned Ephesus with signs and wonders for three years. Through this revival, all of Asia heard the word of the Lord (Acts 19:10; 20:31). Paul even had the authority to turn someone over to Satan for the destruction of his flesh (1 Corinthians 5:1–5). His ministry was far more than a gift of healing or miracles.

Lastly, we should not draw the conclusion that signs and wonders have ceased with the deaths of the apostles. Stephen and Philip were not apostles, but the Lord gave them a ministry of signs and wonders similar to that of the apostles.[6]

---

6. Luke wrote that Philip performed "great signs and miracles" (Acts 8:13; see verse 6) but does not add "wonders." Acts 8:7 gives the only specific examples of what constitutes signs in the book of Acts: many impure spirits came out of people with great shrieks, and many people who were paralyzed or lame were healed. The emphasis is on both the quality and the quantity of the miracles. The whole region of Samaria was converted through Philip's preaching, exorcisms, and healings. The leading sorcerer of Samaria, Simon, was amazed by Philip's "great signs and miracles" (8:13). The conversion of Samaria is unique, for God withheld the Holy Spirit from the Samaritans at their conversion. There was nothing defective in Philip's preaching or in the Samaritans' faith. There was much defective in the history of the Samaritans' relationship to the people of God. They had refused to submit to God's government through Israel. They developed

There is also nothing in the New Testament that would preclude future outpourings of revivals accompanied by signs and wonders. In fact, it is biblical to long for and pray for such revivals. Consider the prayer of Acts 4:29–30: "Now, Lord, consider their threats and enable your servants to speak your word with great boldness. Stretch out your hand to heal and perform signs and wonders through the name of your holy servant Jesus." God signaled his approval of their prayer by shaking the house and filling them all with the Holy Spirit so that they all spoke the word of God boldly (Acts 4:31).

Signs and wonders did not authenticate the apostles. Signs and wonders grew the first-century church. If the modern church in the Western world were to take this prayer seriously, who knows what kind of outpouring of signs and wonders in revival God might be pleased to give us?

I have never experienced a signs and wonders revival like the one in the book of Acts, but I have experienced small foretastes of what it might be like.

I spoke at a Wimber conference in Perth, Australia, in March 1990. At the end of a workshop in the afternoon, I asked the people with bone and joint problems to stand up, and others gathered around them to pray. There were twelve hundred people

---

their own center of worship, not recognizing Jerusalem. They edited Israel's Pentateuch to create the sectarian Samaritan Pentateuch to support their distinctive theology. They rejected the rest of Israel's Scripture. Now that they had become Christians, God showed them that they must submit to the authority of the Lord's apostles, by withholding the Holy Spirit until Peter and John came down from Jerusalem to pray for them to receive the Holy Spirit (8:14–17). They received the Holy Spirit and spoke in tongues after the apostles laid their hands on them and prayed. We know they spoke in tongues because "Simon saw that the Spirit was given at the laying on of the apostles' hands" (8:18). If the Samaritans hadn't spoken in tongues, just as the Jewish Christians had done when the Holy Spirit first came on them, the Jerusalem church would not have received them or would have regarded their conversion as inferior to their own.

in the room. It seemed like everyone we prayed for was healed. I saw a crooked ankle straighten in seconds right before my eyes. The whole room was shouting, "Hallelujah! Praise God!" These healings began suddenly, lasted for ten minutes, and then stopped abruptly. I told John Wimber about it, and he just smiled and said, "That was your first time, wasn't it?" He had witnessed this sudden outburst of healing many times in places as diverse as Africa and England.

For the last thirty years, I've prayed for healing in private homes, in churches, and on conference stages. And I've seen enough healing to give me hope to pray Acts 4:29–31 every single day. There are places in the world today where the Holy Spirit is producing signs and wonders revivals. He tends to pour out his power on the poorest of the poor and on the most persecuted brothers and sisters of the Lord. These are the ones who can't survive without the power of the Lord rescuing them.

nine

JOHN CALVIN FORMULATES CESSATIONISM

B y 1500, the church of Augustine and Aquinas had become filled with corruption. Roman Catholic priests were openly sleeping with their concubines and neglecting pastoral duties. The leaders of the church created schemes to exploit its members. Archbishops licensed priests to sell indulgences—certificates that removed the temporal penalty for a specific sin. The price of the indulgence was determined by the church member's social position and financial worth.

In 1476, Pope Sixtus IV expanded the indulgence market to cover the dead in purgatory. The Roman Catholic Church taught that purgatory was a place of temporary, purifying torment for those not pure enough to enter heaven. The sellers of indulgences preached heartrending sermons describing the pain of loved ones suffering in purgatory and how heartless it would be not to buy their way into heaven. These schemes were possible because the Catholic Church taught good works were necessary to enter heaven.

Martin Luther (1483–1546), a lowly monk in Wittenberg, Germany, preached and wrote against the corrupt doctrine and practices of the Roman Catholic Church. He taught that the Bible was the final authority for believers, not the pope or church tradition, that people are justified by faith in Christ alone and not by good works, and that all believers are priests. Luther became the prophet of the Reformation, the movement that gave birth to the Protestant Church.

John Calvin (1509–1564) was the theologian of the Reformation. He taught these same cardinal doctrines in Geneva, Switzerland. He wrote the first edition of the *Institutes of the Christian Religion* when he was only twenty-six. He expanded the final edition to four volumes, and it became one of the most influential systematic theologies of all time.

These two great men had their flaws, but they will forever be heroes of the Protestant faith. I first read and profited from their works when I was a seminary student, and I still enjoy their writing today.[1]

The Catholics maintained that their doctrines went back to Peter and were supported by fifteen hundred years of miracles. They charged the Reformers with inventing new doctrines not supported by tradition or miracles.

Calvin could have replied that miracles authenticate Jesus as the Messiah and the message about Jesus, but they don't ratify the truth of other doctrines. Only Scripture can do that. He would

---

1. The best book I have read on the Reformation is Eric Metaxas's *Martin Luther* (New York: Viking, 2017).

have been on safe ground. Instead, this superb and normally careful teacher stepped into quicksand. He answered his Catholic critics by giving the doctrine of cessationism its modern form.

His three main points were that the purpose of miracles was evidential (they authenticate the apostles as trustworthy teachers of doctrine); miracles have ceased; and the miracles of the Catholics are satanic delusions because God would never do a miracle in support of false doctrine. He does not offer a systematic discussion of the ceasing of miracles. His comments are diffused throughout his *Institutes* and biblical commentaries and are sometimes contradictory.

Calvin claims that miracles confirm the teaching of the apostles.[2] Then he undercuts the evidentialist purpose of miracles when he says of the miraculous *charismata* ("spiritual gifts"), "All such gifts . . . were given for the edification of the church, and unless they contribute to this they lose their grace."[3] This truly is the main purpose of the *charismata* according to the apostle Paul. If the spiritual gifts were needed to build up the church in the first century, they would be needed to do the same in all the following centuries.

Regarding the ceasing of miracles, Calvin writes:

> But that gift of healing, like the rest of the miracles, which the Lord willed to be brought forth for a time, has

---

2. John Calvin, *Institutes of the Christian Religion*, vol. 1, ed. John T. McNeill, trans. Ford Lewis Battles (Philadelphia: Westminster, 1960), 16–17. He also claims that miracles confirm Scripture and demonstrate the authority of leaders like Moses (1.8.4–5). In his commentary on Acts 14:3, he maintains that miracles confirm the gospel and "show to us the power and grace of God" (*Calvin's Commentary on the Bible*, www.studylight.org/commentaries/cal/acts-14.html).

3. Calvin, *Institutes*, 3.2.9.

vanished away in order to make the new preaching of the gospel marvelous forever. Therefore, even if we grant to the full that anointing was a sacrament of those powers which were then administered by the hands of the apostles, it now has nothing to do with us, to whom the administering of such powers has not been committed.[4]

In this quote, Calvin asserts what is assumed by the cessationists who follow him, namely, that only the apostles healed and performed miracles in the first-century church.

James commanded the elders of the church to pray for the sick and promised that the prayer offered in faith would make the sick well (James 5:13–16). Calvin even takes this prayer away from the church. He writes:

That is, James spoke for that same time when the church still enjoyed such a blessing of God. Indeed, they [Calvin's Catholic opponents] affirm that the same force is still in their anointing, but *we experience otherwise* . . . Therefore they make themselves ridiculous when they boast that they are endowed with the gift of healing. The Lord is indeed present with his people in every age; and he heals their weaknesses as often as necessary, no less than of old; still he does not put forth these manifest powers, nor dispense miracles though the apostles' hands. For that was a temporary gift, and also quickly perished partly on account of men's ungratefulness.[5]

---

4. Calvin, *Institutes*, 4.19.18; see also 4.19.6.
5. Calvin, *Institutes*, 4.19.19, emphasis added.

Calvin does not offer scriptural evidence that miracles "perished partly on account of men's ungratefulness." Nor does he offer any historical evidence, but just a naked assertion. In this quote, Calvin reveals his real reason for not believing in contemporary miracles: "we experience otherwise." No cessationist has ever been able to produce a single verse of Scripture that says God has withdrawn the miraculous *charismata*.

In book 4 of the *Institutes*, Calvin demolishes his cessationist argument. In his discussion of Ephesians 4:11, he claims that the offices of apostle, prophet, and evangelist were temporary, but the offices of teacher and pastor were permanent. But he leaves the door open for the former three when he says that the Lord "now and again revives them as the need of the times demands." Of prophets he says, "This class either does not exist today or is less commonly seen." Of apostles he says, "I do not deny that the Lord has sometimes at a later period raised up apostles, or at least evangelists in their place, as has happened in our own day." Calvin often praised Luther and even called him a "distinguished apostle of Christ."[6]

If there is any contemporary need for the workers of miracles or for apostles, there is no way to argue that miracles fulfilled their purpose in the first century. Calvin envisioned God "reviving" miracles in an area where the gospel had not been preached. Following Calvin, many modern cessationists would not quibble if God decided to revive apostolic signs and wonders in "cutting-edge missionary situations." Calvin did not see, nor do his modern disciples see, that this concession undercuts the

---

6. The discussion on Ephesians 4:11 is found in 4.3.4–9 of the *Institutes*. The reference to Luther as an apostle is found in Calvin's *Defensio adversus Pighium* cited by McNeill in note 4 in 4.3.4.

whole cessationist argument. If signs and wonders are necessary for evangelism in some far-off place ruled by spiritual ignorance, superstition, false religion, and demonic power, why wouldn't they be necessary in a place like Manhattan that is ruled by the same powers, even if Manhattan's dark powers are a little more polished than the far-off powers?[7]

Calvin's third point was that since miracles confirm the person and doctrine of the miracle worker, God would never do a miracle to confirm prayer to the saints or pilgrimages to shrines or any other superstition.[8] The benefit to the Reformers of believing this was that it relieved them of having to investigate Catholic miracles. They could dismiss all Catholic miracles, as well as the miracles of anyone else who disagreed with them doctrinally, as delusions or works of Satan.

Calvin offers no scriptural proof of this assertion. Most cessationists tend to hold the same assumption. But the Bible teaches that God sometimes works miracles through groups that have spiritual abuses, doctrinal error, and even immorality.[9]

Calvin was normally a great student of Scripture, but in the heat of the battle, he was careless in the area of spiritual gifts. This shouldn't diminish our gratitude for the man God used to give back to the church the priesthood of all believers, justification by faith alone in Christ, and the absolute authority of Scripture.

---

7. Calvin even claimed that God was doing miracles among the Reformers. "Well, we are not entirely lacking in miracles, and these very certain and not subject to mockery," he wrote to King Francis (*Institutes*, vol. 1, p. 17).

8. See *Calvin's Commentary on the Bible*, Acts 14:3, www.studylight.org/comment aries/cal/acts-14.html.

9. See chapter 22 in this book.

ten

CONYERS MIDDLETON FORMULATES THE HISTORICAL CRITICISM OF MIRACLES

Less than two hundred years after John Calvin's death, the Anglicans in England fought with each other over miracles. The primary argument was not over what the Scriptures taught, but over the historical witness to miracles after the death of the apostles. In 1749, Conyers Middleton published *A Free Inquiry into the Miraculous Powers, Which Are Supposed to Have Subsisted in the Christian Church, from the Earliest Ages through Several Successive Centuries.* Middleton argued that a careful reading of history showed that God had withdrawn miraculous powers after the apostles. He was a Cambridge-educated clergyman considered to be one of the finest stylists in the English language, even praised by

Alexander Pope. He was also known for his harshness and was seldom out of controversy.[1]

Middleton is important because he gave skeptics a systematic framework for denying any historical report of a miracle. His treatment of early, godly martyrs for the Lord Jesus is a good example of his method.

Ignatius was born around AD 35 and was martyred around AD 107 in Rome. He was the bishop of Antioch and held in high esteem in the early church. In his letter to the church in Philadelphia, Ignatius claimed that the Holy Spirit showed him the divisions going on in the church:

> Howbeit there were those who suspected me of saying this, because I knew beforehand of the division of certain persons. But He in whom I am bound is my witness that I learned it not from flesh of man; it was the preaching of the Spirit who spake on this wise; Do nothing without the bishop; keep your flesh as a temple of God; cherish union; shun divisions; be imitators of Jesus Christ, as He Himself also was of His Father.[2]

Middleton rejected Ignatius's claim that the Holy Spirit had revealed to him the division in the church in Philadelphia: "Yet I do not find, that any other Commentator has ventured to build

---

1. See Leslie Stephen, "Middleton, Conyers," in *Dictionary of National Biography*, 1885–1900, 37:343–48, https://en.wikisource.org/wiki/Middleton,_Conyers_(DNB00). The whole article is basically a recitation of his controversies, including a charge of plagiarism regarding his most famous work, *The History of the Life of M. Tullius Cicero* (1741).

2. See *Ignatius to the Philadelphians* 7:2, www.earlychristianwritings.com/text/ignatius-philadelphians-lightfoot.html.

anything miraculous or supernatural upon it."[3] It was easier for Middleton to believe that this godly martyr was lying than to believe that the Holy Spirit would give Ignatius revelation to help him shepherd the Lord's church.

So the first interpretive key to dismiss supernatural reports is to claim that *the smart authorities don't believe this was supernatural.* But a lot of smart people did believe this was supernatural, and they wrote refutations of Middleton.[4]

Polycarp was born around AD 70 and was martyred around AD 155.[5] He was the bishop of Smyrna. He was universally believed to have been a disciple of the apostle John. His Christlike character, powerful preaching, extensive evangelism, and prophetic gift were extolled in the ancient church.[6]

Three days before Polycarp was arrested, "while praying, he fell into a trance, and he saw his pillow burning with fire. He turned and said to those that were with him: 'It must needs be that I shall be burned alive.'"[7] Middleton's response was that Polycarp knew he was being hunted, and he could have figured

---

3. Conyers Middleton, *A Free Inquiry into the Miraculous Powers, Which Are Supposed to Have Subsisted in the Christian Church, from the Earliest Ages through Several Successive Centuries* (London: Manby and Cox, 1749), 8.

4. Many of these refutations are cited in the article mentioned in footnote 1 in this chapter. One that I like is by William Dodwell, *A Free Answer to Dr. Middleton's Free Inquiry into the Miraculous Powers of the Primitive Church* (London: S. Birt, 1749). The University of Oxford conferred a DD (Doctor of Divinity) on Dodwell for his service to religion by refuting Middleton (*Dictionary of National Biography*, 1885–1900, 15:182–83, https://en.wikisource.org/wiki/Dodwell,_William_(DNB00)). At the time, the DD was a higher degree than a PhD.

5. His dates are debated, but the general consensus favors these dates.

6. "In the number of these latter [the elect] was this man, the glorious martyr Polycarp, who was found an apostolic and prophetic teacher in our own time, a bishop of the holy Church which is in Smyrna. For every word which he uttered from his mouth was accomplished and will be accomplished" (*The Martyrdom of Polycarp* 16:2, www .earlychristianwritings.com/text/polycarp-smyrnaeans.html). This letter was written shortly after Polycarp was martyred, about AD 155.

7. *Martyrdom of Polycarp* 5:2.

by common sense that his death was near "without recurring to any thing miraculous."[8] So Middleton's second interpretive key is that *if something could have a natural explanation, then the miraculous explanation should be discarded.* Middleton believed that a man who was about to lay down his life for Jesus lied about how he knew the manner and time of his death. In the New Testament, God sometimes prepared his faithful children for martyrdom by warning them ahead of time. Jesus told Peter what kind of death he would die (John 21:19). Paul knew that the time of his martyrdom had come, and he asked Timothy to come to him soon (2 Timothy 4:6–9).

Eyewitnesses of Polycarp's death testified to its supernatural character. When Polycarp was led into the stadium, a voice from heaven said, "Be strong, Polycarp, and take courage. I am with you."[9] The believers in the stadium heard the audible voice. The proconsul did not want to burn an old man. He asked Polycarp to deny Jesus so that he could set him free. Polycarp chose the flames instead. As he lay on the pyre, the flames formed a vault over his body and did not touch his body but baked it like bread. A sweet aroma like incense came out of the flames.

---

8. Middleton, *A Free Inquiry*, 9.

9. *Martyrdom of Polycarp* 9:1 (my translation). They are seven extant manuscripts of *The Martyrdom of Polycarp*, dating from the tenth to the thirteenth centuries. The early church historian Eusebius (ca. AD 260–340) reproduced most of the text in his *Ecclesiastical History.* Four Greek manuscripts and Eusebius add, "I am with you." The editors tend to omit "I am with you" from their final version of the text. The reason for this is that it's easy to see why someone would add it and difficult to see why any scribe would omit it. But the best witness to the original text of *The Martyrdom of Polycarp* is the Mosquensis manuscript, especially when it agrees with Eusebius. And Mosquensis is one of the four manuscripts that has "I am with you," and Eusebius also agrees that "I am with you" belonged in the original text. The verb translated "take courage" can also mean "be a man." When it is used in the compound phrase with "be strong," it means "take courage." This usage is illustrated in the Septuagint translations of Psalm 27:14 (LXX Psalm 26:14) and Psalm 31:25 (LXX Psalm 30:25).

The executioner stabbed Polycarp with a dagger. "When he had done this, there came forth a dove and a quantity of blood, so that it extinguished the fire; and all the multitude marveled that there should be so great a difference between the unbelievers and the elect."[10]

Middleton devoted three pages to Polycarp's martyrdom not to refute the supernatural elements but to ridicule them. A third interpretive key of skeptics is that *some supernatural stories are so incredible that they are not worthy of refutation.* Yet all the signs that are said to have happened in Polycarp's martyrdom happened during the life and death of Jesus. Just before Jesus' hour approached, he prayed in front of a crowd, "'Father, glorify your name!' Then a voice came from heaven, 'I have glorified it, and will glorify it again'" (John 12:28). Some heard the voice and were amazed. Others heard only thunder. When Stephen went before his murderers, his face shone like an angel (Acts 6:15). On the day of Jesus' crucifixion, "darkness came over all the land" from noon until 3:00 p.m. (Matthew 27:45). There was no eclipse on April 3, AD 33. It was a supernatural darkness. When Jesus died, the curtain of the temple was torn in two from top to bottom. At the moment of his death, an earthquake shook Jerusalem. "The tombs broke open. The bodies of many holy people who had died were raised to life. They came out of the tombs after Jesus' resurrection and went into the holy city and appeared to many people" (Matthew 27:52–53). When a soldier pierced Jesus' side with a spear, blood and water flowed out (John 19:34). This was a supernatural sign. Dead bodies do not bleed, for the heart no longer pumps blood. People in the first

---

10. *Martyrdom of Polycarp* 16:1.

century knew this because they frequently handled dead bodies. Water does not flow out of dead bodies. John presents this as a miracle sign. That's why he makes such a point of having been an eyewitness (19:35). In John's gospel, Jesus used water as a symbol of eternal life and of the Holy Spirit (John 4:10–14; 6:35; 7:37–39). Out of his death (blood) flowed eternal life (water) for all who believe in him.

The God I believe in presides over a world in which his servant can split seas and make water flow out of rocks, and even a world in which a donkey can see an angel and talk.[11] So strange and weird can't be criteria for withholding belief.

Do I believe the story of Polycarp's death as it has been handed down to us? I do. Do I believe the part about the aroma, the dove, and the blood coming out of his body? I do. We mustn't lose sight of the greatest miracle here. There was a man named Polycarp who loved God so much and God's people so much that he chose to be burned alive rather than to go free by dishonoring God and letting down the people of God. And he thanked God for granting him the honor of being burned alive for him. Is it unseemly that God would honor such a man with the dove and the blood? Jesus began his sacrificial ministry with the dove and ended it with the blood. Maybe God was testifying to the stadium crowd that Polycarp had lived his life by the power of the Spirit and that the power of the Spirit had now enabled him to shed his blood for Jesus. And maybe Polycarp's sacrifice rose up to heaven like sweet incense.

These early Christians lived in a world that would put them to death for doing nothing other than claiming to be a Christian.

---

11. See Exodus 14:15–31 for the Red Sea; Exodus 17:5–7 and Numbers 20:9–11 for rocks giving water; and Numbers 22:22–35 for the talking donkey.

There are places like that today. There have always been places like that. And there have always been fantastic stories coming out of places like that because these people are forced to depend on God for everything, and God honors their faith and suffering for him in miraculous ways.

Middleton also writes off any historical witness to miracles who (1) puts forward a fanciful interpretation of Scripture, (2) believes in the report of a miracle that turns out to be a false report, and (3) believes a false doctrine or something else that today we know is manifestly false.

Justin Martyr (AD 100–165) was one of the first Christian apologists and was beheaded for his faith. Besides some fanciful interpretations, Justin believed that resurrected saints would reign with Jesus for a thousand years on the earth before the end of history (Revelation 20:4). This doctrine is called premillennialism. It is a cardinal doctrine of the seminary where I taught. Middleton calls the doctrine "absurd and monstrous," as well as "impious and heretical."[12] This and some other interpretations allow him to conclude that Justin's writings are "the pure flights of an enthusiastic fancy and heated brain."[13] William Dodwell replied that Middleton's strictures required a witness to be infallible before he could be believed, and in that case, he made historical inquiry into miracles an impossibility.[14]

Cyprian (AD 200–258) was the bishop of Carthage and considered the most learned church father in Latin until Jerome and Augustine. The Roman proconsul, Galerius Maximus, did not want to execute Cyprian, but when the bishop refused to sacrifice

---

12. Middleton, *A Free Inquiry*, 31.
13. Middleton, *A Free Inquiry*, 30.
14. Dodwell, *A Free Answer*, 70.

to Roman gods, the proconsul had Cyprian beheaded. Middleton dismisses Cyprian's testimony to God's supernatural works by claiming that Cyprian was power-hungry, so that his "character would tempt us to suspect, that he was the inventor, rather than the believer of such idle stories."[15] There is no godly, brilliant martyr that Middleton wouldn't mock if they committed the sin of believing that God was doing miracles in their lifetime.

If the one testifying to a miracle did not do the miracle themselves, did not see it with their own eyes, or did not give the names of the persons involved, Middleton claims that their report is not credible.[16] If this were actually a canon of historical research, we would have to dismiss Luke's gospel. Luke did not do any of the miracles recorded in his gospel; he didn't see them with his own eyes; and most of the people who are healed in his gospel are in nameless crowds—and even many of the individuals healed remain nameless.

---

15. Middleton, *A Free Inquiry*, 101.
16. Middleton, *A Free Inquiry*, 22–24.

eleven

B. B. WARFIELD PRODUCES THE FINAL FORM OF CESSATIONISM

The cessationist argument reached it apex when the "Lion of Princeton," Benjamin Breckinridge Warfield, entered the fight with his book *Counterfeit Miracles* in 1918. At the end of his life, Warfield used his immense learning and formidable intellect to prove that God had not worked a miracle since the days of the New Testament apostles. Warfield adopts John Calvin's three main points: (1) the purpose of miracles was evidential; (2) miracles have ceased; and (3) the miracles of the Catholics are delusions because God would never do a miracle in support of false doctrine.

Warfield squeezed these three doctrines into a far more rigid system than any cessationist before him. And he laid the groundwork for all cessationists after him. No one would improve on his arguments.

He divided the spiritual gifts into the "ordinary" and the "extraordinary." The latter, the "distinctly miraculous," were given only to the apostles and those on whom the apostles laid their hands. He maintained that the purpose of the miraculous gifts of the Spirit was to confirm the apostles as trustworthy teachers of doctrine, and since we have their doctrine in the New Testament, there is no longer a reason for God to do miracles. He asserted that the history of the church after the death of the apostles contained no true miracles, for most miraculous reports came from Catholics, and Warfield was certain that God would never do a miracle to support Catholic doctrine or practice.[1]

The fact that so many people continued to believe in miracles throughout the history of church Warfield attributes to "the curious power which preconceived theory has to blind men to facts."[2]

Regarding the New Testament doctrine on spiritual gifts, Warfield was Calvin's disciple. He offered not even a sliver of scriptural evidence to prove that the purpose of the spiritual gifts was to authenticate the apostles as trustworthy teachers of Scripture. He simply asserted it, for Warfield had fallen victim to "the curious power which preconceived theory has to blind men to facts." He was on a mission to save people from the Roman Catholic Church and from the faith healers of his day and to protect the authority of Scripture. Warfield did not search Scripture or history to find truth. He already knew the truth. Miracles had to cease. Otherwise the Catholics and faith healers might be right, and the Scriptures might be compromised by some new revelation.

---

1. See B. B. Warfield, *Counterfeit Miracles* (1918; repr., Edinburgh: Banner of Truth, 1972), 6; see www.biblestudytools.com/classics/warfield-counterfeit-miracles.

2. Warfield, *Counterfeit Miracles*, 15.

If you want to know what the Scriptures teach about the miraculous gifts, you won't find out by reading Warfield. Here's what you do. You open up your Greek New Testament and look up every occurrence or teaching about the miraculous. You make a list of all the verbs of healing, then the nouns of healing, every reference to anything miraculous, all the spiritual gifts, every reference to the demonic, and so on. You let nothing fall through the cracks. Then you take your list and make notes about the content and purpose of each supernatural act or each teaching about the supernatural. And you do it with an open mind. And you will be overwhelmed with how little you really know about the miraculous ministry of the Spirit of God.

Then you pray, "Father, open thou mine eyes, that I may behold wonderous things out of thy law."[3] And I can guarantee you that you will never believe that the purpose of the gifts of the Spirit was to authenticate the apostles as trustworthy teachers of doctrine. I did this at the beginning of 1986, while still a professor of Old Testament Exegesis and Semitic Languages at Dallas Seminary. Warfield had been one of my heroes for fifteen years. Four months later, I knew I had been duped. I cannot find any evidence in the writing of Warfield that he has ever done a thorough study like this, nor can I find a single story in Warfield's writing of him ever praying for a sick person. No theologian in the history of the church has done more to discourage prayer for the sick than the Lion of Princeton.

Warfield repeatedly speaks of the apostles having the "*charismata.*" This is a massive blunder. The Greek word *charisma* is not even used in the Gospels or Acts. The New Testament

---

3. Psalm 119:18 KJV.

does not ascribe the healing ministry of the apostles to their possession of the miraculous *charismata*, but to the ministry of signs and wonders.[4] Warfield does not produce a single verse that teaches the *charismata* would cease with the death of the apostles. Scripture tells us that the gifts like tongues and prophecy will cease when Jesus brings the final perfect form of his kingdom (1 Corinthians 13:9).

Warfield alleges that the only times the miraculous *charismata* were given without the laying on of hands by an apostle were at Pentecost and in Cornelius's house. But Ananias laid his hands on Paul (Acts 9:17) so he could be healed and receive the Holy Spirit. Warfield claimed that this "is no exception, as is sometimes said; Ananias worked a miracle on Paul but did not confer miracle-working powers. Paul's own power of miracle-working was original with him as an Apostle, and not conferred by any one."[5]

This is a dishonest reading by Warfield. He is not explaining Scripture; he is explaining Scripture away. Even Warfield's explanation contradicts his theory that only the apostles worked miracles and those on whom they laid their hands. There is no record of any apostle laying their hands on Ananias, yet Warfield admits that he worked a miracle on Paul. Acts 9:17 says more than that. When Ananias laid his hands on Paul, he said, "Brother Saul, the Lord—Jesus, who appeared to you on the road as you were coming here—has sent me so that you may see again and be filled with the Holy Spirit." Paul was filled

---

4. For the contrast between spiritual gifts and the ministry of signs and wonders, see the section titled "The Ministry of Signs and Wonders Is Greater Than the Gift of Healing" in chapter 8.

5. Warfield, *Counterfeit Miracles*, 143n48.

with the Holy Spirit—a filling that included both prophetic and miracle-working power, like the blinding of the sorcerer Elymas (Acts 13:11). And Paul both received the Spirit and was filled with the Spirit through Ananias. Luke could not have made it any clearer. Only a person blinded by a "preconceived theory" could fail to see it.

The New Testament teaches that every single Christian receives at least one spiritual gift (1 Corinthians 7:7; 12:7, 11; 1 Peter 4:10). The miraculous gifts of the Spirit were already in operation in the church in Rome before any apostle visited there (Romans 12:6–8). It's true that Paul could impart spiritual gifts (Romans 1:11; 2 Timothy 1:6), but so could the elders of the church (1 Timothy 4:14). I've seen people with spiritual authority and prophetic gifts impart spiritual gifts. Years ago, a prophetic person told Leesa she would begin to have prophetic dreams. Those dreams started that night and have been a huge blessing to us.

The bulk of Warfield's book is his application of Conyers Middleton's historical method of debunking nineteen hundred years of testimonies to miracles. His conclusion is that since the death of the generation on whom the apostles laid their hands, God has not done a single miracle. Warfield admits that God can heal sickness in answer to prayer, but this kind of healing is not miraculous. A miraculous healing would be the healing of a broken bone.[6]

Pierre de Rudder was a Belgian peasant, a Catholic believer, who lived in the small city of Jabbeke. A falling tree broke the tibia and fibula of his left leg. When the physician removed the

---

6. See Warfield, *Counterfeit Miracles*, 112–13.

bone fragments, the upper and lower bones were more than an inch apart. Eight years later, the bones had not joined. The lower part of the leg swung in all directions, and de Rudder hobbled about on crutches. He had to dress the suppurating wound several times a day.

Multiple surgeons pronounced the wound incurable, and Professor Thiart of Brussels advised amputation. Instead, de Rudder went to Lourdes in 1875—to the Oostakker Grotto, where he prayed before the statue of Notre Dame de Lourdes, Our Lady of Lourdes, the virgin Mary. As he prayed, he felt power moving through his whole body. He walked away from the statue completely healed.

Dr. Van Hoestenberghe, the physician who removed the bone fragments initially and treated de Rudder many times over the eight years, testified that it was an inexplicable miracle. Twenty-eight physicians, both Catholics and unbelievers, examined all the evidence. They questioned De Rudder's physicians and neighbors and unanimously concluded that it was a miracle.[7]

All of this information, and more, was available to Warfield. Here is his response.

> We have never seen a satisfactory natural explanation of how this cure was effected . . . We prefer simply to leave it, meanwhile, unexplained . . . After all, inexplicable and miraculous are not exact synonyms . . . We are only beginning to learn the marvellous behavior of which living tissue is capable, and it may well be that, after a while, it may seem very natural that Pierre de Rudder's case happened

---

7. The full story is told by Ruth Cranston, *The Miracle of Lourdes Updated and Expanded Edition by the Medical Bureau of Lourdes* (New York: Doubleday, 1988), 161–64.

just as it is said to have happened . . . We are willing to believe that it happened just as it is said to have happened. We are content to know that, in no case, was it a miracle.[8]

It is now one hundred years after Warfield wrote this explanation, and we do know a great deal more about "the marvellous behavior of which living tissue is capable." We now know with absolute certainty that bone cannot regenerate itself instantly. Twenty-eight physicians called this a miracle. But Warfield refused to call it a miracle because of a prior belief, a certainty that God stopped doing miracles after the death of the last apostle. And Warfield is equally certain that God would never honor the faith of one of his children praying for healing at a Catholic shrine.[9]

Warfield brought this prejudice against Catholics into his examination of church history. Most of *Counterfeit Miracles* is Warfield's evaluation of the reports of miracles down to his day. But it is not a real evaluation, for Warfield's theology rules out the possibility of miracles after the apostolic age.

Here is a brief look at how Warfield handled the earlier historic testimony to miracles. He acknowledged that from the fourth

---

8. Warfield, *Counterfeit Miracles*, 71–72.

9. C. S. Lewis, a believer in miracles, demonstrates why evidence alone can't persuade a person to believe in miracles: "Seeing is not believing. For this reason, the question whether miracles occur can never be answered simply by experience. Every event which might claim to be a miracle is, in the last resort, something presented to our senses, something seen, heard, touched, smelled, or tasted. And our senses are not infallible. If anything extraordinary seems to have happened, we can always say that we have been the victims of an illusion. If we hold a philosophy which excludes the supernatural, this is what we always shall say. What we learn from experience depends on the kind of philosophy we bring to experience. It is therefore useless to appeal to experience before we have settled, as well as we can, the philosophical question" (*Miracles* [1947; repr., New York: Macmillan, 1960], 3).

century on there are numerous eyewitness reports of miracles and that these eyewitnesses were not obscure neurotics but were "rather the outstanding scholars, theologians, preachers, organizers of the age."[10] In this connection Warfield mentions Jerome, the leading biblical scholar of his day; Gregory of Nyssa; Athanasius; Chrysostom, the greatest preacher of the day; Ambrose, the greatest churchman of the day; as well as Augustine, whom Warfield credits as the greatest thinker of the day.[11] Warfield uses Middleton's methodology to dismiss these respected scholars as unreliable witnesses to miracles. And when he is forced to admit that a healing did take place, he attributes it to natural means or psychological forces. Others have noted his biased treatment of the historical evidence and criticized him severely.[12]

Here's how Warfield dismisses the leader he respects the most. Initially, Augustine believed that the miraculous gifts had been withdrawn from the church. At the end of his life, he wrote a series of retractions, and one of the statements he retracted was this belief that miracles had ended. In *The City of God* (book 22:8), he said that in less than two years, he knew of more than seventy recorded and verified instances of miracles

---

10. Warfield, *Counterfeit Miracles*, 23.

11. Warfield, *Counterfeit Miracles*, 23.

12. For example, Max Turner ("Spiritual Gifts Then and Now," *Vox Evangelica* 15 [1985]: 41–42, https://biblicalstudies.org.uk/pdf/vox/vol15/gifts_turner.pdf) observes that Warfield's "book swings violently from a confessionalist, and somewhat naïve evidentialist, treatment of miracle in the apostolic age, to an extreme scepticism towards *any* claims of miracles in the church in the *post*-apostolic period, quite clearly dependent on Conyers Middleton. Had he shown the same openness—some would say credulity—towards post-apostolic claims that he evinced when discussing New Testament miracles, which of the miracles of the saints would not have received his defence, if not indeed his approbation?! And, had he turned the degree of scepticism manifest in his treatment of post-apostolic writers onto the New Testament accounts, what scant few miracles of the apostles (or of the Lord himself) would have escaped his sharp wit and criticism!"

in his city of Hippo. That is a miracle in Hippo about every ten days. And those miracles included raisings from the dead.

Warfield believed that Augustine had made a great contribution to the history of doctrine, but he would not accept Augustine's testimony on the miraculous. One of the reasons he rejected Augustine's testimony was the fact that some of the healings Augustine reported were wrought through relics, specifically the bones of Stephen.[13] Warfield never bothered to prove that these alleged healings through the bones of Stephen did not take place or could not have taken place. He never considered that the bones of Elisha actually raised a man from the dead (2 Kings 13:21). He never considered that God does much in Scripture that is strange. The prophet Isaiah, for example, went naked and barefoot for three years as a sign against Egypt and Cush (Isaiah 20:3). The prophet Hosea was commanded to marry a prostitute (Hosea 1:2). Peter's shadow healed the sick people on whom it fell (Acts 5:15). Handkerchiefs and aprons that touched Paul's body healed the sick and drove out demons (Acts 19:12). If any of these things had happened after the apostolic age, Warfield would have written them off as superstition, products of a deranged mind.

When I parted company with Warfield, Leesa and I began to have supernatural experiences, and so did our friends who joined us. People in our church told us stories of angelic encounters that they had kept secret from me because they were afraid I'd think they were crazy. Angels first came to Leesa in her dreams. Our daughter, Alese, could see angels. This shouldn't seem strange, for God sends angels to serve those who pursue the Lord (Hebrews 1:14).

---

13. See Warfield, *Counterfeit Miracles*, 24.

In August 2000, we lived in our dream home high up on the side of a mountain in Whitefish, Montana. Leesa was lying on our bed in the afternoon praying for God to change her. Suddenly, an elderly woman dressed in blue stood beside her bed. She placed her hands on Leesa's forehead and pressed three times. Then she laid her hands on Leesa's cheeks and did the same.

She said, "If you want to change, now is the time to change." Leesa was overwhelmed by the love and authority she felt from the woman. Then the woman said, "I have to go now." And Leesa watched her float up through the ceiling and out of our house.

When I came home, she told me what had happened. Neither of us knew what it meant.

That fall, we had dinner one night at the home of our close friends John and Ingrid. Ingrid said, "I don't understand this, but this week the Lord told me to begin praying about your departure from Whitefish because you are going to leave here in great pain." Even though Ingrid had on occasion spoken impressive prophetic words that had come true, I didn't give much thought to this word. I didn't think I would ever leave the paradise of Whitefish.

At the beginning of December 2000, we were in the mountains of Moravian Falls, North Carolina, at a conference. I left our cabin early in the morning, and Leesa slept in. Leesa was awakened by a young woman standing at the foot of the bed massaging her feet through the covers. She was dressed in a beautiful, multicolored robe. Leesa said, "Would you leave a piece of your robe here so I can show Jack?" The angel smiled and disappeared. We understood none of this.

We lost our second-born son, Scott, to a drugged-out suicide in our home in the dark morning hours of December 27, 2000. We left Montana three days later and fell into a new world that was darker and more unforgiving than any we had ever known. Leesa sank into an abyss of grief and demonic condemnation. Just about everything that could go wrong went wrong. God did not take away our pain. He came down into it with us and redeemed it little by little.

Years later, I understood the purpose of Leesa's angelic visits in those months before we lost Scott. The angel pressed her hands on Leesa's forehead to impart protection against the devil's assault on Leesa's mind following Scott's death. Her hands on Leesa's cheeks imparted protection to limit the damage Leesa's tears could do to her. The angel who massaged her feet imparted strength to Leesa to walk through the greatest darkness she would ever know. And the Lord called Ingrid, one of our closest friends, to pray for grace for us to walk through our greatest trial months ahead of that trial. The Lord prayed for Peter before his greatest trial so that Peter's faith would not fail (Luke 22:31–32). When the devil came to sift us, the Lord did the same for us by sending angels and prayers ahead of time so that our faith might not fail.

twelve

CONCLUSIONS REGARDING CESSATIONIST ARGUMENTS

This is my last chapter on cessationism. I have covered four hundred years of theological controversy in three chapters. In this chapter, only one scriptural text and one argument need to be evaluated. Before doing that, here is a summary of my critique of cessationism thus far.

SUMMARY OF THE ARGUMENTS AGAINST CESSATIONISM

The major biblical problem for the cessationists is that there is not a single verse of Scripture stating that God will withdraw the miraculous gifts of the Spirit before Jesus returns to establish his kingdom on the earth.[1] This means they are reduced to using a theological argument to prove that the miraculous gifts had a temporary purpose and once that purpose was fulfilled, there was no reason for God to leave the miraculous gifts in the church.

Here is their main argument. God empowered the apostles to do miracles, and those miracles authenticated the apostles as trustworthy teachers of doctrine. We have their doctrine in the completed New Testament, so there is no longer a need for miracles. Therefore, miracles ceased with the death of the apostles and those on whom they laid their hands. This means the ultimate purpose of miracles was to authenticate Scripture, to prove it is from God.

Here are the problems with that argument. No verse of Scripture says that miracles "authenticated" the apostles.[2]

---

1. Hebrews 2:3–4 is frequently used by cessationists to prove that miracles ceased with the apostles. The author of Hebrews asks us, "How shall we escape if we ignore so great a salvation? This salvation, which was first announced by the Lord, was confirmed to us by those who heard him. God also testified to it by signs, wonders and various miracles, and by gifts of the Holy Spirit distributed according to his will." The author of Hebrews is not limiting this text to the apostles. He does not say the message was confirmed by the apostles, but that the message was confirmed "by those who heard" the Lord. The apostles were not the only ones who heard the Lord. Others heard him also, and others did miracles and received the gifts of the Spirit. The writer of Hebrews is saying that neither he nor his audience heard the Lord directly or saw his miracles directly. They first heard the message about the Lord Jesus through "those who heard him" directly. When they heard this message, God confirmed it by working signs and wonders through the group that preached to them. It could have been the apostles who preached to them, but it also could have been others who had originally heard the Lord. It is certain that the recipients of Hebrews had experienced miracles, for they had tasted "the powers of the coming age" (Hebrews 6:5). Thus, miracles were happening at the time of the writing of Hebrews. The translation "gifts of the Holy Spirit" in the NIV and ESV is misleading. The writer did not use *charisma*, the normal word for spiritual gifts. He used the rare word *merismos*, which means "distribution." By using the phrase "distributions of the Holy Spirit," the writer includes not only spiritual gifts but other powerful works of the Spirit as well.

2. When Luke described the ministry of Paul and Barnabas at Iconium, he said that the Lord "confirmed the message of his grace by enabling them to perform signs and wonders" (Acts 14:3). The Lord did not confirm the apostles, but rather "his word"

If the primary purpose of miracles was to authenticate the apostles, why did God let so many other people do miracles? Jesus sent out the seventy-two to do miracles. Stephen and Philip did signs and wonders. The gifts of prophecy, tongues, healing, and miracles were distributed all over the first-century church.[3] This makes no sense if the primary purpose of miracles was to authenticate the apostles.

Only three of the original twelve apostles wrote Scripture, and almost half of the New Testament was written by people who were not apostles and have no recorded miracles. If apostolic miracles confirmed Scripture, this would mean that almost one half of the New Testament is unconfirmed and therefore inferior to the part written by the apostles.[4]

Miracles do not authenticate the Bible. Scripture is self-authenticating and judges the authenticity of miracles.[5] The Scriptures lists ten to twelve purposes of miracles, none of which have anything to do with authenticating Scripture or smoothing the historical transition from the Old Testament way of worshiping God to the New Testament way of worshiping

or "the message" that the apostles were preaching. The miraculous confirmation of the preaching of the gospel message was the major factor in the rapid growth of Christianity in the first three centuries.

3. For the scriptural references showing the wide distribution of the miraculous gifts across the first-century church, see footnote 2 in chapter 8.

4. The books that weren't written by apostles are the gospels of Mark and Luke and the books of Acts, Hebrews, and Jude. These constitute 40 percent of the New Testament.

5. This is what the Westminster Confession of Faith teaches: "The authority of the Holy Scripture, for which it ought to be believed, and obeyed, dependeth not upon the testimony of any man, or Church; but wholly upon God (who is truth itself) the author thereof: and therefore it is to be received, because it is the Word of God" (1.4). Moses confirmed this when he wrote that if a prophet or a dreamer of dreams gave a sign or a wonder and it came to pass, they were to ignore that miracle if it contradicted what had already been revealed to them (Deuteronomy 13:1–5). Scripture is not confirmed by miracles. Scripture judges miracles.

God. The purpose of the New Testament miracles is rooted in the eternal character of God, demonstrating that miracles will continue until Jesus returns.[6]

Some argue that 2 Corinthians 12:12 teaches that signs and wonders authenticate the apostles, but the context of the verse makes that interpretation unlikely. Paul defended his apostleship and ministry to the Corinthians in 2 Corinthians 10:1–12:21. False apostles had turned some of the Corinthians against Paul. They said that Paul's "speaking amounts to nothing" (10:10). They preached a different Jesus than the Jesus Paul preached, and the false apostles took advantage of the church financially. Paul reminded the Corinthians that he took no money from them (11:7–12). The main proof of his apostleship was the sufferings he endured for Christ and the gospel (11:16–33). His second proof was the "surpassingly great revelations" the Lord gave him (12:7).

Paul summarizes his defense with 2 Corinthians 12:12. The NIV's translation here is misleading: "I persevered in demonstrating among you the marks of a true apostle, including signs, wonders and miracles." I believe the ESV renders the verse more accurately: "The signs of a true apostle were performed among you with utmost patience, with signs and wonders and mighty works." In this passage, Paul uses *sign* (*semeion*) in two different ways. The first use of *sign* in the phrase "signs of a true apostle" cannot refer to miracles, for then Paul would be saying that "the miracles of an apostle were done among you with signs and wonders and miracles." What would be the point of saying the miracles of an apostle were done with . . . miracles? The first use

---

6. For a discussion on the purposes of miracles, see chapter 13.

of *sign* means "what is characteristic" of an apostle. Paul does not say that "the signs of a true apostle" are miracles, but rather that "the signs of a true apostle"—those things that are characteristic of an apostle—are *accompanied by* signs, wonders, and miracles.[7] If Paul had meant that the signs of his apostleship were the signs and wonders and miracles, he would have used a different construction in the Greek language.[8]

So what were the signs of Paul's apostleship? In the immediate context, Paul's suffering was the number one sign (2 Corinthians 11:16–33). The false apostles did not suffer for Jesus. When Jesus called Paul to be an apostle, he showed Paul that lifelong suffering would characterize his apostolic ministry (Acts 9:16). Paul frequently appealed to his suffering as a vindication of his apostleship (1 Corinthians 4:9–13; 2 Corinthians 6:3–10; Galatians 6:3–10). His second appeal was the great revelations he had received from God (2 Corinthians 12:1–10). The false apostles did not have heavenly revelations. The sense of 2 Corinthians 12:12 is that the things that demonstrated Paul's apostolic authority—suffering for Christ and heavenly revelations—were displayed among the Corinthians with great endurance and accompanied by signs, wonders, and miracles.[9]

---

7. "Signs, wonders, and miracles" are in the dative case and are meant to be taken as datives of accompaniment.

8. He would have used the nominative case rather than the dative case. See Ralph R. Martin, *2 Corinthians* (Waco, TX: Word, 1986), 436.

9. The commentators suggest a number of things that could be contained in "the signs of a true apostle." Paul does appeal to his blameless life, the call of God to be an apostle, and the effectiveness of his ministry. All of these are characteristic of his apostleship, but in the immediate context, he has singled out extraordinary suffering and revelations as the signs most relevant that will contrast him with false apostles. The commentators also point out that signs and wonders are not likely to be seen as the sign of his apostleship in this context because false apostles can perform "all sorts of display of power through signs and wonders" (2 Thessalonians 2:9; see Mark 13:22). One commentator argues that signs and wonders are the sign of Paul's apostleship because

WERE MIRACLES NEEDED TO LAUNCH THE CHURCH?

Some teach that miraculous ministry was the rocket booster to launch the church. The booster was jettisoned when the church became a major player on the world stage. Thomas Edgar expresses this view:

> The beginning Church was in a different situation from that of the Church after the first century. By the end of the first century the Church and Christianity were established in the major centers of the known world . . . The initial stages of Christianity, however, had no background from the human perspective. The message was unusual and astounding. A man executed in a very small country was presented as the Son of God, who came to die for all men; to those who trusted in Him, God would surely by grace forgive their sins. Few people outside Israel had ever heard of Jesus. He died before the Church was established. He was executed after a brief career. Such facts at least show the difficulty faced by the early evangelists. Who could accept such a message?
>
> However, the miraculous sign gifts put this whole message in a different perspective, since the miracles were evidence that the message was from God. The situation since the first century has never been the same. Missionaries

otherwise Paul would have left "the signs of a true apostle" undefined (see Murray J. Harris, *The Second Epistle to the Corinthians* [Grand Rapids: Eerdmans, 2005], 876). But Paul hasn't left the signs of his apostleship undefined, for 12:12 is the conclusion to the immediately preceding two lengthy discussions of the two most relevant signs for the context of this defense, namely, his extraordinary suffering and revelations.

going to jungle areas are referring to an individual with a reputation in the world, to a recognized religion and religious Figure, as far as the world is concerned. These missionaries come from groups of believers in countries where this religion is prevalent. It may be considered helpful by many to have miraculous confirmation of this gospel today. This may or may not be true, since full and well-testified confirmation has already been given by Christ and the apostles and is still ignored by those who live in countries where it is well known. There can be little doubt, however, that the need for confirmation at the beginning was greater than the need for this today.[10]

Edgar does not cite a single verse of Scripture to support his argument and fails to notice a contradiction in it. If miracles were beneficial for the growth of the church in the first century, why would they not also benefit the church in the twenty-first century?

Edgar maintains that after Christianity had become a *recognized* group with some *reputation*, it no longer needed the power of miracles. Who would trade the miraculous power of God for worldly reputation?

Finally, this theory demeans the power of the gospel. Although miracles do testify to Jesus and the message about him, miracles were never necessary in order for people to believe in the gospel. Edgar writes as though they were, at least in the beginning of the church. According to Edgar, the historical obscurity and novelty of the gospel message seemed to have required miracles to prove it. He asks, "Who could accept such a message?"

---

10. Thomas Edgar, *Miraculous Gifts: Are They for Today?* (Neptune, NJ: Loizeaux, 1983), 263–64.

For one, Lydia and her family had no trouble at all accepting this message as they heard Paul preach it without any accompanying miracles (Acts 16:14–15). In the first century, the Holy Spirit was perfectly capable of producing conviction and belief without miracles (John 16:8). John the Baptist's ministry also brought conviction and repentance to huge crowds, but John did no miracles (John 10:41). The gospel is the power of God that brings salvation and does not require other miracles to capture the hearts of sinful people.

The greatest miracle in the world is that God loves us and his Son died for us. His love for us is, and forever will remain, an inexplicable mystery. The most amazing supernatural event ever to occur was the incarnation and then the death of the eternal Son in the place of sinful humanity, followed by his bodily resurrection. The greatest gift is eternal life by faith alone in Jesus Christ. The greatest power any human will ever know is the power of the cross of Jesus Christ.

I believe that miracles can open doors wide for preaching the gospel and can bring people to repentance. However, the simple preaching of the gospel could do all of these things *without* miracles at any time in history and can still do them today. When miracles are given by God to authenticate gospel preaching, they are given on the basis of grace, not out of a divine necessity to make up for a deficiency in the gospel message. Miracles are a gracious gift from God that serve many functions. Sometimes the only reason given for a New Testament healing or miracle is that God had compassion on the suffering one.

On October 2, 2005, I sat at a balcony bar in a restaurant in downtown Fort Worth waiting for my dinner guests. My cell rang. It was my friend Bill Jolly, one of the board members of the

New Canaan Society. He was standing in the kitchen of another board member, Hal Rosser, who was suffering from a severe case of Bell's palsy.

Bell's palsy paralyzes and disfigures one side of the face. In rare cases, it can paralyze both sides of the face. Its cause is unknown, and there is no reliable treatment for it. Additional anxiety is created by its unpredictable duration. It can last weeks or forever. Hal had been tormented by it for eight weeks. When he tried to work, he drooled on his papers.

"Jack, Hal is suffering. Would you pray for him?" asked Bill.

"Sure. Bill, put your phone on speaker. Now put your hand on Hal's cheek," I said.

I prayed a simple prayer for Hal's healing.

Hal felt the left side of his face heat up. He was instantly healed.

The compassion of God had flown sixteen hundred miles to the kitchen of Hal Rosser in New Canaan, Connecticut. Or as the psalmist said, the Lord "sent out his word and healed them" (Psalm 107:20).

thirteen

WHY GOD HEALS

Why did God heal? It's a simple question, but sometimes we professional Christians have a habit of making simple things complicated. We kick up a cloud of dust and then complain that we can't see. Healing must have been important to Jesus because he did a lot of it. He taught his disciples to heal, and they taught their disciples to heal. God loves to make wrong things right in our bodies, souls, and spirits, regardless of where we are in our spiritual journeys.

When I first studied every healing and miracle story in the New Testament, I was overwhelmed by the purity and simplicity of the supernatural ministry of the Holy Spirit. God did not heal to show that the apostles were trustworthy teachers of doctrine so we could have confidence in the Bible and make the transition to a new way of worshiping God. The reason for healing did not lay in a historical transition, but in the eternal character of God.

Sometimes Jesus heals just because he is asked. It can be that simple.

Mark told the story of Jesus healing a deaf and mute man

(Mark 7:31–37). The only reason given in the story for Jesus' healing of the man was that some people had asked him to do it.[1]

GOD HEALS BECAUSE HE HAS COMPASSION

Jesus heals because he has compassion on the sick and hurting. A typical incident is recorded in Matthew 14:13–14:

> When Jesus heard what had happened, he withdrew by boat privately to a solitary place. Hearing of this, the crowds followed him on foot from the towns. When Jesus landed and saw a large crowd, he had compassion on them and healed their sick.

Compassion motivated Jesus to heal a man who had leprosy (Mark 1:41–42), a boy possessed by an impure spirit (Mark 9:22), and two men who were blind (Matthew 20:34), and even to raise a widow's son from the dead (Luke 7:11–17). In Matthew, the feeding of the four thousand is motivated not by a desire on Jesus' part to demonstrate that he is the bread of life, but by his compassion for the multitude (Matthew 15:32).[2] Likewise, Jesus healed those who were blind (Matthew 9:27–31; 20:29–34), possessed

---

1. The Gospels and Acts teach theology through stories. For example, in Acts, Luke doesn't offer sermons on prayer. He tells stories that demonstrate the power of prayer in eighteen of his twenty-eight chapters. Some of those chapters have multiple references to prayer. Acts 10 has six explicit references to prayer. Over and over, Luke shows us what happens when the people of God pray. The healing and miracle narratives show us a variety of reasons why God heals and the different ways in which he displays his supernatural power.

2. The feedings of the five thousand and four thousand demonstrate that Jesus is the bread of life, but this is not how Matthew uses these miracles. The feeding of the five thousand (Matthew 14:15–31) is set in a context that emphasizes Jesus' compassion

by demons (Matthew 5:22–28; 17:14–21), and had leprosy (Luke 17:13–14) in response to their cries for mercy. Even the healing of the most severely demon-possessed person in the New Testament is attributed ultimately to God's mercy (Mark 5:19).

In Hebrew, the word for "compassion" is derived from the word *womb*. God feels about his people the way a mother feels about her unborn baby. She has tender longings for that baby and would die to protect her child. Like a mother carrying her child, God longs for his helpless children and is moved by our pains, and he waits for us to cry out to him for help (Isaiah 30:18–19). The sheer number of the texts listed in the previous paragraph demonstrates that God's compassion and mercy were major factors in the healings of the New Testament.[3] Jesus was touched by the pains and the sicknesses of people all around him. He felt the pain of a widow as he watched the funeral procession carrying

---

(Matthew 14:14), and the feeding of the four thousand is directly attributed to his compassion for the crowd (Matthew 15:32).

3. The most common verb used in the Greek New Testament to refer to God's compassion is *splanchnizomai*. This verb is used twelve times. Once it is used of the Samaritan's compassion for the wounded man (Luke 10:33); the other eleven uses refer to God's compassion. In two separate parables, Jesus uses this verb to refer to God's compassion in saving and forgiving sinners (Matthew 18:27; Luke 15:20). The remainder of its uses all refer to compassion as the major motivation for Jesus' healing and miracles. In nine out of eleven occurrences where this verb is used of God's compassion, it refers to the compassion of the Lord Jesus Christ as his motivation for healing. The nominal form of the verb *splanchnizomai* originally referred to the inner parts of a person—the heart, liver, and so on. It could be used of the inward parts of a sacrificial animal, but it became common to use this word in reference to the lower parts of the abdomen, the intestines, and especially the womb (see Helmut Köster's entry in the *Theological Dictionary of the New Testament* 7:548). Some theologians have felt that this term was too rough or graphic to be used in reference to God's compassion. Using the word for "intestines" to refer to God's compassion is akin to our using the word *guts* in modern English. Sometimes when we feel the pain of someone we love, we say, "I felt like I was kicked in the guts." Sometimes we actually feel a sharp pain in the abdomen when those we love suffer. I think the New Testament writers meant to convey in the same graphic manner how God feels about our misery. They were impressing on us the power and the force of God's compassion, which is rooted in his deep love for us and his sensitivity to our pain.

the body of her only son, and that compassion moved him to raise the son from the dead (Luke 7:11–17).

If the Lord healed in the first century because he was motivated by his compassion and mercy for the hurting, why would we think he has withdrawn that compassion after the death of the apostles? Why would we think he no longer feels compassion when he sees lepers or those dying from AIDS? Why would we think he is now content to demonstrate that compassion only by giving grace to endure the suffering rather than by healing the condition? When someone tells me that God no longer heals or gives gifts of healing, I ask them to tell me what happened to God's compassion. It is far more likely that we have stopped asking for healing than it is that God has withdrawn his compassion and mercy for the sick and hurting.

GOD HEALS FOR HIS GLORY

Sometimes the stated purpose for a healing is to bring glory to God. That was one of the primary purposes in raising Lazarus from the dead. Jesus told the disciples, "This sickness will not end in death. No, it is for God's glory so that God's Son may be glorified through it" (John 11:4). And then he said to Martha, "Did I not tell you that if you believe, you will see the glory of God?" (John 11:40). When Jesus raised Lazarus from the dead, he demonstrated that he was the resurrection and the life, and this demonstration brought great glory to God and to the Son of God.

This same purpose is also seen in the apostolic healings. Peter explained the healing of the lame man at the temple gate called Beautiful in the following way:

When Peter saw this [the people's wonder and amazement over the miracle that had just taken place], he said to them: "Fellow Israelites, why does this surprise you? Why do you stare at us as if by our own power or godliness we had made this man walk? The God of Abraham, Isaac and Jacob, the God of our fathers, has glorified his servant Jesus. You handed him over to be killed, and you disowned him before Pilate, though he had decided to let him go."

Acts 3:12–13

When Peter said the lame man was not healed "by our own power or godliness," he not only gave God the glory for the healing, but he set healers free from condemnation. Most of us who pray for the sick know that the power for healing comes from God, not us. We are less clear about the role of our own godliness in the healing. Almost every time I pray for someone, whether in front of a crowd or in a home, an evil voice attacks me, saying things like, "You should have been fasting; you should have been praying more . . . ," and it reminds me of specific sins. That articulate darkness is trying to rob me of faith by persuading me that someone's healing rests on my goodness instead of God's goodness. But Peter's words set me free from that trap. Every time evil speaks to me in this way, my mind goes back to Acts 3:11–12, and I'm free of that condemnation.

The healing of the lame man achieved its intended effect, for Luke later says that "they were all glorifying God for what had happened" (Acts 4:21 NASB). This was a normal response among people who observed the miraculous ministry of Jesus. They frequently responded by praising and glorifying the God of Israel. For example, Matthew tells us, "Large crowds came to [Jesus], bringing with them those who were lame, crippled, blind, mute, and many others, and they laid them down at His feet; and He healed them. So the crowd marveled as they saw the mute speaking, the crippled restored, and the lame walking, and the blind seeing; and they glorified the God of Israel" (Matthew 15:30–31 NASB).

This is also a major theme in Luke's gospel. The people glorified God when they saw Jesus heal the paralytic lowered through the roof (Luke 5:24–26), when Jesus raised the widow of Nain's son from the dead (Luke 7:16), when he healed the woman bent over double by a spirit (Luke 13:13, 17), and when he healed the blind man (Luke 18:42–43). Luke brings this theme to a fitting conclusion at the triumphal entry of the Lord Jesus: "When he came near the place where the road goes down the Mount of Olives, the whole crowd of disciples began joyfully to praise God in loud voices for all the miracles they had seen" (Luke 19:37).

Jesus expected people who received the healing power of God to glorify him. After healing the ten lepers and seeing that only one returned to give thanks, Jesus said, "Were there not ten cleansed? But the nine—where are they? Was no one found who returned to give glory to God, except this foreigner?" (Luke 17:17–18 NASB). These texts demonstrate that miracles were given not only to authenticate Jesus and his message but also to bring glory to God the Father and God the Son.[4]

This theme of glorifying the Lord through healings and miracles was prominent in the ministry of William Duma, a famous black South African preacher who was used in many notable miracles and healings until his death in 1977.

---

4. There was a similar connection in the Old Testament between the miraculous and the manifestation of God's glory (see Numbers 14:22).

Duma's reputation was so great that white people visited his church seeking to be healed by Jesus Christ. This was significant because it happened in a time when it was not acceptable for whites to visit black churches in a country controlled by apartheid.

Duma went on an annual twenty-one-day fast in complete solitude to gain direction from the Lord for his ministry in the coming year. Yet he would not credit his holiness as the secret to his healing ministry. The title of his biography, *Take Your Glory Lord*, reveals the real secret of his healing power. When Duma laid his hands on the sick to pray for them, his dominant thought was that the Lord would be glorified. And the Lord honored that desire with many notable miracles, including raising a young girl from the dead.[5] Like God's compassion, the purpose of bringing God glory is not rooted in temporary historical circumstances. God has always been concerned to bring glory to himself and to his Son. And healed people are still glorifying God today.

GOD HEALS IN RESPONSE TO FAITH

A woman who had a hemorrhage for twelve years sneaked up behind Jesus, touched the edge of his cloak, and then was instantly healed of her hemorrhage. Jesus felt power leave his body and turned to find the woman. When he found her, he said, "Take heart, daughter . . . your faith has healed you" (Matthew 9:22). It was the faith of a Canaanite woman that moved Jesus to heal her demonized daughter. He said to her, "Woman, you have great

---

5. See Mary Garnett, *Take Your Glory Lord: The Life Story of William Duma—A Man Who Lived in Agreement with the Holy Spirit* (1979; repr., Kent, UK: Sovereign World, 2000), 40–48.

faith! Your request is granted" (Matthew 15:28). What motivated the Lord Jesus to heal the paralytic who was lowered through the roof at Capernaum? The Bible says that "when Jesus saw their faith" (Matthew 9:2), he healed the paralytic.[6]

This same principle of God's healing in response to faith is found in the ministry of the apostles. Luke records that "in Lystra there sat a man who was lame. He had been that way from birth and had never walked. He listened to Paul as he was speaking. Paul looked directly at him, saw that he had faith to be healed and called out, 'Stand up on your feet!' At that, the man jumped up and began to walk (Acts 14:8–10).

GOD HEALS IN RESPONSE TO HIS OWN PROMISE

Another reason for believing that healing ought to be a primary ministry of the church today is God's promise to heal through the elders of the church. In James 5:14–16, God commissioned the whole church to heal:

> Is anyone among you sick? Let them call the elders of the church to pray over them and anoint them with oil in the name of the Lord. And the prayer offered in faith will make the sick person well; the Lord will raise them up. If they have sinned, they will be forgiven. Therefore confess your sins to each other and pray for each other so that you may be healed. The prayer of a righteous person is powerful and effective.

---

6. Technically, their faith led Jesus first to forgive the man's sins, and then, as proof that those sins were forgiven, he healed the man.

Why would God command the church to pray for the sick and promise the church healing if they prayed unless God intended healing to be a normative part of church life? Many Christians who believe in the infallibility of their Bibles hardly know that James 5:14–16 is in their Bibles. I taught seminary classes for ten years before I ever encouraged students to apply James 5:14–16.

Church members will never ask their elders for healing prayer unless they are taught to do so, and they will never have confidence in God to heal unless they are taught that God does heal and the reasons that he heals. As soon as we began to teach and practice James 5:14–16 with a little anticipation, God began to heal in our church. Ruth Gay, the woman I mentioned in chapter 4 who was healed of an aneurysm, was one of the first for whom we prayed. It is not only the elders who pray for the sick. In verse 16, James commands all Christians to "pray for each other so that you may be healed." If the whole church were to take God's command seriously, we would see a great deal more healing than we see presently.

In this chapter, I have cited Scripture showing that God heals:

- because he is asked
- because he has compassion and mercy on the sick
- to bring glory to himself
- in response to his promise to the elders
- in response to faith

The Scriptures also give other reasons that God heals. Although I discuss these in appendix 2, I will mention them briefly here:

- He heals to lead people to repentance and open doors for the gospel.
- He heals to remove hindrances to ministry and service.
- He heals to teach us about himself and his kingdom.
- He heals to demonstrate the presence of his kingdom.
- And he heals for sovereign purposes known only to himself.

None of these reasons are based on the changing historical circumstances of the first-century church. They are rooted in the character and eternal purposes of God.

I have learned these reasons by heart, and they have given me confidence to pray for the sick, even to hold the dead in my arms and ask God to bring them back to life. To the degree that any individual or church will align themselves with these purposes when they pray for the sick, they will see healings take place in their ministry.

fourteen

UNBELIEF

Unbelief is the major reason some Christians don't see healings and miracles today. Some unbelief is based on a theology that teaches God has withdrawn the gifts of healing and miracles. That's the form of unbelief I've been addressing in this book. But those who believe God still heals are susceptible to other forms of unbelief.

DOES GOD PROMISE HEALING TO ALL?

People in the Pentecostal tradition tend to believe it is always God's will to heal. They maintain that anyone who has enough faith will be healed. They use Isaiah 53:5 as a basis for this: "But he was pierced for our transgressions, he was crushed for our iniquities; the punishment that brought us peace was on him, and by his wounds we are healed." They feel this proves that the cross of Jesus guarantees healing to all who have faith. They point out that after Jesus spent a whole evening healing all the sick and demonized people who were brought to him, Matthew wrote that Jesus' healing ministry fulfilled Isaiah 53:4: "Surely he took up our pain and bore our suffering" (see Matthew 8:17).

It is not only healing that comes through the cross, but all of the blessings of God come through the cross. All of God's family will be completely healed and perfected in heaven. The question is whether the cross guarantees healing to all in this life. I cannot find this promise in Scripture, but I can find examples that seem to disprove this idea. Next to Jesus, the apostle Paul is presented as the most gifted healer in the Bible. Paul was imprisoned in Rome at the end of his life and needed Trophimus, but he had to leave him sick in Miletus because he could not get him healed (2 Timothy 4:20). Before he went into prison for the last time, Paul wrote this to Timothy: "Stop drinking only water, and use a little wine because of your stomach and your frequent illnesses" (1 Timothy 5:23). The apostle whose handkerchiefs healed the sick and who sent demons flying out of people back into the darkness (Acts 19:11) could not heal his spiritual son who was plagued by frequent illnesses and stomach problems. If Paul believed that anyone could be healed if they had enough faith, he would have encouraged Timothy to "fan into flame" the gift of faith. This is what Paul said to Timothy when his faith had so weakened that he was not using the spiritual gift Paul had imparted to him (2 Timothy 1:6). Instead, Paul writes as though he knows what most of us know as well: not everyone will be healed in this life.

Pentecostals also point out that in Scripture everyone who came to Christ was healed, so they conclude it is always Jesus' will to heal. I think they underestimate the uniqueness of Jesus. He was given the Holy Spirit without limit (John 3:34). No one in the New Testament, not even the apostles, healed like Jesus. If it really was Jesus' will that everyone should be healed, then why hasn't he raised up healers like himself who can bear the power of the Spirit without limit and inspire the necessary amount of faith in people for them to be healed?

There is a pastoral problem that is difficult to avoid if we tell people that God will heal them if they have enough faith. This puts the burden for healing on the sick person rather than on the wisdom and mercy of God. It can force a person to "whip up" psychological certainty for a healing that God may not be giving.

I spoke at a conference long ago in Centralia, Missouri, and I remember two things about the conference: it was a healing conference, and I was sick the entire conference. I had a miserable case of pink eye, a cold, and terrible insomnia. I can only remember one person I prayed for—a beloved man in the church, bedridden, in the last stage of cancer. He was lying on a hospital bed in his den, and a bunch of young people and I surrounded his bed. We laid our hands on his body. I prayed something like this: "Lord, would you heal our brother. Strengthen his immune system. Kill every cancerous cell in his body . . ."

After we prayed, I stood outside in the yard to talk with the young people.

One of them said, "Wow! That is the first time that's ever happened."

"What do you mean?" I asked.

"That's the first time anyone has ever mentioned cancer in his presence. He forbids people to say 'cancer' because he believes that God has healed him," said the student.

The man's skin and eyes were yellow. He was too weak to sit up. He had embraced a theology that forced him to live in denial and call it faith. I have heard it said to unhealed people, "God has the power. I have the faith. You didn't get healed, so there must be unbelief or sin in your life." Some have called this response "tough love"; I call it cruelty.

The responsible people I know in the Pentecostal tradition would never say anything like this to an unhealed person. They demonstrate that it's possible to believe that God wants to heal everyone and still treat the unhealed with kindness and sympathy. Many, many people have been healed and are being healed in the Pentecostal movement. I am grateful for this move of God, though I think there is a better approach to healing faith.

DOUBTING GOD'S POWER

For Christians, unbelief is doubting God's power, wisdom, or goodness. When I first began to pray for the sick, one of my church members brought a relative who had a large tumor next to her esophagus. It was thought to be malignant, but she hadn't had a biopsy. She was the wife of a local judge who had come to the church with her that night. Seven of us gathered around her to pray, while the judge stood off to the side, his back to us, enduring our prayers for his wife. I prayed silently, asking God what to do. *She doesn't believe I can heal her*, was the sentence that popped into my mind. I stopped the prayer.

"Do you think God has the power to heal you?" I asked gently.

"Well, I suppose God can do anything. He's God, right?" she answered.

"Yes, that's true, but do you think he has the power to heal your tumor?"

Tears welled in her eyes, and she said, "Not really. Maybe if we'd caught this sooner, he could have healed me."

I told her some recent healing stories and explained that God could heal at any stage of an illness. I saw a little light come into her eyes, and we prayed again. I think the outcome was good, but this happened more than thirty years ago, and I can't be sure. The reason I remember the story at all is that it is one of the few times I prayed for a person who doubted that God had the power to heal her.

DOUBTING GOD'S GOODNESS

For those of us who believe God heals, the most common form of unbelief we struggle with is doubting God's goodness. When someone prays for us to be healed, we begin to think of our sins, all the reasons why God shouldn't heal us. This happens even in our private prayer times, especially when we lay a big request before God. The bigger the request, the faster our sins besiege our minds. The Holy Spirit took John to heaven and showed him the key to this attack against our minds and hearts:

Then I heard a loud voice in heaven say:

"Now have come the salvation and the power
    and the kingdom of our God,
    and the authority of his Messiah.
For the accuser of our brothers and sisters,
    who accuses them before our God day and night,
    has been hurled down.

> They triumphed over him
>> by the blood of the Lamb
>> and by the word of their testimony;
> they did not love their lives so much
>> as to shrink from death."

Revelation 12:10–11

Satan accuses us "before our God day and night." He doesn't stand before God pointing out my failures. That would have no effect on God. He accuses me directly when I go before God to pray. Anytime I pray, a demonic power assigned to me points out my sins. Every time I stand before a group to pray for healing, I hear a voice saying things like, "You should have prayed more before this meeting. You don't care about people. You just want people to think you're awesome. Why didn't you fast? Why didn't you fast more? If you really cared about God's people, you would have . . ." That nasty voice will continue to speak as long as I'm willing to listen to it.

Some of the things the accuser says are true; some are partly true. Who has ever prayed enough or loved purely enough? When have our motives ever been completely pure? What the accuser is attacking is the goodness of God. He wants us to believe that God's goodness is contingent on our goodness. The accuser doesn't care if we believe that God heals, as long as he can get us to think that God only heals good people, not weak, immature, inconsistent people like us. The truth is that every time we ask God for anything, we are asking for something we don't deserve. We are asking for a favor that we can never pay back.

We overcome the accuser by placing our confidence in the blood of Christ. I can ask God for anything because I am a blood-bought child of God, and I am loved by him, regardless of the quality of my performance. When we come before God confident in the blood of his Son, he will often give us a "word of testimony" like the following.

In October 2017, I was a speaker at a conference in Oklahoma City, Oklahoma, sponsored by Bridgeway Church, where Sam Storms serves as lead pastor. One afternoon, after I finished my talk, several pastors came onto the stage to lead in a time of prayer. A large prayer team stood at the front of the auditorium. I silently asked God what we should pray for. The voice of the accuser said, "God won't heal anybody. You should have prayed more before you walked out onto this stage." I told the voice to be quiet and thanked God that I had been bought by the blood of Jesus and that no one's healing depended on my goodness.

Then I had an impression that we should pray for couples who hadn't been able to conceive.

Couples came forward, and the prayer team gathered around them to pray. I prayed silently for the couples. Out of nowhere the name "Rachel" popped into my mind. My first thought was, *Great. God is going to give someone named Rachel a child.* My next thought was, *You just made that up. If you call out the name "Rachel," no one will respond, and you will look foolish before all these people, and you will be the cause of people not believing in healing. You're just trying to look awesome.* I knew the second voice was the devil. God never warns me about looking foolish. I wasn't 100 percent sure that "Rachel" was spoken by God, but there was only one way to find out.

"There is someone here named Rachel. You haven't been able to conceive. God wants to give you a child. Please come forward and let us pray for you."

No one came forward.

A small group of folks had come from a church that was skeptical of the healing ministry. Rachel Gonser was in that group and had not been able to conceive. Her group gathered around her to pray. She didn't expect much until she heard her name called out. The group was so blown away that God knew Rachel's name that they did not come up to the prayer team until we pastors left the stage.

Nine months later, on June 28, 2018, Silas Gonser was born. I will never forget Silas's birthday, for he was born on the same day of the month as our firstborn, Stephen Deere.

fifteen

HEALING FAITH

Thirty years ago, I was on the pastoral staff at the Vineyard Christian Fellowship of Anaheim. I answered the phone in my office and was overwhelmed by a torrent of hysteria. I figured out the caller was Karen Hersom, a gifted member of our healing team and also our friend. Karen was in her first trimester of pregnancy and had just come home from an appointment with her physician. Her sonogram had shown that her baby had only one kidney. The doctor assured her that her baby would be able to function well with one kidney. Karen was so upset that she forgot to ask the sex of her baby. Then she found out that her husband's sister had been born with only one kidney and had some other severe complications. By the time Karen called, she was headed for the dark side.

I said to her, "Don't worry, Karen. We will pray for you, and God will heal your baby."

"Do you really think so?" she said.

"Yes," I said. "Just come into the office and everything will be okay."

"All right," she said. "Thank you so much, Jack."

As soon as I hung up the phone, I wondered if I had lost my mind. I was the leader of the healing teams in a famous church that prayed effectively and responsibly for the sick. I forbid the members of the healing teams to promise healing. Many people have been hurt by healers who promised a healing that didn't happen. Cardinal rule for all healing team members: Do not promise healing. I had just promised Karen Hersom healing.

"Lord," I said, "I hope that was you speaking to Karen and not me." And then I felt a peace about what I'd said.

When Karen came into my office the next day, my friend Steve Zarit and I prayed for her. She shook the whole time we prayed for her. Later she said it felt like popcorn was popping inside her womb.

Two weeks later, she went to the same doctor and had a second sonogram, and her baby had two normal kidneys. Sarah Hersom was born August 2, 1991, in perfect health. My internist said to me, "Jack, if there was only one kidney in the first sonogram, there is no way a second kidney could have formed later. This was a first-rate miracle." Today, Sarah is a nurse in labor and delivery at a hospital in Southern California.

HEALING FAITH IS NOT PSYCHOLOGICAL CERTAINTY THAT SOMEONE WILL BE HEALED

I had only been praying for people for four years when I told Karen that God would heal her baby. Back then, it was rare for me to know that God would heal someone before I prayed for them. That kind of certainty is a gift from God. No one can manufacture it. And the New Testament doesn't require it for people to be healed.

When two blind men requested healing, Jesus asked them, "Do you believe that I am able to do this?" They said yes, and Jesus touched their eyes and said, "According to your faith let it be done to you," and they went away seeing (Matthew 9:27–31). Faith for healing is confidence in Jesus' ability to heal. A man with leprosy said to Jesus, "Lord, if you are willing, you can make me clean." Jesus touched him and said, "I am willing" (Matthew 8:2–3). This story shows that faith is not psychological certainty that we will be healed. Although the leper had confidence in Jesus' ability to heal, he did not assume he would automatically be healed. When we ask for healing or anything else, we must always ask in the spirit of "if you are willing." I know that sometimes people use this phrase to mask their unbelief, but it really is the only attitude that is appropriate when we approach "the King eternal, immortal, invisible, the only God" (1 Timothy 1:17) with a request.

IT DOESN'T TAKE MUCH FAITH TO BE HEALED

Every time I speak to a group about healing, someone will ask, "How much faith does it take to get healed?" The short answer is, "Not much." Twice Jesus told his disciples that if they had faith as small as a mustard seed, they could do miracles (Matthew 17:20; Luke 17:26). I think Jesus was pointing his disciples away from confidence in their ability to follow him to simply having confidence in him.

For several months in 2003, I did weekly meetings in the

Dallas–Fort Worth metroplex with three hundred people. I taught them how to pray for the sick and how to hear God's voice. The sessions were a mixture of lectures and hands-on training. One night at the end of a session, I said, "I think God will heal bone and joint pain. If you have any joint pain, stand up and we'll pray for you."

A lady with severe carpal tunnel pain in her wrists and pain in her shoulders had come to the meeting at the request of a friend. She had never been to a meeting of Christians who prayed for healing. Her pain was so severe that it hurt her shoulder and her wrist just to carry her purse. She thought, *I doubt I will be healed, but I'll stand up anyway.* She stood up. No one came over to pray for her. She felt nothing. She wasn't disappointed because she hadn't expected much. She sat back down. I dismissed the meeting. She stood up and picked up her purse, but before she got to the door, she noticed that it did not hurt to carry her purse. There was no pain in her right shoulder or right wrist. Her left side was also pain-free. She realized she had been completely healed. How much faith did she have? Just enough to stand up during a prayer, but not enough to believe she would be healed.

While her faith was miniscule, those of us leading the meeting that night were confident that Jesus would heal people. He led us to pray for bone and joint pain, but he did not show us which individuals he would heal. He did not heal everyone that night, but he healed some. This is a common way that healing faith works for me.

When people don't get healed, I say, "I don't know why God didn't heal you. Let's pray for you next week and every week after that until you get healed or until God tells us to stop praying because he is going to give you grace to endure this." People aren't hurt by this approach. They feel loved and important because we care enough to keep praying for them.

IT IS GOD'S WILL TO GIVE US GRACE IN EVERY SITUATION

Faith is confidence in Jesus to do what he promised he would do. If he doesn't promise everyone healing in this life, what does he promise us? The promise I live by, the promise I pray by, the promise that has never failed me, is Hebrews 4:16: "Let us then approach God's throne of grace with confidence, so that we may receive mercy and find grace to help us in our time of need."

There is a throne of grace from which the world is ruled. The One who sits on it always gives what none of his followers can ever deserve—perfect mercy and grace to carry us through the worst times and the best times. We receive that mercy and grace by coming to the throne with confidence, believing that he will give us exactly the grace we need. Sometimes he will give us grace to shut the mouths of lions. Sometimes he will give us grace to be sawn in two (Hebrews 11:33, 37).

When I'm praying for myself, I rarely know which kind of grace he's going to give me. And from one perspective, it doesn't matter whether I get the miracle or the power to endure suffering. This life is only a vapor, a short series of trials personally designed by our Father to turn us into lovers who bring him glory and give him the right to honor us for all eternity.

God is a perfect Father. If he doesn't take away my pain but instead gives me the grace to endure the pain, it's because I need that pain. I have had pain I did not deserve. I've never had pain that I did not need. There are depths in the abyss of divine love that can only be reached by suffering for Christ.

I've shut the mouths of lions, and I've been sawn in two. And I've had deeper experiences of God's compassion and love in my worst sufferings than in my victories. If we stay with him in our pain, he redeems our pain and gives us the power to bring his compassion to those in anguish. I go into homes where families have been devastated and into hospital rooms where the prognosis is bleak. I don't go with a plan or a prepared speech. I go to listen to the hurting and to listen to my God and to bring his light into the darkness.

On May 16, 2003, I was the speaker for a men's ministry called the New Canaan Society. This group is all about friendship with God and friendship with men who are pursuing God. On that Friday morning, two hundred men huddled in Jim Lane's house in New Canaan, Connecticut, to worship God and enjoy each other. Afterward I met Adam Siburn, whose newborn son, Addison, was in the neonatal ICU. Addison was born on April 21, 2003, after only twenty-four weeks and six days in his mother's womb. He weighed one pound, five ounces. He did well for the first two weeks. Then on May 7, at two weeks, two days old, Addison crashed. His oxygen level fell, and his physicians put him on a ventilator at high settings. His lungs filled with fluid, and he was put on a diuretic. One lung collapsed, and he had pneumonia. Nine blood transfusions, a staph infection, weight loss—Addison was shutting down.

On Tuesday morning, May 13, Addison was three weeks and one day old. His nurse and doctor sat down with Adam and Meredith to tell them that their firstborn baby was very sick, and though they were doing everything possible to save him, they might lose Addison. The medical professionals who run the ICU and see death regularly have this talk with you when they're pretty sure your loved one is going to die. I've been in the ICU a lot and have been given this talk several times. No one in that ICU thought Addison would make it.

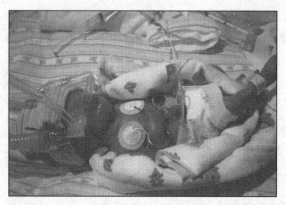

Addison wearing his father's wedding ring on his wrist

On Friday morning, May 16, Adam and his father, George, had come to the men's meeting hoping for help because the prognosis was so grim. As soon as I heard the story, I felt like God would heal Addison. I volunteered to go to the hospital to pray for him. Bill Jolly, one of the leaders of the ministry, went with me.

At the hospital, we put on robes and gloves. Addison was enclosed in an oxygen tent. He was the tiniest person I've ever seen. The physicians were kind and sympathetic. I reached through sleeves into the tent, placed my finger on Addison's heart, and prayed for God to heal him. Then Bill did the same. I said to Adam and George, "I think the Lord says that Addison is a miracle baby. He's going to be fine. He is going to improve.

If there is a setback, don't worry. He will recover and steadily improve and be healed." Then we left.

On Sunday, George, Addison's grandfather, was on his tractor mowing his field. He was so distraught over the possibility of losing his grandson that he got off his tractor and knelt down in his field to plead with God for the life of Addison. He heard an audible voice say, "Addison will be healed. Worship God and give him thanks." Today (2019), Addison is a healthy teenager.

Addison at age sixteen with two of his neonatal nurses

I don't think my prayers healed Addison. I think our great God looked down and heard the cries of a young mother and father, of his grandparents, of Addison's church, and of his father's men's group, and those prayers moved God to give them a miracle baby. My role was to bring some hope from the Holy Spirit into the neonatal ICU on Friday. And on Sunday, the day of resurrection, God sealed that hope with an audible voice from heaven.

By the time I met Addison, I had been praying for healing for seventeen years as a way of life. It had become common for God to speak to me about the people I prayed for. By then, it was not unusual for me to know that someone I was about to pray for would be healed. Everyone who finds joy in praying for the sick will see their faith for healing grow the more they pray for the hurting.

sixteen

DEMONIZATION

Right from the beginning, we saw demons manifesting in people we prayed for. This wasn't learned behavior. We had no one to learn from. We didn't look for demons. Like most conservative Christians, we tended to think all the demons had gone to Africa and China. We were only trying to get people healed of emotional and physical pains. Sometimes when the power of the Lord came on a person, they would feel something moving around in them or would choke and gag. Sometimes a spirit would speak through a person, but in a different voice. A sweet person would spew out vulgarities. We witnessed other supernatural displays that we don't talk about. From the beginning, Jesus warned us not to study "Satan's so-called deep secrets" (Revelation 2:24; see Ephesians 5:11–12).[1]

---

1. For a long time, the secular scholarly world has disbelieved in the reality of evil spirits. Genuine demonization has been explained away with various psychological diagnoses. That has changed. The *Journal of Mind and Behavior* 39, no. 4 (Autumn 2018), devoted the whole issue to proving the reality of demonization. In the first article—"On the Psychology of Demon Possession: The Occult Personality"—Mark Crooks demonstrates the inadequacy of purely psychological explanations. But he has written his almost ninety-page article in an academic style that makes for slow reading. The second article—"Crooked Spirits and Identity Theft: A Keener Response to Crooks?"—by Craig S. Keener, is superb and easy to follow. Both bibliographies are impressive.

I complained to my mentor, John Wimber, that since we set sail on this sea of prayer, demons came from all over our city to sink us. "No, Jack," he said, "those demons have been there all along. They were quietly ruining the lives of some of your people. When you all launched out in prayer, God gave you power to make wrong things right in their lives. Look at it like this: you all are cleaning a house that has been soiled through years of neglect. Eventually you will cleanse the house, and things will settle down. I see this pattern all the time. In the meantime, you're going to see some things you've never seen. Do not become fascinated with the devil's power. We are the ones with the power, not the demons."

When we couldn't make a demon leave a person, I called John Wimber. He always knew what to do. I studied every passage in the Bible that mentioned Satan or demons. I read some classic books on demonization.

If you pray for the sick as a way of life, you will encounter demonic resistance. There are some things you should know at the outset.

NEVER FEAR SATAN OR DEMONS

First of all, neither Jesus nor the apostles ever showed the slightest fear of Satan. No Christian should fear Satan. We are to fear only God. "Submit yourselves, then, to God. Resist the devil, and he will flee from you" (James 4:7; see 1 Peter 5:8–11). The key to overcoming the devil is submitting to God. Satan is not God's opposite. God created a beautiful and powerful angel who later rebelled against God and became Satan (Ezekiel 28:11–19).

Satan's opposite is Michael, the archangel (Revelation 12:7–9). *Satan* means "adversary."

We are never to mock or revile Satan (2 Peter 2:10–12; Jude 8–10). When people disrespect this powerful adversary, they give up some divine protection and suffer needless pain. Satan has become the god of the age we live in (2 Corinthians 4:4–6; 1 John 5:19). Demons are fallen angels who followed Satan in his rebellion (Matthew 25:41). Satan's ultimate enemy is God, but he can't hurt God directly, so he hurts what God loves. He sets traps for us in hopes of gaining ultimate control over us.

DEMONIZED, NOT DEMON-POSSESSED

Unfortunately, the English translations of our Bible do not recognize that there are various levels of demonic influence over humans. They use *demon-possessed* to translate the verb in Greek that meant "demonized," that is, "subject to the influence of a demon." Like English, the Greek language has different ways to turn a noun into a verb. Linguists classify these verbs as "denominatives," which is Latin for "from a noun." In English, if we want to turn *theology* into a verb, we add *ize* to the end of the noun and get *theologize*. The word translated "demon-possessed" is a denominative and should have been translated "demonized." The context of each passage specifies how much influence the demon(s) has over the person.[2]

---

2. The English translations and linguistic scholarly literature offer us no help here because most scholars have no practical experience in setting people free of demonic influence. In appendix 5, I list all the ways the New Testament expresses demonic influence and the ways demons can torment people.

DEMONIC TEMPTATION

Think of demonic influence on a sliding scale from one to ten. At one, I would place temptation. Satan and demons tempt Christians (1 Corinthians 7:5; 1 Thessalonians 3:5), but not all of our temptations come from demons. Our fallen human nature likely accounts for most of our temptation (James 1:13–18). But if a temptation persistently resists our prayers and often arrives with "supernatural" timing, it may have a demonic base.

From 1984 to 1985, I lived in Germany, and I was shocked to see how omnipresent pornography was and how openly it was displayed. After the shock wore off, my soul was assaulted by the desire for porn whenever I walked into a supermarket, train station, or news kiosk by myself. A force seemed to pull me to the table loaded with porn. Sometimes I stood by that table for a full five minutes, not opening a magazine, but unable to leave. After I had become a Christian, I had lived free from the desire for porn, but during my German year, the desire for pornography never left me. When I came back to the States, the desire left me. I now believe I was demonized for that entire year.

DEMONIC ILLNESS

I think most of our illnesses come from living in a fallen world. But some of our sicknesses may come from demons. I move demonic illness farther up the sliding scale of one to ten to a level four or five. Jesus freed a woman who was bent over by a demon for eighteen years (Luke 13:10–17). A physician would have diagnosed her with severe arthritis or a bone deformity. But Jesus saw the demon locked to her back.

During a conference in the United States, a leader of a mission organization in another country asked me to pray for him. He had a gastric condition similar to irritable bowel syndrome but worse, and his doctors could not find the cause of it. They worried that it might end his life. I laid my hand on his shoulder and prayed for him. Power came on him. He shivered and said to me, "Something just ran across my chest." When I heard that, I "knew" a demon was trying to kill him. I said in a calm voice, "I speak in the name of the One who has all authority in heaven and earth, the Lord Jesus Christ. You have to come out of him now." The man began to retch. I said, "I forbid you to make him throw up. Leave him now." Sometimes when an evil spirit leaves a person, they can feel it coming up their esophagus and out their throat. Sometimes they feel nothing. This leader felt the demon leaving, and I knew the evil spirit was gone.

After it left, I went into an automatic pilot mode, where I am speaking for God but the words don't originate in my mind. They seem to come out of nowhere. I said, "You are healed. The symptoms will take six weeks or so to go away. Don't worry about that. You are healed."

Four years later, I was leading a healing conference in another country. There were hundreds of people in the room. During the ministry time, I pointed to the back of the room on my right and said, "There's a woman back there who has something like irritable bowel syndrome. You have severe diarrhea that won't go away. Please come down to the front so we can pray for you." We prayed for her and many others that night.

After most of the people left, a man with a big smile walked toward me. "Do you remember me?" he asked. It was the leader of the mission I had prayed for years earlier at the conference. "I sure do. How's the mission work going, and how are you doing?" I said. He told me he was completely healed. It had taken about six weeks for the symptoms to go away, and they never came back. Then he told me that the woman I had called out with the severe diarrhea went to his church and had the same illness that had almost killed him.

DEMONIC MENTAL ILLNESS

Sometimes demons can cause a combination of severe mental and physical illness. I think of this as an exceptionally strong influence, maybe a seven or eight on the sliding scale. The biblical story of the boy who had seizures and often tried to commit suicide is an example of this kind of demonization. The disciples were not able to drive out this demon, even though earlier, Jesus had sent out the Twelve and empowered them to drive out demons (Matthew 10:7). The father brought the boy to Jesus, who asked how long the boy had been like this. The father said, "From childhood" (Mark 9:21). The word translated "childhood" can be used for a baby up to a child seven years of age.[3] Jesus rebuked the demon, and the boy was immediately healed. The disciples asked Jesus privately why they were not able to drive out the demon. Jesus told them that "this kind can come out only by prayer" (Mark 9:29).

"This kind"? What did Jesus mean by that?

---

3. The Greek word is *paidiothen*. Philo, the first-century AD Jewish philosopher, quoted Hippocrates, the father of medicine (fifth century BC), saying that the word could be used of a child up to seven years of age (Henry George Liddell and Robert Scott, *A Greek-English Lexicon* [1819; repr., Oxford: Clarendon, 1940], 1287).

DEMONIC INFLUENCE IN CHILDREN

In any army there are different kinds of soldiers with different assignments and different levels of authority. Just as there are rules of engagement in modern warfare, there are also rules of engagement in spiritual warfare. Demons can't just enter any person they please. Adults give demons a legal right to enter them by prolonged voluntary sin in certain forbidden areas.[4] Some demons are more wicked than others, and they have power to do more damage than others (Matthew 12:45). The demon that enters a child does so without the child's permission, and that demon is especially powerful. I have seen this happen, especially after a child has been traumatized by abuse.

A four-year-old girl began to wet the bed and have nightmares. The mother brought her to our prayer team after she found out that the babysitter was sexually abusing her daughter. We prayed gently for the child without mentioning demons or Satan. We held her hand and prayed something like this: "Father, thank you that you love Debbie so much. Would you please send the nightmares away and help her not to wet the bed anymore? We speak in the name of Jesus to these bad dreams and command them to go away." One of us prayed aloud, and the others prayed silently. The prayer lasted not much more than a minute. The child was healed.

Most of the time, a simple prayer like this will be enough to get rid of the demon imparted to a small child if the team fasts regularly and prays for the child right after the abuse started. The absence of the symptoms is usually evidence of the absence

---

4. I call these sins "demonic inroads," and I'll discuss them in the next chapter.

of the demon. One of the keys is to pray for the child soon after the trauma has taken place. If the demon is allowed to remain and integrate itself with the child's personality, then the story may turn out differently.

The young woman's life had been a disaster. She had come to us after her third stay in a mental institution, and she was so desperate for help that she had decided she would not hide anything from us. Her sexual immorality had begun early in her childhood. After the initial interview, we prayed, "Lord, show us where this began and what the entry point was for the evil one." Then we waited silently for the Lord to speak to us. These words came into the mind of one of the team members: *one, uncle, seventeen*. The team member asked her, "Do you have an uncle who is sixteen or seventeen years older than you?"

"Yes. How did you know?" she asked.

"It was just an impression. Is your uncle a good person?" asked the team member.

"No. Not at all," she said.

The team member told her he believed the impression meant that her uncle had sexually abused her when he was seventeen and she was only a year old. If this were true, it would explain why the sexual immorality had started so early in her life. An evil spirit had been imparted to her by an evil man when she was defenseless. We led her in a prayer of renunciation, confession, and repentance. Then we commanded the evil spirit to leave. It did not leave peacefully, but it left. It took several weeks of intense sessions to get the demon to leave. For the first time in her life, she felt consistent peace and joy. People who knew her were amazed by her transformation. I stayed in contact with her for almost a year, and she remained free and joyful that whole time.

Jesus said "this kind" does not go out except by prayer (Mark 9:29). The King James Version has "prayer and fasting," and the majority of Greek manuscripts also have "prayer and fasting," while the earliest, most reliable manuscripts have only "prayer." The majority of textual critics today reject the addition of "fasting" because the early church placed a high value on fasting. They believe a scribe or scribes sneaked "fasting" into the Greek manuscripts.

Though I'm not a textual critic, this is one place where I think the experts are wrong. The sober, biblically based literature I've read on driving out demons, written by people with practical experience in doing this, demonstrates that fasting increases our authority and power in driving out demons. I can confirm this by my own experience. When I know ahead of time that I will be confronting a demonic power, I fast.

DEMON-POSSESSED

In the next chapter, I'll offer practical help in driving out evil spirits. But I want to close with one last level of demonization on our sliding scale from one to ten. I would place the biblical story of the Gerasene demoniac at a level of nine or ten. Like the account of the suicidal boy with seizures, this story is told by all three Synoptic Gospels (Matthew 8:28–34; Mark 5:1–20; Luke 8:26–39). The man in the story lived naked among the tombs, cried out night and day, and had the supernatural strength to break chains. He often cut himself.[5] This case could legitimately

---

5. I think there is often a demonic power in the widespread practice of young children cutting themselves.

be called "demon-possession," for thousands of demons lived in the man. But even here, the demons did not have complete control of the man. When the demon-possessed man "saw Jesus from a distance, he ran and fell on his knees in front of him" (Mark 5:6). The last place those demons wanted their victim was on his knees at the feet of Jesus. The man still retained enough willpower to resist the demonic pressure to run away from Jesus.

He fell at the feet of Jesus, the safest and most powerful place on earth. When I pray for people to be healed and freed, I seek to do it from my knees at the feet of Jesus, and my goal is to bring people to that same place with me.

seventeen

DEMONIC INROADS

At a conference, someone asked John Wimber, "Can Christians have a demon?" "Sure," answered Wimber. "Christians can have anything they want, but who'd want a demon?" It was vintage Wimber. He always waded into controversy with a joke.

CHRISTIANS CAN BE DEMONIZED

The argument against Christians being demonized is based on the belief that Christ and demons can't inhabit the same home. Some claim that light and darkness can't dwell together. This is not a valid argument. Christ and sin dwell together in the heart of every Christian. Jesus is not defiled by the sin in our heart or by a demon that has found a way to hitch a ride in one of his children. Some say that demons can be "on" or "around" but not "in" Christians. This is silly semantics. Demons are not spatial beings. They are spiritual, personal, evil beings that look for open doors in believers and unbelievers. They are equal opportunity haters.

The woman who was bent over double by a demon for eighteen years was a believer. Jesus called her "a daughter of Abraham" (Luke 13:16), and when Jesus called someone a daughter or son of Abraham, he meant they were believers (Luke 19:9). A church member in Corinth was living in sin with his father's wife. Paul rebuked the church for not doing anything about this, and he told them that even pagans don't do such things. The apostle handed the man over to Satan; that is, he gave Satan permission to kill the man, that "his spirit may be saved on the day of the Lord" (1 Corinthians 5:5). This is a difficult passage to understand on a number of levels, but it surely refers to a believer who loses his life to demonic power.

Regardless of the position one takes on this issue, everyone would agree that demons can gain influence in our lives when we give them open doors of access. So what are these open doors or demonic inroads? The New Testament mentions seven specific inroads.

ANGER AND UNFORGIVENESS

"'In your anger do not sin': Do not let the sun go down while you are still angry, and do not give the devil a foothold" (Ephesians 4:26–27; see Matthew 6:14–15; especially 18:21–35; Mark 11:25; 2 Corinthians 2:9–11). The kingdom of Jesus Christ is founded on love and forgiveness (Christ's own example in Luke 23:32–34). Hell runs on the fuel of hatred and unforgiveness. When we consistently refuse to forgive, we give demons a place in our lives because we are agreeing with hell against heaven. The majority of demonization that I see can be traced back to a person's refusal to forgive.

In 1993, I did a series of conferences in the five major coastal cities of Taiwan. In one of those cities (I believe it was Hsinchu), the prayer team brought a twenty-four-year-old woman to me. Arthritis had crippled her hands. I took her hands in mine to pray for her, and before I prayed, I thought, *She is too young to have arthritis. Lord, what is the cause of this?* Two thoughts popped into my mind: *failed romance; fired.* I let go of her hands and asked, "How long have your hands been like this?"

"I don't know. Maybe three and a half years," she said.

"About four years ago, did something traumatic happen to you?" I asked.

"No. Nothing I can think of," she said.

"Did you go through a breakup with a boy back then?" I asked.

"Oh, I forgot about that. I did," she said.

"Who did the breaking up?" I asked.

"He left me," she said.

"About that same time, did you lose a job?" I asked.

She broke into tears. Her two best friends were her pastor and her pastor's wife. She had been the church secretary, and they had fired her for incompetence. She regarded that as the greatest betrayal of her life. This couple was at the conference, and it killed her even to look at them.

I quoted Scripture to her and explained that she had to forgive them. She had to stop wanting something bad to happen to them. I told her I didn't know who was right or wrong in this quarrel, but it was wrong of her to hold this unforgiveness in her heart. She argued with me for a while.

Finally, she said, "Okay, I'll forgive them. How do I do it?"

"First, ask God to forgive you for hating them all these years.

Then tell God that you forgive them. Ask him for grace to keep choosing forgiveness," I said.

She did exactly what I told her to do, through a lot of tears, in front of the five of us. Then I took her arthritic hands in mine and prayed, "Father, please uncurl these fingers." Within seconds, her fingers straightened, perfectly healed. We all laughed and cried and said, "God, you are so amazing!" I never recovered from that night. I have become a lifelong student of forgiveness. Forgiving is a skill that is not native to our hearts. We have to be taught to forgive and then empowered by God to forgive from the heart.

When I was a brand-new professor and preacher, an elder said to me after one of my sermons, "Jack, don't ever do that again."

"Do what?"

"Don't stand up in front of church and tell everyone you hated somebody. When the church hears that their pastor hated someone, they will think it's okay to hate people as well," he said.

"I told them I was wrong and that I was miserable while I was trapped in hatred," I said.

"Jack, that is not what they will hear. They will just come away with permission to hate. Besides, you didn't really hate the guy; you were just irritated with him," said my elder.

"Well, look at it this way. While I was irritated with that guy, if he had dropped dead suddenly of a heart attack, I would have praised God for his righteous judgments. If that is not hatred, it will do until hatred comes along." The elder thought he was a better judge of my heart than I was.

Many people in the church don't want to admit they are capable of hating others. I once listened to a fifty-year-old man raised in the church rant about his sister for ten minutes. I said,

"You need to repent of your hatred for your sister. It's going to make you sick."

"What do you mean?" he said. "I don't hate my sister. I just never want to see her again."

He wasn't joking.

Don't try to figure out whether it's hatred or only advanced loathing. If it's unforgiveness, it's hatred. Be inclusive. Call it "hatred," and everything beneath hatred will be forgiven. When I refuse to forgive, I want something bad to happen to that person; I feel spiritually superior to that person; I write them off as unredeemable; and I usually defile my friends by trying to persuade them to join me in wishing ill on that person. This is hatred.

Jesus said that saying the words of forgiveness is not enough. We have to forgive from the heart, or we will be tormented in a spiritual prison (Matthew 18:32–35). Sometimes the hurt inflicted on us by another is so great that we forgive in stages. Like peeling an onion, unforgiveness may come off in layers. As long as we keep choosing to forgive and seeking the grace to forgive, we stay out of prison. But harboring prolonged, voluntary unforgiveness and ill will is one of the surest ways to become demonized. I have seen it for thirty years.

Forgiveness means I surrender my wish for something bad to happen to a person, that I stop telling others how badly that person treated me, that I give up my desire for that person to admit his sin to me and ask for my forgiveness or make some other form of restitution, and that I ask God to forgive me for hating that person. Forgiveness does not mean I have to enter back into the same relationship with the person. Some people are too toxic for us to be around, or we may need more time to be healed of our wounds. The God who empowers us to forgive will show us how to relate to those we have forgiven. Forgiveness does not mean we should tell the person we have forgiven them. This is usually a bad idea that provokes another round of conflicts.

I pray the Lord's Prayer every day. I pray the version found in Matthew 6:9–13. Every clause of that prayer is indispensable for our friendship with the Lord. When I pray, "Father, forgive us our sins, as we also have forgiven those who sin against us," I also pray, "Father, show me whom I need to forgive." I pray this because the only sin that hides better than unforgiveness is pride. These two sins lie in the rocky depths of our deceitful hearts and usually can be detected only in the light of God's supernatural revelation. They are hard to detect, not because they are so small, but because they are such a characteristic part of our personalities.

SEXUAL IMMORALITY

Her home group leader brought her to our prayer team in the late afternoon. She was in her early twenties. Every single night for the last three months, she'd had nightmares. Her home group had prayed for her, but the nightmares would not leave. Sometimes she woke up from a nightmare and felt an evil presence in the room. She was terrified and paralyzed, pinned to the bed. She wanted to pray, but she couldn't open her mouth. She tried praying in her head, but her mind was confused. Finally, in her head she could think, *Jesus.* Each time she called out to Jesus in her mind, she grew a little stronger. At last, she could say his name out loud, and the evil presence receded.[1]

---

1. This experience is so universal that in the psychological and psychiatric literature, it is given the name "ghost crushing." Sometimes the bed will actually shake.

We bowed our heads and prayed silently, asking God to show us how to begin. The name "Don" floated through my mind.

"Does the name Don mean anything to you?" I asked. The shock on her face told me that it did and that it was not good.

"Yes, but I don't think I can talk about it," she said.

She looked down at the floor and sighed.

"That's okay. I understand. It would probably be better if we waited to pray for you. Sometimes the key to making nightmares leave is knowing how they started. This is my team. We're here all the time. We don't judge anyone. All of us fall into traps. When you feel like you can talk about it, call me, and we'll pray for you," I said.

I didn't know if we would see her again, but I was sure nothing would happen until she could confess her secret.

Two weeks later, she came back. She had gone with a girlfriend to hang out with a guy she had never met. They went to his apartment. He was good-looking, funny, and considerate. The girls were not big drinkers, but the guy got them drunk and then got them drunker. They both ended up together with him in his bed for the night. She left early the next morning, covered with shame. Evil spirits followed her home. The guy was in the occult.

She confessed. We prayed. A demon left, and her nights became peaceful. James said, "Therefore confess your sins to each other and pray for each other so that you may be healed" (James 5:16). It's that simple.

Sexual impurity is a major inroad for demonic influence. A whole class of demons is devoted to seducing and holding people captive in sexual immorality. They are called "unclean spirits."[2] Perversion led to the Corinthian church member being handed

---

2. Both the adjective, *akathartos*, "impure" (Ephesians 5:5), and the noun, *akatharsia*, "impurity" (Colossians 3:5), mainly refer to various forms of sexual impurity.

over to Satan for the destruction of his body (1 Corinthians 5:5). And not only perversion, but all forms of sexual immorality can open doors for demons to influence us. We live in a world that has lost the power to blush. This is all part of the demonic plan for taking the world captive.

In the last days, John saw a great prostitute with whom "the kings of the earth committed adultery, and the inhabitants of the earth were intoxicated with the wine of her adulteries" (Revelation 17:2). However we interpret the "great prostitute" in Revelation 17–18, behind the imagery of this prostitute is a demonic general who has organized an army of unclean spirits to make the world drunk with sexual insanity.

When I was ten years old, I heard Mom talking to Dad about seeing the movie *Cat on a Hot Tin Roof*, starring Paul Newman and Elizabeth Taylor. I walked into the kitchen and said, "I want to see *Cat on a Hot Tin Roof*." In 1958, my non-Christian, unchurched mom, who could out cuss any sailor, said to me, "No son of mine will ever see a movie like that." I knew better than to ask her why she thought it was okay for her to see it. Her answer would have been a backhand to my smart mouth. That day, a secret lust was birthed in my heart to see *Cat on a Hot Tin Roof.*

When I was twenty-one, I finally saw the movie. There was no nudity and hardly any profanity, and I thought, *What is the big deal?*

Today, I know what the big deal is. Sixty years after that conversation with Mom, I pray for the sweetest Christian teenage girls who are trapped in a world of phone sex and porn. Elementary school teachers in my church tell me about catching first graders performing oral sex on each other in the restroom. One out of every three little girls is sexually abused. Hard-core porn is a click away. The "big deal" is that it has only taken the army of unclean spirits sixty years to make the world drunk with sexual insanity, and it is worsening.

A world drunk with sexual insanity has some obvious benefits to Satan. Marriages and families are weakened. Children are traumatized. But I think there is a more profound benefit to the cause of evil. Christians who are trapped in some form of sexual immorality are shamed away from praying. And praying is the most powerful thing we do. God governs the world through the prayers of his saints.

When Jesus told his apostles how the world would end, he finished with a personal warning.

> "Be careful, or your hearts will be weighed down with dissipation, drunkenness and the anxieties of life, and that day will close on you unexpectedly like a trap. For it will come upon all those who live on the face of the whole earth. Be always on the watch, and pray that you may be able to escape all that is about to happen, and that you may be able to stand before the Son of Man."
>
> *Luke 21:34–36 (NIV, 1984 ed.)*

The Lord looked at his A-team that day and said, "Peter, you're the rock, but if you don't pray, dissipation will take you down, and you will waste your life on the pursuit of pleasure." Jesus said, "John, you're my best friend, but you will become a drunk if you don't pray." Not even the apostles could escape dissipation, drunkenness, and anxieties unless they prayed continually. Defiled people find it hard to pray. That is why it is the devil's plan to drown the world in a sea of sexual insanity, dissipation, drunkenness, and the anxieties of life.

VIOLENCE

A Samaritan village refused to welcome Jesus because he was on his way to Jerusalem. "When His disciples James and John saw this, they said, 'Lord, do You want us to command fire to come down from heaven and consume them?' But He turned and rebuked them, [and said, 'You do not know *what kind of spirit you are of*; for the Son of Man did not come to destroy men's lives, but to save them.'] And they went on to another village" (Luke 9:54–56 NASB, emphasis mine).[3]

That same murderous demonic power had found a home in the heart of the religious elite. They were determined to kill Jesus (John 8:40). Jesus said to the religious leaders, "You belong to your father, the devil, and you want to carry out your father's desires. He was a murderer from the beginning, not holding to the truth, for there is no truth in him. When he lies, he speaks his native language, for he is a liar and the father of lies" (John 8:44). Violence and murder are the marks of another type of demonic spirit.

She had dark circles under her eyes. She hadn't been able to sleep for months. She had violent dreams and was sometimes paralyzed at night by an evil presence. She hadn't committed any secret sin. She hadn't gone through any trauma she could remember. Her childhood was unremarkable. She had become a Christian in her teenage years. She was in her twenties, attended

---

3. The majority of the Greek manuscripts have some version of "And he said, 'You do not know what kind of spirit you are of, for the Son of Man did not come to destroy men's lives, but to save them,'" but the earliest manuscripts do not. Therefore, textual critics don't feel that this sentence was in Luke's original manuscript. Even if these sentences weren't in the original text, the fact that Jesus rebuked the brothers for wanting to kill the Samaritans for their rudeness suggests that their desire came from the evil one.

our church, and was in one of our home groups. The home group had prayed for her, but her insomnia was intractable. No one could find any physical or spiritual reason for the nightmares or sleeplessness. Her home group leader had brought her to my team.

After the interview, the five of us closed our eyes and prayed silently, asking God to give us the key to the young woman's freedom, and then we waited. I like to pray with a team of four or five people who are not only gifted to heal but also gifted at hearing God's voice. This multiplies our chances of hearing from God. It also takes the pressure off a single individual.

During the silent time, *horror movies* sailed into my mind. My first thought was, *That makes no sense.* But then it came out of nowhere, like most of the impressions that God gives me when I'm praying for people and don't know the cause of their pain.

"Do you watch horror movies?" I asked her.

"Well, yes, but they don't scare me or have anything to do with my insomnia," she said.

She was addicted to the most violent, graphic movies on the market. I told her I thought God was telling us that the horror movies were the inroad for the demonic nights. I asked her if she would be willing to give them up. She wasn't. The movies were her main source of entertainment.

"I don't think you can be free until you give up the graphic movies. If we prayed for you today, nothing would happen, and it would be harder for you to believe that God wants to heal you. Pray about giving up the movies, and when you're ready to do that, come back and we'll pray for you." Eventually, she came back and was set free in a single prayer time.

Movies influence us for good or evil. Who can watch *The Help* and not come away hating racism? Who can take in a steady diet of graphic violence on film and not become desensitized to it and eventually develop a taste for it?

Movies also reflect what's going on in the culture. The reason there are so many graphic films and sequels today is that we have developed a taste for violence. These movies could not have been made when I was a kid. We are growing more violent and more immoral, and it is all part of a diabolic plan to enslave us to evil.

The church can warn people about the trap, but our warnings don't prevent much evil. The church that prays for the sick and demonized can set people free one by one. But our world will grow more and more evil unless churches come together to pray. The promise God gave to Solomon is still in force: "If my people, who are called by my name, will humble themselves and pray and seek my face and turn from their wicked ways, then I will hear from heaven, and I will forgive their sin and will heal their land" (2 Chronicles 7:14).

We preachers can use our Sunday stages to rail against the evil of our world all we want, and the evil will grow stronger. Or we preachers can come together to lead our churches into the presence of God to pray and to repent, but that will take a miracle of the first order.

Four Additional Demonic Inroads

Four other demonic inroads are also mentioned in Scripture. I'll cover these quickly, but each of them is a topic worthy of careful study and attention.

First, there is the special hatred that makes us joyfully trample others. It comes in three versions: envy, jealousy, and selfish ambition. Envy is feeling discontent with our situation and resenting another who has what we want. Jealousy is stronger than envy. It is anger toward another who has what we feel we deserve but they don't deserve. Selfish ambition is the excessive desire that drives us to ignore the rights of others in order to achieve a status that we think will fulfill us. All three of these are ultimately anger at God for not giving us what we think we deserve. They are the opposite of gratitude and love. Illustrations of this hatred and its connection to evil spirits are found in 1 Samuel 18:8–11 and James 3:13–18.

Second, an obvious demonic inroad is found in all kinds of occult practices (see Leviticus 19:31; 20:6; Deuteronomy 18:9–13; Acts 16:17–18). Included in this area are imaginary friends. We have driven demons out of adults that entered those adults as imaginary friends when they were young children. I'm not saying that all imaginary friends lead to demonization, but some do. I tell all my young friends not to play this game with their children.

Third, the worship of anything other than God is called idolatry, and if persisted in long enough, it will give demons power over us (1 Corinthians 10:18–22). Greed is a form of idolatry (Colossians 3:5; 1 Timothy 6:9, where "trap" means the trap of the devil; see 1 Timothy 3:7; 2 Timothy 2:26; for a vivid illustration, see Acts 5:1–11). The trap of deferred joy—"I'll be happy when . . ."—is a form of idolatry. Looking to anything other than God for our ultimate happiness is a form of idolatry. The opposite is to learn the mystery of contentment. Paul wrote, "I know what it is to be in need, and I know what it is to have plenty. I have learned the secret of being content in any and every situation, whether well fed or hungry, whether living in plenty

or in want. I can do all this through him who gives me strength"
(Philippians 4:12–13). Paul found his ultimate joy in his friendship with Jesus, and in that friendship, he also found power over
life's circumstances.

The fourth is blasphemy, which is attributing evil to God
or slandering him in some other way. Paul handed Hymenaeus
and Alexander over to Satan to teach them not to blaspheme
(1 Timothy 1:20).

I think drug addiction is another inroad, though I don't know
of any unequivocal scriptural support for drugs as a point of entry
for demons. There is a good deal of practical experience to support this idea. When a person is drunk or high, the unacceptable
becomes acceptable. When we lose control of ourselves, an evil
power may try to usurp control.

SETTING A DEMONIZED PERSON FREE

How do we know if a person is demonized? The best way is
through the spiritual gift of "discerning of spirits" (1 Corinthians
12:10 KJV).[4] If a person has walked down one of the demonic
inroads long enough, it is likely that they will come under demonic
influence. I don't look for demons. I don't assume demons are
behind most of our pain.[5] My goal is to hear God and bring the

---

4. See "Discerning of Spirits" in appendix 1.
5. There are ministers who see demons behind everything. They usually believe
it is God's will to heal all our pain. These kinds of positions can be attractive because
they seem to simplify our lives and remove the mystery of our pain. Don't write off these
kinds of ministers as useless, even though this kind of theology can cause confusion and
controversy in the church. One of these ministers set a friend of mine free who was in
secret sexual torment. As long as we are in this broken world, every spiritual gift will

person we're praying for into the presence of Jesus so that he heals them. If a demon is behind the pain, it will usually have to reveal itself in the presence of the power of Jesus and the Holy Spirit.

I always use a team of three to five people to pray over the demonized. Each team should have a leader who starts with the interview. Five people all asking questions can be confusing and overwhelming. Team members can take turns leading or ask God to show them who is to lead in each time of prayer. One person should take notes of everything that is said or happens. Sometimes we will miss something important, but when we read over the notes, we may catch it. The notes can also serve as a legal protection.[6] The team needs to be unified. Demons will exploit strife on a team. Set a reasonable time limit for the session— sixty minutes or ninety minutes. Long sessions wear people out. Usually that demon has been there for a long time. Don't panic and think it has to leave in the first session.

If the demon resists repeated commands to come out, I assume it has a legal right to be there. The demonized person has been influenced by a demonic inroad for too long. We stop telling the demon to leave and ask God to show us what allows the demon to stay there. When we find out, we try to lead the person to repent. After the person's repentance, the demon will normally leave.

How do you know if a demon has left? In the New Testament, they frequently leave with some sort of physical manifestation. Sometimes they come out with shrieks (Acts 8:7) or

---

be abused. We should be patient with that kind of abuse and remember that we are not above misusing our spiritual gifts.

    6. In rare cases, a demonized person may threaten legal action against those praying to set them free. Keeping accurate notes and always praying with a team—never being alone with a demonized person—will protect you against bogus legal action.

with convulsions that can throw a person to the ground (Mark 9:26–27). I've had prophetic people on my prayer team who could see demons leave. Sometimes a demon will leave quietly, and you will know by the gift of discerning of spirits that they have gone. When we are driving out spirits, we are not on our own. We depend on God for revelation, and he usually guides through the whole process. Another way to know that a spirit has left is that the trouble the demon caused has ceased.

The more we pray over the demonized, the better we will become at it. Everyone makes mistakes in praying for the demonized, especially at the beginning. Overzealous people try to drive out demons that aren't there. People mistake mental illness for a demonic power. If we are loving, kind, and patient, these mistakes aren't a big deal. No one learns anything without making mistakes. Like every spiritual gift, the gift of discerning of spirits has to be cultivated to become consistently useful.

Don't pray for a demonized person alone. Never, never take a demonized person into a back room alone to pray for them.

Fasting increases our authority and power over demons. If we are not willing to fast, we probably shouldn't pray over the demonized.

Do not study the occult. The deep things of Satan can defile us (Revelation 2:24).

Do not get into a wrestling match with a demonized person. Neither Jesus nor the apostles ever tried to physically restrain a demonized person. I was once speaking at a conference abroad and walked into a gym where the prayer teams were praying for crowds of people, and I saw three big men on the floor trying to pin a small woman down. She was winning.

"Guys, stop it," I said.

"She's got a demon," one of the guys said.

"If she does, you can't make it leave with physical force," I said.

When they let her go, she rolled up into a fetal position and closed her eyes. I knelt down beside her, and without touching her, I said softly, "We really want to help you. If you want our help, you need to get up and sit in a chair. Or if you'd rather lie on the floor here and be left alone, you can do that as well."

She got up and sat in the chair, and we were able to pray for her.

I have prayed for a lot of demonized people, and although some of them have threatened me with violence, I've never had to block a punch or restrain anyone. Our power lies in Christ's authority, and the person who does not have confidence in that authority should not try to drive out demons.

In setting the demonized free, you may be exposed to some strange things, as well as to depths of evil behavior that have defiled demonized people. Don't talk about these things. Never talk about demons or Satan in a way that makes people fear Satan or makes them fascinated with Satan.

When the session ends, pray a cleansing prayer over each team member. Once I was driving a demon out of a woman brought to me by two of my seminary students. I listened to the most defiling things I had ever heard. My team wasn't with me, and I forgot about the cleansing prayer. I took home an evil residue from that encounter, and for the next week, I was tormented by the most hideous thoughts. Then my team prayed over me and freed me from that defilement.

In each session, be guided by the Lord, not by a paradigm. Our power lies in our friendship with God, not in formulas.

Getting rid of the evil spirit is usually the easy part of the healing. Healing the trauma caused by the demon and addressing the conditions that gave the demon access to the person can take much longer. No one gets healed or stays healed without being in healthy relationships with people who are pursuing God.

Setting demonized people free is a subcategory of healing in the New Testament (Acts 10:38). Most likely there are specialized gifts of healing for various illnesses (see "Gifts of Healing" in appendix 1). There may be a gift of healing that specializes in healing the demonized. John Wimber was exceptionally gifted in freeing people of demons. Yet he refused to call himself a "deliverance minister."

I've not had good experiences with people who consider themselves "deliverance ministers." Freeing people of demonic power is only part of the healing process, and people who think they are specialists in this area frequently fall into demonic traps.

When John Wimber taught about setting the demonized free, he used to caution his hearers about glorifying ministry to the demonized. He said, "Doing battles with demons is like cleaning out toilets. Someone has to do it, but no one in their right mind would brag about it."

eighteen

FILLED WITH THE SPIRIT IN THE GOSPEL OF LUKE

Christians have been trying forever to discover a paradigm, a formula, or a secret that will lead us to perfection in this life, or at least to a path that greatly minimizes the struggle of the Christian life. When I was a student in seminary, one of our graduates who had become a household name in the evangelical world told me that once I learned the secret of letting the Holy Spirit empower my daily living, I would find it harder to sin than to obey God. All I had to do was find the right button or lever to push, and I could enjoy life with God on cruise control.

A current, popular version of "cruise control" Christianity rests on "the filling of the Holy Spirit," which is sometimes used interchangeably with "the baptism of the Holy Spirit." According to this version, our early Christian walk is a series of struggles and failures. Then the Holy Spirit overwhelms us, either by baptizing us or by filling us, and we speak in tongues and then enjoy a new level of power. We love more. Our prayers are more powerful. We have more peace.

The New Testament picture of life with God is the opposite of this dream of easier obedience. Jesus' hardest struggles came at the end of his life. The night before he died on the cross, he was in such agony that he sweat blood, and God had to send an angel from heaven to strengthen his Son (Luke 23:43–44). At the beginning of the apostle Paul's new life, Jesus showed him "how much he must suffer for my name" (Acts 9:16). Paul's life in Acts is the story of overcoming increasingly painful trials. The reward for overcoming a trial is to be given a more difficult trial. The ultimate joy in this life does not come from a better performance, but from experiencing the affection of our God (Ephesians 3:16–19). Jesus did not fill his friends with his Spirit to make their lives better or easier.

As I read theology today, I am struck by how little clarity there is about the filling of the Holy Spirit. It doesn't matter to what theological tribe the writer belongs or to what level of scholarship the writer has climbed. I have yet to see anyone set out all the New Testament examples of the filling of the Spirit and draw the obvious conclusions.[1] It is not difficult. Is the filling of the Spirit the same thing as the baptism of the Spirit? Are these the same as the indwelling of the Spirit, the sealing of the Spirit, the anointing of the Spirit, the receiving of the Spirit, or the Spirit coming on someone? Do all these things happen the

---

1. The *Theological Dictionary of the New Testament*, one of the standard scholarly sources for the last sixty years for elucidating the meaning of Greek words and phrases, devotes only one confused paragraph to the meaning of "filled with the Holy Spirit" (*TDNT* 6:129–30).

moment we become Christians, or do they happen later after we fulfill certain conditions?

How would we know the answer to these questions? Just ask the Bible. Look up every single reference to the filling of the Spirit. Read every reference in context. Make a list of what each passage teaches about the filling of the Spirit. Then do the same for the baptism of the Spirit and so on. They may all be different descriptions for the same work of the Holy Spirit. Or they may be different works, serving different functions in our spiritual journeys. There may be some overlap between these works. Or they may be completely distinct. But we'll never know unless we study each work individually, carefully looking up each example of the Holy Spirit's work.

The most surprising thing is that all the New Testament examples of the filling of the Spirit occur in Luke and Acts. The only mention outside of Luke and Acts is in Ephesians 5:18, which is really not an example, for it is not the same Greek word used in Luke and Acts. Another technical detail needs to be kept in mind. Luke has two descriptions for the filling of the Spirit. He uses an adjective, "full of the Spirit," and he uses a verb, "filled with the Spirit." We'll start by looking at every use of the verb—*pimplemi* in Greek.[2]

The first reference comes in a promise from the angel Gabriel to Zechariah the priest. Gabriel told Zechariah that in

---

2. In Ephesians 5:18, the verb translated "be filled" is not *pimplemi* but *pleroo*. Paul is writing about a different experience of the Spirit than Luke is describing. There are a number of technical grammatical problems in Ephesians 5:18–21 that make it difficult to know what these verses mean. And Paul never tells us how to be filled with the Spirit. Apparently 5:19–21 lists the results of being filled with the Spirit. Maybe Paul means that we are daily to depend on the Spirit to draw us close to the Lord and that this dependence will produce the results of Ephesians 5:19–21.

his old age he and his barren wife, Elizabeth, would give birth to a son who would grow up to be "the voice" of one calling from the wilderness prophesied in Isaiah 40:3 and the "messenger" of Malachi 3:1. Their son would have the honor of being the forerunner of the Messiah. He would be unique from every child ever born before him, for, among other things, while he was still in his mother's womb, he would be "filled with the Holy Spirit" (Luke 1:15). How is that possible? We may as well ask how a virgin could give birth. Gabriel's simple answer was, "For nothing will be impossible with God" (Luke 1:37 ESV).

Zechariah doubted Gabriel and wanted proof that old people could have kids. Gabriel responded by taking away Zechariah's ability to speak for nine months. Gabriel didn't say what it might mean for a child in the womb to be filled with the Spirit. But the story doesn't end here. Six months later, Gabriel paid his most famous earthly visit to a teenage girl in a little hick town called Nazareth. What he said to her was even more unbelievable than what he had said to Zechariah. But unlike Zechariah, she believed Gabriel. So Mary was still able to have a conversation with her elderly relative, Elizabeth, when she visited her several months later. Elizabeth was six months pregnant, just as Gabriel had said. Here is Luke's record of the beginning of that visit:

> At that time Mary got ready and hurried to a town in the hill country of Judea, where she entered Zechariah's home and greeted Elizabeth. When Elizabeth heard Mary's greeting, the baby leaped in her womb, and Elizabeth was filled with the Holy Spirit. In a loud voice she exclaimed: "Blessed are you among women, and blessed is the child you will bear! But why am I so favored, that the mother of

my Lord should come to me? As soon as the sound of your greeting reached my ears, the baby in my womb leaped for joy. Blessed is she who has believed that the Lord would fulfill his promises to her!"

Luke 1:39–45

Here are some of the things we learn from this visit.

We now discover what it meant for John the Baptist to be filled with the Spirit while he was yet in his mother's womb. John's leap in Elizabeth's womb was caused by joy. John's joy was caused by the presence of his Lord, who also was in his mother Mary's womb. But we ask, "How in the world could a baby still in the womb recognize another baby in the womb, let alone recognize that the other baby was his Lord, the Messiah?"

In the world, of course, it could never happen. But John was not in the world when he made the connection to Jesus. He was *in the Spirit*. He was, in fact, filled with the Spirit, just as Gabriel had said. John was simply doing what all the prophets before him had done. The Holy Spirit would come on them, and they would speak about the One to come. The One no human could have imagined. The One whom the holiest person on earth could not have recognized. And the first to recognize him was his little cousin still in the womb of his mother. And John did this by the Holy Spirit—the only way anyone has ever recognized the way and the truth and the life. John did this earlier and better and with more authority than any prophet before him.

Beholding the Son of God is better than speaking in tongues. It's better than praying with power. It's better than serving effectively. It's better than doing miracles. I wonder how much joy the Holy Spirit got from showing baby John the Lord of the universe for the very first time. Seeing the Lord—what could be better? Maybe, just maybe, showing the Lord to someone else for the very first time. And that is why we are filled with the Holy Spirit—to show people an infinite Love that can't be seen with their natural eyes.

Elizabeth was happy too. Why? Because the power that created the universe had just entered her house. Never mind that this power was compressed into the womb of her teenage relative. That did not make the power any less real to her or diminish the honor of hosting that power. In fact, it made the honor greater, much greater. Mary was the first person to know that the Messiah had entered the world. The angel had told her that her womb would be his first home. John was the second to know because the Holy Spirit came into Elizabeth's womb to tell John. And now, the old barren woman who had lived all these years under the shadow of shame, the old woman God had forgotten, the young woman who grew old while her deepest daily prayer went unheard until one day it ceased to be spoken at all, the old woman for whom it was too late—that woman, Elizabeth, was the third person on the planet to know that the Light of the world had arrived. He had come into her home, and now his light was shining on her heart through the filling of the Holy Spirit. She was carrying his herald, the point man for the kingdom of God, in her womb.

A baby in the womb, a teenage girl, and an old woman were the first to know. No one would have thought God would come that way—to the small before the great. Like his Father, Jesus showed the same preference for babies and women, even women of questionable character whom religious people avoided. If the history of revelation teaches us anything, it teaches us that God loves to look at the overlooked, like an elderly priest living in retirement in the hill country of Judea.

That's where we pick up the story again, three months after Mary's visit to Elizabeth. Zechariah hasn't spoken for nine months. And now, the son Gabriel promised to Zechariah has been born. Gabriel said that this son would be great in the sight of the Lord. So great, so unique, that he was filled with the Holy Spirit of God while he was still in his mother's womb. He will belong to God in a way that no one before him has. He will be the Prophet's prophet. He will have the honor of introducing the Messiah. They will have met before either was born. There will never be another like him.

He will bring a nation back to their God. Elijah could shut and open the heavens, call down fire from those same heavens, heal the sick, and raise the dead. This son will do something greater. He will open the human heart and set it on fire. He will turn the hearts of fathers back to their children. He is a gift from the Father. He is the only prophet the other prophets prophesied about. His name was decided in heaven before he was even conceived. Every son born to barren women in the Bible was special, but this son is in a different realm of special. Could Zechariah believe this part? He has had nine very quiet months to meditate on it.

Eight days after John the Baptist's birth, it is time for the baby boy to be circumcised and formally named. It's a party. All the neighbors, friends, and relatives are gathered for this event. They know children born to the barren are special. They've come to celebrate his circumcision and naming. Everyone assumes the baby will be named Zechariah, honoring his father and carrying on his name. But Elizabeth says, "No! He is to be called John" (Luke 1:60). His name will not honor his father Zechariah.

The crowd thinks this is nonsense. They appeal to the still mute Zechariah, who writes on a tablet, "His name *is* John" (Luke 1:63, emphasis added). Heaven had already named the son in honor of *the* Father, for the name John means "the LORD is gracious." In John, the Lord has been gracious to Zechariah and Elizabeth. Now John will introduce to the world the One who is full of grace and truth. And now Zechariah can speak.

In naming his son "John," Zechariah showed that at last he believed Gabriel's words. Then Zechariah became the third person in the age of the Messiah to be filled with the Spirit (Luke 1:67). When he is filled, he does not speak in tongues or pray in power, but he prophesies. He does what John did in the womb, what Elizabeth did when Jesus entered the room in Mary's womb. By the revelatory power of the Holy Spirit, he testifies about Jesus. He is speaking of the mystery that has been hidden from human intelligence, the mystery that can only be known by divine revelation. Paul, echoing Isaiah, said it like this: "'What no eye has seen, what no ear has heard, and what no human mind has conceived'—the things God has prepared for those who love him—these are the things God has revealed to us by his Spirit" (1 Corinthians 2:9–10; see Isaiah 64:4; 65:17).

God's goodness is so far beyond our ability to even imagine it, let alone deduce it, that he must reveal it if we are ever going to enjoy it. And one way he does this is by filling us with his Spirit.

In Luke's gospel, only three people are "filled with the Holy Spirit": a baby in his mother's womb, that baby's elderly mother, and an elderly priest—the baby's father. And they all do the same thing when they are filled. They see what no eye can see. They are dazzled by the beauty of what they see. And the Holy Spirit empowers them to show us that Jesus is the Christ.

nineteen

FILLED WITH THE SPIRIT IN ACTS

In Acts, we find five examples of people being filled with the Holy Spirit. Do not confuse these with examples of people "receiving the Holy Spirit" (Acts 8:17) or "the Holy Spirit coming on" people (Acts 10:44; 19:6). Luke is a theologian who uses stories to teach us about the ministry of the Spirit, and he is precise in the language he uses to explain the work of the Holy Spirit.

ACTS 2:4

There are three great onetime celebrations in Scripture when the Spirit of God moved into a new residence on the earth. When God's presence came to dwell in the tabernacle, the glory of the Lord appeared to all the people, and fire came down from heaven and consumed the sacrifices (Leviticus 9:23–24). When God's presence came to dwell in the temple, the glory of the Lord filled the temple, and fire came down from heaven and consumed the sacrifices (2 Chronicles 7:1–3). And now, fifty days after Jesus was crucified at nine in the morning, the fire and the glory of God descend at nine in the morning on living sacrifices, and the Holy Spirit takes up residence in a new temple—the hearts of God's born-again children.[1]

The 120 were praying together in a room when the Holy Spirit filled them and enabled them to speak in languages they had not learned (Acts 2:1–13). If this were the only example of being filled with the Spirit, we would be justified in concluding that speaking in tongues is intrinsically linked to the filling of the Spirit, maybe even serving as the sign of being filled with the Spirit. But we have four more examples in Acts (4:8, 31; 9:17; 13:9), and no one speaks in tongues in those examples. Therefore, speaking tongues is a legitimate spiritual gift, but it is not intrinsically connected to being filled with the Spirit.

Thousands of people gathered to hear the disciples. Peter defined the experience for the crowd as the fulfillment of Joel 2:28–32. From now on, all the people of God will be prophetic. "In the last days, God says, I will pour out my Spirit on all[2] people. Your sons and daughters will prophesy, your young men will see visions, your old men will dream dreams. Even on my servants, both men and women, I will pour out my Spirit in those days, and they will prophesy" (Acts 2:17–18).

---

1. In the Old Testament, only the king could be assured of the permanent presence of the Spirit. When Saul turned away from God, the Holy Spirit left him and came on David (1 Samuel 16:13–14). After David committed adultery and tried to cover it up with murder, he asked God not to take away the Holy Spirit (Psalm 51:11).

2. The Greek word for "all" is used with a variety of meanings just like the English word. It can mean "all without exception, the totality of . . . ," or it can mean "the majority of," or it can mean "all without distinction, all kinds of." The context shows that "all people" means "all kinds of people," that is, without distinction for gender or age.

The Holy Spirit empowered the 120 to prophesy, for they were "declaring the wonders of God" (Acts 2:11). Then the Spirit empowered Peter to prophesy to the crowd of people who do not yet believe in Jesus. After Peter explained to the crowd that they were witnessing the prophetic ministry of the Holy Spirit in the last days (2:14–21), he preached Jesus to the people who crucified Jesus (2:22–40), and three thousand people accepted the Lord that day (2:41). Therefore, to be filled with the Spirit is to be prophetically empowered to reveal Jesus to unbelievers.

ACTS 4:8

The apostles did signs and wonders and taught in the temple every day. At night they ate together in their homes, rejoicing in God. Every day the Lord saved more people and added them to the church. The church had grown to five thousand men, and the religious leaders of the Jews felt threatened. They brought Peter and John before the Sanhedrin to question them about one of their recent miracles—the healing of a man crippled from birth. "By what power or what name did you do this?" they asked (Acts 4:7). The religious leaders thought Peter and John were ignorant and could be easily intimidated. They did not know they had just picked a fight with the Holy Spirit.

Jesus warned the Twelve that the religious authorities would persecute them and drag them before kings and governors, but he promised them that the Holy Spirit would give them words and wisdom that their adversaries could not resist (Luke 12:11–12; 21:12–15). This is the first fulfillment of that promise. Here is how it played out:

Then Peter, filled with the Holy Spirit, said to them: "Rulers and elders of the people! If we are being called to account today for an act of kindness shown to a man who was lame and are being asked how he was healed, then know this, you and all the people of Israel: It is by the name of Jesus Christ of Nazareth, whom you crucified but whom God raised from the dead, that this man stands before you healed. Jesus is

"'the stone you builders rejected,
    which has become the cornerstone.'

Salvation is found in no one else, for there is no other name under heaven given to mankind by which we must be saved."

Acts 4:8–12

The rulers were astonished and let them go.

Peter was empowered by the Holy Spirit to give supernatural prophetic testimony to Jesus to an audience of hostile unbelievers.[3] This example proves that the filling of the Holy Spirit does not necessitate speaking in tongues. It is not some generalized power to live a better Christian life. It is a temporary experience of power. The power comes on Peter *when he needs it* and then lifts off from him when he is no longer speaking. Peter was filled with the Holy Spirit on Pentecost and then again weeks later in

---

3. Peter's words were supernatural because they were given to him by the Holy Spirit. They were prophetic because, just like Elijah did, he confronted the religious leaders of his day. This is often referred to as the "forthtelling" ministry of the prophets. They were also prophetic because the Spirit guided him to the perfect text, Psalm 118:25, to define what was happening at that very moment.

front of the rulers.[4] Thus, the filling of the Spirit is a temporary, repeatable, prophetic empowering to testify about Jesus to hostile unbelievers.

ACTS 4:31

After Peter and John were released, they gave a report to the leaders of the church. Luke summarized their report in one verse (Acts 4:23), and then the meeting erupted into spontaneous prayer for the next eight verses. Luke uses his storytelling skill to show us where the power of the first-century church lay. It was not in their purity or in their intelligent strategies, but in their prayers. The biggest difference between the first-century church and the modern church in the Western world is that the first-century church was a praying church. We are a talking church.

There is a part of this prayer that I pray every day. It's Acts 4:29–31:

> "Now, Lord, consider their threats and enable your servants to speak your word with great boldness. Stretch out your hand to heal and perform signs and wonders through the name of your holy servant Jesus."
>
> After they prayed, the place where they were meeting was shaken. And they were all filled with the Holy Spirit and spoke the word of God boldly.

---

4. Luke used the same tense for *pimplemi*, "filled," that he did in Acts 2:4. If he had wanted his readers to understand that this was the same filling of the Spirit that had happened on Pentecost, he would have used a pluperfect to say, "Then Peter, who had been filled with the Holy Spirit . . ."

They did not pray to be filled with the Holy Spirit. They prayed for boldness to speak the word of the Lord to a hostile audience. And it's as if God said back to them, "The only way you can speak my word boldly is to be filled with my Spirit." The filling of the Spirit is not speaking in tongues. It is not a onetime encounter with the Holy Spirit that gives us permanent power to live the Christian life on a higher plane. It is the temporary empowering of the Spirit to give prophetic testimony to Jesus. God shook the building where they prayed as a sign that he was going to answer their prayer with power that would shake the world.

In 1949, a small group of believers huddled in a granite house to pray for revival on the treeless, rocky Isle of Lewis in the Scottish Hebrides. Suddenly, the granite house shook like a leaf with wave after wave of divine power sweeping through it. Starting that night, a historic revival swept through the Scottish Hebrides.[5]

When I lived in Southern California on two different occasions, I began to pray Acts 4:29–31, only to be interrupted by an earthquake. The first time happened as I sat alone on my living room sofa. I took this as a sign, maybe even a promise, that if I would keep praying Acts 4:29–31, God would let me speak his word with miraculous power to unbelievers before I finish my race. The second time happened in front of a prayer group of 120 people as I was reading Acts 4:29–31. I took this as a sign that the Lord will shake the world again when enough of his church is praying night and day.

---

5. The preacher who became a leader in that revival was in the granite house the night God shook it (see Duncan Campbell, *Revival in the Hebrides* [Detroit: Kraus House, 2016]).

ACTS 9:17

The Lord brought one of his most powerful enemies down to the dust of the earth by blinding him with the glory of God. The first lesson the Lord taught Saul was that the church is the Lord's body. The one who persecutes the church is persecuting the Lord. The second thing the Lord taught Saul was that he would always need the body of Christ for his own spiritual health and for his own ministry. Saul couldn't regain his sight until Ananias prayed for him. The third thing the Lord taught Saul was that his great learning would not convert darkened hearts. Ananias said to Saul, "Brother Saul, the Lord—Jesus, who appeared to you on the road as you were coming here—has sent me so that you may see again and be filled with the Holy Spirit" (Acts 9:17). The text does not tell us when Saul was filled with the Spirit, but it shows a similar result as the other times when believers were filled with the Spirit. The next thing we see Saul doing is astonishing the whole synagogue by proving that Jesus is the Messiah. His enemies couldn't refute him, so they tried to kill him (9:19–25).

ACTS 13:9

On their first missionary journey, Paul and Barnabas proclaimed the gospel to the proconsul Sergius Paulus at Paphos on the island of Cyprus. An attendant of the proconsul, a Jewish false prophet and sorcerer named Elymas, kept interrupting them.

> Then Saul, who was also called Paul, filled with the Holy Spirit, looked straight at Elymas and said, "You are a child

of the devil and an enemy of everything that is right! You are full of all kinds of deceit and trickery. Will you never stop perverting the right ways of the Lord? Now the hand of the Lord is against you. You are going to be blind for a time, not even able to see the light of the sun."

Immediately mist and darkness came over him, and he groped about, seeking someone to lead him by the hand. When the proconsul saw what had happened, he believed, for he was amazed at the teaching about the Lord.

Acts 13:9–12

This is the last reference in Acts to the filling of the Spirit.[6] It confirms what we have already seen, namely, that the filling of the Spirit in Acts is a temporary (repeatable) empowering by the Spirit to produce a prophetic (i.e., miraculous) testimony that Jesus is the Christ. Acts 9:17 promised that Paul would be filled with the Holy Spirit. This is the first explicit incidence of Paul being filled with the Spirit, though Acts 9:19–30 gives implicit evidence of Paul being filled with the Spirit after Ananias's prayer. The filling of the Spirit in Acts always happens in the presence of an unbelieving audience. It is an evangelistic ministry of the Spirit.

In the gospel of Luke, three people are filled with the Spirit. The first person to be filled by the Spirit is John the Baptist in the womb of Elizabeth, then Elizabeth, and finally Zechariah on the eighth day after John's birth. All give supernatural prophetic testimony that Jesus is the Messiah. In Acts, the 120 are filled

---

6. The verb in Acts 13:52 is not *pimplemi*; it is *pleroo*. Although the English translation is the same, "filled with the Holy Spirit," the phrase with *pleroo* means that one's life is characterized by the fruit of the Spirit. See more under the discussion of "full of the Spirit." So Acts 13:52 means that disciples were joyful and bore the fruit of the Holy Spirit (see Galatians 5:22–23).

with the Spirit on Pentecost, Peter before the Sanhedrin, all the believers who prayed together after the Sanhedrin released Peter and John, and Paul twice—first in the synagogue and then at Paphos preaching the gospel to the governor.

How do we persuade God to fill us with the Holy Spirit today? The believers in Luke and Acts who were filled with the Spirit had given their lives to testifying that Jesus is the Messiah. They were empowered by the Spirit because apart from the supernatural power of God, no one can believe in Jesus (2 Corinthians 4:4–6). The human heart is that sick. All we have to do to be filled with the Spirit is to dedicate ourselves to reaching the lost. If we pray and reach out to the lost, God will empower us and our words.

The first time I was filled with the Spirit, I didn't know it because I had no clue what it meant to be filled with the Spirit. I had never thought about it or prayed for it. But I was a Young Life leader dedicated to reaching the lost. My senior year in college, I was on a plane bringing high school kids home from a Colorado ski trip in December. My rowdy kids were on a spiritual high, and they had taken over the plane, laughing and singing songs of praise to God. I sat next to a girl who was a junior at a Colorado college. She wasn't part of our group, and she wanted to know why the kids were so happy. She had no experience with God and thought she could have a meaningful life without God, if there even was a God. She told me her favorite book was *Toward a Psychology of Being* by Abraham Maslow.

I had read and critiqued Maslow's book for one of my philosophy classes. My specialty was apologetics—logically defending the Christian position and the Scriptures. I knew God had placed me beside her so I could lead her to Christ. I thought, *This is going to be so easy.* Ninety minutes later, I was so frustrated that I wanted to change seats. She had sweetly challenged everything I said and could not understand my brilliant explanations of the cross and justification by faith. We were ten minutes from landing at Love Field in Dallas, and this experience would go down as my worst failure at witnessing. Then the pilot announced that because of a snowstorm, traffic was backed up over Love Field, and we would have to circle the airport for forty-five minutes.

I had been given a reprieve. I thought, *I'd better try something new,* so I decided to pray. *Lord, please grant me power to show her that you love her.* Then I said to her the next thing that popped into mind.

"You know what your problem is?" I asked her.

"No," she said.

"It's the same as mine," I said. "You're a sinner, and you need a Savior."

She burst into tears. "I know. I know it's true, but what can I do?" she said through her tears.

I had been filled with the Spirit, the same as Peter was on the day of Pentecost when, at the conclusion of his message, three thousand people cried out, "What shall we do?" (Acts 2:37). I thought the power of God was in those three sentences. "You know what your problem is? It's the same as mine. You're a sinner, and you need a Savior." The next time I tried out those sentences, the person shot back to me, "I'm not a sinner, you self-righteous know-it-all." I tried out those lines a few more times, but they never worked again. It turned out that I was like everyone else, searching for a formula to make my service easier when what God really wants to give me is a friendship to make life more joyful.

I had been given the key to evangelism, but it would be years before I found out that the key was the filling of the Holy Spirit.

twenty

FULL OF THE SPIRIT IN LUKE AND ACTS

Luke is the only writer who uses the adjectival phrase "full of the Holy Spirit." Normally the phrase "full of . . ." is a character description. In the Greek text of Acts 9:36, Luke writes that Dorcas was "full of good works"; the NIV translates this as Dorcas was "always doing good," which is a good rendering.

When a dispute over the distribution of food broke out in the early church, the apostles said to the church, "Brothers and sisters, choose seven men from among you who are known to be full of the Spirit and wisdom" (Acts 6:3). Wisdom is skill at living life. A person who is "full of wisdom" is a person who is exceptionally wise. By analogy, a person in this context who is "full of the Spirit" is exceptionally spiritual; that is, their life is characterized by the fruit of the Spirit (Galatians 5:22–23).

The fruit of the Spirit is love, kindness, patience, and several other qualities, exactly the ones needed to resolve a controversy.[1]

Luke characterized Barnabas in a similar way: "He was a good man, full of the Holy Spirit and faith, and a great number of people were brought to the Lord" (Acts 11:24). The emphasis on evangelism here suggests that in this context "full of the Holy Spirit and faith" probably means not only that Barnabas bore the fruit of the Holy Spirit, but also that he was repeatedly filled with the Spirit to do evangelism with miracles. Luke is flexible in the way he uses "full of the Spirit." It can be a character description, while at other times it is a description of the empowering of the Holy Spirit, and sometimes—as in Acts 11:24—it can be both.

Stephen occupies a special place in Acts. He starts out serving widows, becomes a miracle worker, then a witness for Christ whom no one can refute, and finally becomes the first person to die for Jesus. He is Luke's supreme example of the kind of disciple the apostles produced in the early days of the church. Among the seven men chosen by the church to serve the tables of widows, Luke singles out Stephen. He is "a man full of faith and of the Holy Spirit" (Acts 6:5). Stephen will become a miracle worker, so "full of faith" probably means he had the faith to believe God for miracles, not just that he was exceptionally faithful. And "full of the Holy Spirit" means that his life was characterized not only by the fruit of the Spirit but also by evangelism with miracles.

Like the Lord Jesus, Stephen did "great wonders and signs"

---

1. The word translated "full" in the phrase "full of the Holy Spirit" is the adjective *pleres*. There is a similar description of the disciples at Psidian Antioch: "And the disciples were filled with joy and with the Holy Spirit" (Acts 13:52). The verb translated "filled" here is not *pimplemi*, the verb Luke uses for the empowering of the Holy Spirit to give prophetic testimony about Jesus to unbelievers. The verb in Acts 13:52 is *pleroo*, a cognate with the adjective *pleres*. So Acts 13:52 is a character description like Acts 6:3.

(Acts 6:8). Like the Lord Jesus, Stephen's Jewish enemies "could not stand up against the wisdom the Spirit gave him as he spoke" (6:10), so they persuaded false witnesses to drag him into a rigged trial, but Stephen's face shone like "the face of an angel" (6:15).

Instead of defending himself, Stephen put the nation on trial. Luke gives Stephen the longest speech in Acts, for it is God's fullest indictment of the Jewish nation. When Stephen's enemies kill him, they reveal that their father is the devil, the father of lies and murders, and they consign their nation to a history of oppression like that of no other nation.

At the conclusion of the speech, the mob was ready to rush him. "But Stephen, full of the Holy Spirit, looked up to heaven and saw the glory of God, and Jesus standing at the right hand of God. 'Look,' he said, 'I see heaven open and the Son of Man standing at the right hand of God'" (Acts 7:55–56). This verse uses the phrase "full of the Holy Spirit" to show that the Spirit has empowered Stephen to do battle with the devil and to accomplish more in his death than in his life.

The most quoted verse of the psalms in the New Testament is Psalm 110:1: "The LORD says to my lord: 'Sit at my right hand until I make your enemies a footstool for your feet.'" When Jesus ascended into heaven, God the Father gave him an honor that no one else had ever enjoyed. Jesus was permitted to sit in the presence of God, and he did not have to rise from his throne until the end of history, when God will make everyone bow to his Son.

But Stephen saw a different scene in heaven. The Spirit opened heaven so that Stephen could gaze on the throne in the center of heaven. Stephen saw an empty throne, for the Son of God was standing (Acts 7:55). Did the angels gasp when they saw the Son of God leave his throne at the right hand of God?

The heart of Jesus is so big that he cannot sit on his throne to receive the first one martyred for his name. Jesus left his throne and stood at the edge of heaven to honor Stephen and to be the first to embrace his martyr as he entered heaven.

Luke tells us, "While they were stoning him, Stephen prayed, 'Lord Jesus, receive my spirit.' Then he fell on his knees and cried out, 'Lord, do not hold this sin against them.' When he had said this, he fell asleep" (Acts 7:59–60). The Spirit had led Stephen to die like his Lord.

The Lord heard Stephen's last prayer. I imagine the Son of God smiling and saying, "Oh, Stephen, you have no idea of the power you just released with that prayer. I will honor your prayer. I'm going to save the young architect of your murder, and I will give him power to suffer for my name like no one else."

The devil, great murderer that he is, filled a crowd of his followers with hatred for the Lord's most effective witness. But through Stephen's prayer, the Holy Spirit found a witness among the murderers to replace Stephen. God turned Saul into the apostle Paul, who would carry the gospel around the world.

The use of "full of the Holy Spirit" in Luke 4:1 is similar to Acts 7:55: "Jesus, full of the Holy Spirit, left the Jordan and was led by the Spirit into the wilderness, where for forty days he was tempted by the devil. He ate nothing during those days, and at the end of them he was hungry" (Luke 4:1–2). "Full of the Holy Spirit" is not a character description here. It means that Jesus was completely empowered by the Holy Spirit to do battle with the devil. It is Luke's way of saying what John said about Jesus, namely, that God gave Jesus "the Spirit without limit" (John 3:34). Only Jesus had the character to bear that kind of power.

These are all the references to "full of the Holy Spirit" in the New Testament. The adjectival phrase is more elastic than the verbal phrase "filled with the Spirit." The adjectival phrase ranges from a character description to the ability to consistently work miracles by the power of the Holy Spirit and to the ultimate empowering of Jesus by the Holy Spirit.

Every day, I pray to be like Barnabas—"a good man, full of the Holy Spirit and faith," and through whom "a great number of people were brought to the Lord" (Acts 11:24). Yet no one in Luke or Acts prays to be filled with the Spirit or to become full of the Spirit. Instead they pray for miraculous power to tell a hostile audience that Jesus is the Messiah (Acts 4:29–31).

Everyone who is full of the Spirit in Acts—the apostles, Stephen, Philip, and Barnabas—has been given power to reach the lost. So each morning when I ask God for the grace to be full of the Spirit, I'm really praying, "Please, Father, make me an evangelist again."

twenty-one

PHYSICAL
MANIFESTATIONS

On April 18, 1906, the *Los Angeles Times* reported a strange new revival that was occurring in the city. Under a headline that proclaimed "Weird Babel of Tongues," a reporter from the paper stated:

> Meetings are held in a tumble-down shack on Azusa Street, near San Pedro Street, and the devotees of the weird doctrine practice the most fanatical rites, preach the wildest theories and work themselves into a state of mad excitement in their peculiar zeal. Colored people and a sprinkling of whites compose the congregation, and night is made hideous in the neighborhood by the howlings of the worshippers, who spend hours swaying forth and back in a nerve-racking attitude of prayer and supplication. They claim to have the "gift of tongues" and to be able to comprehend the babel.[1]

---

1. Quoted in Sam Storms, "History of the Pentecostal-Charismatic Movements," www.samstorms.org/all-articles/post/history-of-the-pentecostal-charismatic-movements.

That same day, the great San Francisco earthquake occurred, destroying much of the city. As the tremors from the earthquake were felt by those at Azusa Street, a "spiritual earthquake" shook the meeting, which "in the weeks to come rose to a level of near hysteria."[2]

Although the tremors from the San Francisco earthquake were felt up and down the California coast, the tremors from the spiritual earthquake at Azusa Street began to spread throughout the country. The revival continued day and night for three years and gave birth to modern Pentecostalism. Yet from the very beginning, the physical phenomena that occurred in the revival were ridiculed as a "frenzy of religious zeal," and those who spoke in tongues were said to "gurgle wordless talk."[3]

PHYSICAL MANIFESTATIONS ARE NORMAL IN THE HISTORY OF REVIVALS

Unusual physical manifestations have been common throughout the history of the church, especially during times of revival. Sometimes these manifestations have occurred in the most unlikely settings. During the Evangelical Revival of England in the late 1730s and early 1740s, John Wesley saw numerous "outward signs" occur during his preaching. On June 15, 1739, for example, while Wesley was preaching in the fields and inviting sinners to come to Christ, "many of those that heard began to call on God with strong cries and tears. Some sunk down, and there

---

2. Quoted in Vinson Synan, *The Holiness-Pentecostal Tradition: Charismatic Movements in the Twentieth Century*, 2nd ed. (Grand Rapids: Eerdmans, 1997), 98.

3. Synan, *Holiness-Pentecostal Tradition*, 97.

remained no strength in them; others exceedingly trembled and quaked; some were torn with a kind of convulsive motion in every part of their bodies, and that so violently that often four or five persons could not hold one of them."[4]

When his friend and fellow preacher, George Whitefield, first heard about these signs, he objected strenuously. But on July 7, 1739, Wesley recorded in his journal:

> I had an opportunity to talk with him of those outward signs which had so often accompanied the inward work of God. I found his objections were chiefly grounded on gross misrepresentations of matter of fact. But the next day he had an opportunity of informing himself better: For no sooner had he begun (in the application of his sermon) to invite all sinners to believe in Christ, than four persons sunk down close to him, almost in the same moment. One of them lay without either sense or motion; a second trembled exceedingly; the third had strong convulsions all over his body, but made no noise, unless by groans. The fourth, equally convulsed, called upon God, with strong cries and tears.

Wesley concluded his journal entry that day with the statement, "From this time, I trust, we shall all suffer God to carry on His own work in the way that pleaseth Him."[5]

During that same period, in a staid New England setting, these same kinds of physical manifestations broke out in the church pastored by Jonathan Edwards, considered by many to

---

4. John Wesley, *Journals from October 14, 1735 to November 29, 1745,* vol. 1 of *The Works of John Wesley,* 3rd ed. (Grand Rapids: Baker, 1991), 204.

5. Ibid.

be America's greatest theologian. He was at the center of what is now regarded as one of the greatest revivals in American history, the Great Awakening. In describing one of the meetings in his church, Edwards wrote the following:

> The affection was quickly propagated throughout the room; many of the young people and children . . . appeared to be overcome with a sense of the greatness and glory of divine things, and with admiration, love, joy and praise, and compassion to others that looked upon themselves as in a state of nature [unsaved]. And many others at the same time were overcome with distress about their sinful and miserable state and condition; so that the whole room was full of nothing but outcries, faintings, and such like.[6]

During that fall, Edwards wrote, "It was a very frequent thing to see a house full of outcries, faintings, convulsions, and such like, both with distress, and also with admiration and joy . . . It was pretty often so, that there were some that were so affected, and their bodies so overcome, that they could not go home, but were obliged to stay all night where they were."[7]

On another occasion Edwards described the ministry of a Mr. Buell:

> Mr. Buell continued here a fortnight or three weeks after I returned: there being still great appearances attend-

---

6. Jonathan Edwards, "An Account of the Revival in Northampton in 1740–42 in a Letter to a Minister of Boston," in *Jonathan Edwards on Revival* (Carlisle, PA: Banner of Truth, 1984), 150.

7. Edwards, "An Account of the Revival," 151.

ing his labors; many in their religious affections being raised far beyond what they had ever been before; and there were some instances of persons lying in a sort of trance, remaining perhaps for a whole twenty-four hours motionless, and with their senses locked up; but in the mean time under strong imaginations, as though they went to heaven and had there a vision of glorious and delightful objects. But when the people were raised to this height, Satan took the advantage, and his interposition, in many instances, soon became very apparent: and a great deal of caution and pains were found necessary to keep the people, many of them, from running wild.[8]

These kinds of manifestations cause concern on two different fronts. As Edwards suggested in the last paragraph, even though the manifestations were legitimate reactions to a genuine work of the Spirit, they were capable of being perverted by Satan so that people could be led astray.

On another front, these kinds of manifestations caused a number of conservative Christian ministers to criticize Jonathan Edwards and his meetings as works of the flesh or of the devil.

The Work of God May Cause Physical Manifestations

Edward Gross, who is the coordinator of international disciple renewal for CityNet Ministries in Philadelphia, is an example of someone who would take the side of Edwards's opponents and argue against his understanding of the physical manifestations. In his book *Miracles, Demons, and Spiritual Warfare*,

---

8. Edwards, "An Account of the Revival," 153–54.

Gross cites Charles Hodge, who concluded that "there is nothing in the Bible to lead us to regard these bodily affections as the legitimate effects of religious feeling. No such results followed the preaching of Christ, or his apostles. We hear of no general outcries, faintings, convulsions, or ravings in the assemblies which they addressed."[9]

Contrary to Hodge's statement, there is much in the Bible to indicate that "bodily affections" can be legitimate effects of the Holy Spirit. These physical manifestations occur in both the Old and New Testaments.

According to Scripture, the Holy Spirit's ministry will sometimes produce physical reactions that can vary from trembling, shaking, and trances to even illness and physical collapse. The divine works that produce these reactions may be divided into two categories. First, these responses are caused by spectacular and visible phenomena associated with the work of the Holy Spirit. The physical manifestations mentioned above can be caused by theophanies[10] (Exodus 19:16–25; 20:18), angelic appearances (Matthew 28:2–4), the audible voice of God (Matthew 17:6–7), visions (Daniel 8:17–18, 27; 10:1–17;[11] Acts 10:10–23), reactions to Jesus during his earthly ministry (John 18:6), and the appearance of the glorified Jesus (Acts 9:1–9; Revelation 1:17).

Second, the Scriptures also record physical manifestations to

---

9. Quoted in Edward Gross, *Miracles, Demons, and Spiritual Warfare: An Urgent Call for Discernment* (Grand Rapids: Baker, 1989), 91.

10. *Theophany* is the term used to describe God's appearance to an individual or a group. Theologians generally regard the Old Testament theophanies as an appearance of the preincarnate Christ rather than an appearance of God the Father, since no one has ever seen God the Father (John 1:18).

11. The visionary experience in Daniel 10 is interesting. Only Daniel could see the vision, but the men with Daniel experienced such dread from the presence of God that they ran away and hid (Daniel 10:7).

less visible works of God. People tremble in the presence of God when there are no other visible or tangible phenomena associated with his presence. Sometimes the psalmists trembled when they experienced the presence of God as "the fear of the LORD." The author of Psalm 119 writes, "My flesh trembles in fear of you; I stand in awe of your laws" (119:120). It was not unusual for the people of the Lord to tremble in his presence. The Lord expected this response from his people. Jeremiah wrote, "'Should you not fear me?' declares the LORD. 'Should you not tremble in my presence?'" (Jeremiah 5:22). Humble people tremble when God manifests his presence through his word (Isaiah 66:2). We should expect to tremble in the presence of omnipotence.

Weeping is another manifestation in response to the intangible presence of the Lord. When Ezra was reading the Book of the Law to the people, they began to weep spontaneously as they heard the words of the law (Nehemiah 8:9). Their weeping was not the result of hysteria or psychological manipulation, because the leaders of the meeting did not want the people to weep and attempted to restrain them. The ability to weep over the words of Scripture and over our failure to obey God's commands is something that ought to be cultivated and desired today. It is not a sign of weakness or emotional instability; it is a sign of spiritual and emotional health. The inability to weep over these things, on the other hand, is a sign of a traumatized or hardened heart.

In a trance, a person loses all awareness of their body and surroundings. The Lord brought Paul into a trance during an ordinary experience of prayer. Paul explained his experience in this way: "When I returned to Jerusalem and was praying at the temple, I fell into a trance and saw the Lord speaking to me. 'Quick!' he said. 'Leave Jerusalem immediately, because the people here will not accept your testimony about me'" (Acts 22:17–18). The result of Paul's trance was not to give him any new revelation about the person or work of the Lord Jesus but to save his life and change the course of his ministry.

Sometimes believers may enter into a state that appears to be drunkenness in response to the presence of the Lord. This happened to Hannah during prayer (1 Samuel 1:12–17). And Saul, although the text does not use the term *drunk*, certainly appeared drunk when the Spirit came on him and he stripped off all of his clothes and lay down for the whole day (1 Samuel 19:23–24).

On the day of Pentecost, some of the onlookers assumed that those who were filled with the Spirit were drunk. Their drunken appearance was not due to the fact that they were speaking in foreign languages. That in itself was a sign of intelligence, not drunkenness. Their response to the Spirit evidently produced some characteristics that are normally associated with happy drunkenness.

Finally, there is another category of the work of the Spirit that frequently, though not always, produces a wide range of physical manifestations. When demons are driven out, people may shriek, convulse, or fall down unconscious (see Mark 1:23–28; 9:14–29).

All of these reactions make sense when we realize that a human being is more than just a mind and a will, and that God may touch our emotions and our bodies as well as our minds.

Genuine Physical Manifestations May Appear Chaotic, but They Are Part of God's Work in Restoring Order

In Jonathan Edwards's day, some people failed to see the Great Awakening as a work of the Spirit of God because they said that God is a God of order, not of confusion (1 Corinthians 14:33, 40). They felt that God could not be responsible for the physical manifestations in these meetings because they resulted in confusion. This charge is still being leveled at similar kinds of meetings today. Edward Gross again quotes Charles Hodge:

> The testimony of the Scriptures is not merely negative on this subject. Their authority is directly opposed to all such disorders. They direct that all things should be done decently and in order. They teach us that God is not the God of confusion, but of peace, in all the churches of the saints [1 Corinthians 14:33, 40]. These passages have particular reference to the manner of conducting public worship. They forbid every thing which is inconsistent with order, solemnity, and devout attention. It is evident that loud outcries and convulsions are inconsistent with these things, and therefore ought to be discouraged. They cannot come from God, for he is not the author of confusion.[12]

The reply Edwards gave to the charges of his critics applies to modern-day critics as well:

> But if God is pleased to convince the consciences of persons, so that they cannot avoid great outward manifestations, even to interrupting and breaking off those public means they were attending, I do not think this is confusion, or an unhappy interruption, any more than if a company should meet on the field to pray for rain, and should be broken off

---

12. Gross, *Miracles, Demons, and Spiritual Warfare*, 91.

from their exercise by a plentiful shower. Would to God that all the public assemblies in the land were broken off from their public exercises with such confusion as this the next sabbath day! We need not be sorry for breaking the order of means, by obtaining the end to which that order is directed. He who is going to fetch a treasure, need not be sorry that he is stopped, by meeting the treasure in the midst of his journey.[13]

We are not to evaluate something by how strange it may seem to us. Strangeness is not a scriptural rule to determine whether a ministry is from God. Suppose we were to see a man who was an alcoholic, a wife-beater, and a God-hater shrieking at the top of his voice and then falling down motionless for twenty-four hours during a religious meeting. What if that man rose never again to drink or to hit his wife but to love her as Christ loved the church and to love God and his Word? Though strange, we would have to conclude that the Holy Spirit had been at work in his life. Neither the devil nor the flesh produces love for God, love for one's family, or freedom from addictions.

Just as these kinds of things happened during the great revivals of the past, so they are happening today where people refuse to quench the fire of the Spirit. It would be a great mistake, then, to use Paul's admonition that "all things should be done decently and in order" (1 Corinthians 14:40 ESV) to such a degree that we actually quench the fire of the Spirit.

---

13. Jonathan Edwards, "The Distinguishing Marks of a Work of the Spirit of God," in *Jonathan Edwards on Revival* (Carlisle, PA: Banner of Truth, 1984), 127.

A Genuine Work of the Spirit Will Produce the Fruit of the Spirit

How can we discern when a physical manifestation is a response to a genuine work of the Spirit? In his classic essay "The Distinguishing Marks of a Work of the Spirit of God," Edwards sets forth the criteria for determining what is a genuine work of the Holy Spirit. His first conclusion is this:

> A work is not to be judged of by any effects on the bodies of men; such as tears, tremblings, groans, loud outcries, agonies of body, or the failing of bodily strength. The influence persons are under, is not to be judged of one way or other, by such effects on the body; and the reason is, because the Scripture nowhere gives us any such rule.[14]

The manifestations prove nothing because Scripture does not give us any universal rule with which to judge these manifestations. The Holy Spirit can do a powerful work where there are no manifestations present. People can be healed or saved without groanings, tremblings, or other observable physical phenomena. It is even possible for demons to be driven out without any of these accompanying phenomena.

The foremost test of any ministry or teaching is whether it agrees with the teaching of Scripture. However, we must be sure that the Scriptures are the standard and not our own particular interpretation of Scripture. At one time it was common among certain fundamentalist groups to claim that women acted immodestly and violated Paul's instruction in 1 Timothy 2:9 if

---

14. Edwards, "Distinguishing Marks," 91.

they used cosmetics. No one today would agree with that interpretation of 1 Timothy 2:9.

Edwards concluded that when the Scriptures do not speak directly to a particular issue, the only test for determining a genuine work of God is whether that work manifests the fruit of the Holy Spirit.[15] This is precisely the test that Jesus gave us to discern between true and false prophetic ministry:

> "By their fruit you will recognize them. Do people pick grapes
> from thornbushes, or figs from thistles? Likewise, every good
> tree bears good fruit, but a bad tree bears bad fruit. A good tree
> cannot bear bad fruit, and a bad tree cannot bear good fruit.
> Every tree that does not bear good fruit is cut down and thrown
> into the fire. Thus, by their fruit you will recognize them."
>
> *Matthew 7:16–20*

Testing the fruit of a work is essential in cases where the Scriptures are silent. This test also applies in cases where people espouse correct doctrine, but the fruit of their lives and ministry shows that they are not submitting to that doctrine. They may be attempting a conscious deception, or they may themselves be deceived. In either case, the fruit of their ministry will give them away.

RESPONDING TO PHYSICAL MANIFESTATIONS TODAY

When God gives physical manifestations today, we should accept them from his hand, but we should not make the mistake of

---

15. Edwards, "Distinguishing Marks," 18.

glorifying them. If we exalt the manifestation rather than the work of the Holy Spirit, we will lead people to fake manifestations. It used to bother me when I saw people faking physical manifestations in meetings. That happened in Jonathan Edwards's day, and it happens today. It will happen anywhere there are genuine physical manifestations in response to a powerful work by the Holy Spirit. The genuine will always be counterfeited. Sometimes the counterfeit is easy to spot, and sometimes it isn't so easy. My experience with these false manifestations has led me to believe they are not nearly as serious as I first imagined.

The kind of people who are led to voluntarily shake their hands or tremble at the beginning of the worship service are not normally "dangerous" people. They are, most frequently, insecure and lonely believers. Throughout the week hardly anyone pays attention to them. Often the only time anyone shows them affection is in a meeting at church when someone walks over to lay a hand on them and pray for them. They often use trembling or shaking or some other physical sign as a means of attracting attention to themselves and receiving ministry from other people in the body of Christ. Hardly anyone is fooled by it, and the only people who are really put off by it are visitors who are observing the service with little or no understanding of these matters. If the visitors are sincere and have not come only to criticize, they could always ask someone who understands the dynamics of these "false responses" and receive an adequate explanation for what is troubling them.

In the few cases where a person's behavior is truly bizarre and exhibitionist, pastoral leaders should approach that person and gently but firmly stop that behavior. I have found that when we talk about the scriptural significance of the physical manifestations and discuss them openly, there is very little abuse in this area.

An equally significant mistake would be to try to suppress the manifestations. Imagine a person who is under such intense conviction by the Holy Spirit for his sins that he has an acute sense of the torments of hell and is trembling as a result of that conviction. It would be foolish to tell him to snap out of it. If we attempt to suppress a real physical manifestation of the Holy Spirit's work, we are in danger of putting out the fire of the Spirit.

Finally, we should never be disappointed when God does not give physical manifestations to accompany a genuine work of the Spirit, nor should we ever try to produce them through suggestion or any other natural means. God does not need the manifestations in order to accomplish his purposes.

twenty-two

ABUSES

Cessationists have maintained that God would not do miracles among those who have spiritual abuses, doctrinal error, or immorality. The Bible teaches the opposite. Samson did not acquire his great strength by long, arduous workouts in a local gym. His strength came from the empowering of the Holy Spirit (Judges 14:6, 19; 15:14). On one occasion in the city of Gaza, Samson spent the night with a prostitute (16:1). We would expect that sexual immorality would cause him to lose the power of the Holy Spirit. Yet when his enemies surrounded the city to capture him, God granted him the strength to uproot the gates of the city and carry them up to the top of a mountain in mockery of the Philistines (16:2–3).

The church at Corinth was so rich in spiritual gifts that Paul was able to say that they did not lack any spiritual gift (1 Corinthians 1:7). Yet they exhibited such a sectarian spirit that Paul called them "worldly" (3:1). In addition, they had sexual immorality among them that was worse than the practices of pagans—and they tolerated that sexual immorality (5:1–2).

They were even guilty of getting drunk during the Lord's Supper. Some of the Corinthians embraced one of the worst doctrinal errors mentioned in the New Testament—claiming there was no resurrection from the dead (15:12). Here was a church with significant moral abuses and doctrinal error, and yet it was one of the most richly gifted churches in the New Testament.

When Paul wrote to the churches of Galatia (probably in AD 49), doctrinal heresy had so gripped the churches that Paul could say to them, "I am astonished that you are so quickly deserting the one who called you to live in the grace of Christ and are turning to a different gospel" (Galatians 1:6). The seriousness of their condition is revealed in another passage in which Paul asked them, "You foolish Galatians! Who has bewitched you? Before your very eyes Jesus Christ was clearly portrayed as crucified" (3:1). The Galatian churches were on the verge of deserting the gospel that had saved them, and yet at the very time Paul was writing his letter to the Galatians, God was performing miracles among them: "Does God give you his Spirit and work miracles [present tense] among you by the works of the law, or by your believing what you heard?" (3:5).

This brief survey proves two things. First, the presence of impurity or doctrinal error in Christian groups where miracles occur does not prove that their miracles are not from God. Second, miracles neither confirm nor support the distinctive doctrines or practices of individual churches or Christian groups. According to Scripture, there is only one message that New Testament miracles support or confirm, and that is the gospel message concerning the person and work of Jesus Christ.

Much of the cessationist literature from John Calvin on has failed to grasp these two conclusions. Every time miraculous gifts appeared in history, the cessationists looked for abuses or doctrinal errors within the group where these gifts appeared. When they found doctrinal errors or abuses, they immediately concluded that these gifts could not have been real.[1] They may as well have concluded that the gifts in Corinth and Galatia were not real either.

Abuse is the misuse of a strength to harm someone or lead them away from God. All churches are guilty of abuse because all churches are made up of broken leaders and broken followers. The church that thinks it is not guilty of abuse is probably one of the most abusive. Our own abuses are difficult for us to see because we abuse our strengths, not our weaknesses.

When I was a seminary student, one of my professors told us we should study the Bible for an hour a day. Before I did any homework or studied for a test, I studied the Bible for one hour

---

1. This is John MacArthur's approach in *Charismatic Chaos* (Grand Rapids: Zondervan, 1992). Throughout the book, MacArthur cites one example after another of contemporary charismatic abuse. Rather than interact seriously with the Scriptures and the *theological* arguments of his charismatic brothers, he contents himself with enumerating the most bizarre examples of charismatic abuse in chapter after chapter of his book. To cite one example of this practice, chapter 7 of *Charismatic Chaos* is titled "How Do Spiritual Gifts Operate?" (see pp. 184–206). MacArthur never answers his own question! Instead, he cites one abuse after another, naming offenders such as Benny Hinn, Kenneth Hagin, Fred Price, Maria Woodworth-Etter, John and Carol Wimber, Norvel Hayes, and the first-century Corinthian Christians. This chapter would have been better titled "How Spiritual Gifts Don't Operate." MacArthur let himself get so carried away that he actually wrote, "Nowhere does the New Testament teach that the Spirit of God causes Christians to fall into a trance, faint, or lapse into frenzied behavior" (204). Are we reading the same Bible? The Lord caused Peter to fall into a *trance* on Simon's roof (Acts 10:10), and Paul to fall into a *trance* while praying in the temple (Acts 22:17). As for "fainting," John fell like a dead man at the feet of the Lord Jesus in Revelation 1:17. And as for "frenzied behavior," the 120 were doing something besides speaking in foreign languages, which caused many to think they were drunk (Acts 2:13–15)! *Charismatic Chaos* is filled with these kinds of unscriptural assertions and biblical errors. They do not lend credibility to MacArthur's objectivity as a reliable critic of the charismatic movement. With regard to the multitude of abuses listed by MacArthur, he *assumes* that charismatic doctrine itself produces these abuses. Yet he misses the point. No one debates that there are abuses in charismatic churches. The real question is the relationship between these abuses and charismatic doctrine. For the most part, these abuses spring not from wrong doctrines but from wrong applications of right doctrines.

each day. It was a blessing to me. I was the leader of all the college kids who worked in our high school Young Life clubs. I taught them how to study the Bible and told them that they should study the Bible an hour a day, regardless of how much homework they had to do that day. After a couple of months, one of the college girls said, "I have tried and tried to study the Bible for an hour each day, but I just can't do it, and I feel so guilty." I thought, *Well, I could say something comforting, or I could tell her the truth and try to help her.*

I said, "Well, you *should* feel guilty if you can't give God an hour of your day." She burst into tears. It was years before I understood how heartless that abuse was.

When I was at Dallas Seminary, we felt that our strength was our knowledge of the Bible and our "correct" theology. Paul commanded Christians not to forbid speaking in tongues (1 Corinthians 14:39). Our seminary forbid students to speak in tongues. I quoted this verse to the leader of our seminary. He replied, "That's not the word of God for today." Just as the teachers of the law used their tradition to nullify the word of God in Jesus' day (Matthew 15:3–6), this seminary professor taught students to break the commands of God for the sake of his tradition. He never saw the parallel.

At my seminary, we mocked the idea of papal infallibility. Yet we treated our own interpretive and expository tradition as infallible. We dishonored the Scriptures by giving controversial passages the most ludicrous interpretation whenever those passages disagreed with our own tradition. It was inevitable that we would do this. When someone makes studying the Bible the most important thing in life, they will always break the Bible's most important commands for the sake of their tradition.

While I was still a professor at Dallas Seminary, I was having lunch one day with a group of students, and one of them mentioned John Wimber and Peter Wagner. Another replied, "I have a serious problem with those two men."

"Why?" I asked.

"Because they teach at Fuller Seminary."

I asked him what was so bad about Fuller Seminary. He replied that as a faculty and a seminary board, Fuller would no longer unanimously affirm the doctrine of biblical inerrancy, and therefore, nobody who taught there could be trusted. As the discussion progressed, he could not suppress his anger.

Later that day, the same student came into my office privately and confessed that he had been struggling with a fifteen-year addiction to pornography. He also told me that during the time he had been attending seminary, he had visited prostitutes three times.

This young man was married, had children, and also was a pastor in a local church. He did not consider the visits to the prostitutes to be adultery. He showed a far stronger reaction to Fuller Seminary's view of biblical inerrancy than he did to his fifteen years of lies, lust, and adultery. When doctrinal purity becomes our highest value, our hearts will always be hardened.

After I left my seminary, I went to pray for the son of one of our students. He was not much older than a toddler, and he was dying of AIDS. His mother sat on the bed, holding her son. He was so weak that he couldn't hold his head up. She was in such despair that I thought she might be dying with her son. I placed my hands on the boy and prayed for him, and I told them I would come back and pray again. The family went to a prominent conservative evangelical church in Dallas, and I asked them if any of the pastors or elders of the church had come to pray for their boy. They hadn't.

I have held dead children in my arms and asked God to bring them back to life. I have held hysterical mothers in my arms and led them away from the bodies of their children when the doctors could not get the mothers to leave the emergency room. But thirty years later, I am still haunted by the face of the mother whose son was dying of AIDS. I have never been in a room filled with so much gloom. I prayed. And I prayed again. But I could not find any light of God or hope of the Spirit in that room. I hugged the parents and told them I would be back. The boy died before I could go back.

If ever a young mother and father needed their pastor and elders, it was that couple, but at their lowest point, their leaders didn't come to them. Good doctrine doesn't heal dying babies or broken hearts. I witnessed this kind of abuse over and over in conservative churches that claimed to have good doctrine.

The ministers of George Whitefield's day (1714–1770) criticized him for going out into the fields to preach to the miners who would not come into the churches. They claimed he dishonored the gospel of Jesus Christ. But eventually the church came around to seeing that those who opposed Whitefield dishonored the gospel, and they accepted field preaching as a valid means of winning people to Christ.

This mentality goes all the way back to the beginning of the church. The elite religious leaders criticized Jesus for healing on the Sabbath. When the Son of God came to earth, the demons showed him more respect than the people of the Book. The demons called Jesus "Son of the Most High God" (Mark 5:7). The teachers of the law called Jesus demon-possessed (Mark 3:22).

How could students of Scripture call the purest person who

ever lived demonized? Scripture doesn't produce hate, but religious pride does. The teachers of the law and the other religious elite had come to feel superior to all other people. They were supposed to be the shepherds of Israel, but they referred to their sheep as "this mob that knows nothing of the law—there is a curse on them" (John 7:49). Feeling superior to others is not a feeling that comes from God, and it leads to the worst forms of abuse and hatred. As Peter wrote, quoting Proverbs 3:34, "God opposes the proud but shows favor to the humble" (1 Peter 5:5).

We all need a healthy dose of humility. We need to recognize that our hearts are deceitful and desperately sick (Jeremiah 17:9) and that neither our interpretations nor our practices are infallible. As J. I. Packer has said, we all are at once "beneficiaries and victims of tradition."[2]

It is only when we truly believe in our own capacity for being deceived that we can begin to see clearly. David confessed his relentless blindness when he prayed:

> Search me, God, and know my heart;
>> test me and know my anxious thoughts.
> See if there is any offensive way in me,
>> and lead me in the way everlasting.
>
> *Psalm 139:23–24*

If "the man after God's own heart," who wrote a large portion of the Psalms, saw his need for God to reveal his faults and sins, how much more should we seek that revelatory ministry?

---

2. J. I. Packer, *Truth and Power: The Place of Scripture in the Christian Life* (Wheaton, IL: Shaw, 1996), 289.

twenty-three

THE GIFT OF
TEACHING

Toward the end of the Sermon on the Mount, Jesus divided humanity into two groups—those on a wide road and those on a narrow road (Matthew 7:13–14). We are all born on the wide road. We don't have to do anything to stay on the wide road, just do what seems natural and go with the flow. That road leads to hell, and many are on that road. The narrow road leads to heaven, and few are on it. The wide road is a smooth road, but the narrow road is a bumpy road. The narrow road is a road of duty to God and to people. It is filled with obligations, persecution, and other suffering. Evangelists get people onto the narrow road, and teachers guide people down the narrow road.

Teachers explain the obligations, warn about the penalties for failing to fulfill the obligations, and display the rewards for satisfying the obligations. Great teachers like Jesus never ignore the obligations, but they don't major in the obligations. They major in God. They show us how to enjoy the road by enjoying

God, which involves finding our pleasure in him and feeling his pleasure in us.

Great teachers smooth the bumps out of the narrow road by showing us how to enjoy the obligations. The goal is not just to pray, but to enjoy praying. When my main focus is obedience, I am least obedient. When my main focus is enjoying God, I am most obedient.

When we enjoy God, his commands refresh our soul, make us wise, give joy to our hearts, and give light to our eyes (Psalm 19:7–8; see Matthew 11:28–30).

THE SPIRITUAL GIFT OF TEACHING REVEALS THE BEAUTY OF GOD AND HIS KINGDOM

The spiritual gifts are not human abilities energized by the Holy Spirit. A person can be a great college professor but not have the spiritual gift of teaching. A spiritual gift is an endowment of grace empowered by the Holy Spirit to build up the people of God.[1] The gift of teaching is not primarily the ability to explain Scripture. It is the supernatural empowerment to reveal the excellencies of the Trinity and the kingdom of God in a way that leads people into a deeper friendship with God. This is the foundational ministry of all Christians, not just teachers.

The apostle Peter wrote, "You are a chosen race, a royal priesthood, a holy nation, a people for his own possession, that you may proclaim the excellencies of him who called you out of darkness into his marvelous light" (1 Peter 2:9 ESV). Teachers

---

1. See chapter 24 for a fuller discussion of the nature of the spiritual gifts.

use Scripture, historical examples, logic, and, above all, their own experiences of the excellencies of the Trinity to lead the people of God into this great proclamation.

The great danger for teachers is that they will fail to experience the excellencies of the Trinity, so that their teaching devolves into a recitation of scriptural obligations, and finally into the sectarian obligations of their group as they peddle nothing more than the rules of men. This is what happened to the "teachers of the law" in the days of Jesus.

THE TEACHERS OF THE LAW TOOK AWAY THE KEY OF KNOWLEDGE

By the time of the writing prophets, there were three groups of teachers in Israel. The priests taught the law; the wise men taught practical skills for everyday living (Proverbs); and the prophets revealed the future and the present priorities of God for individuals and groups (Jeremiah 18:18; see Ezekiel 7:26). By the time of Jesus, a single group, called *grammateus* or *nomikos* in Greek, had taken over the teaching function of the priests and wise men. The KJV called them "scribes" because originally these men worked out of the temple and made copies of the Scriptures. But they became much more than copiers; they became the scriptural scholars of the day. Modern translations call them "teachers of the law" or "experts in the law."

Greek language, thought, and customs had weakened Jewish religion. In his entry on *didasko* ("teaching") in the *Theological Dictionary of the New Testament*, Karl Rengstorf wrote, "Scribal learning was a reaction by conservative Judaism to the disintegrating force of Hellenism."[2] But the problem for Judaism was that their scriptural experts adopted the methods of the Hellenists. The teachers of the law emphasized exegesis—drawing the meaning out of the original language of the law—over obedience to the law. Learning and studying the law became the highest value of the teachers of the law. The intellectual triumphed over the moral.[3]

There is another fault inherent in the scriptural scholars' approach to Scripture. When anyone studies Scripture to protect and prove the superiority of their theology and way of life, they lose the ability to hear Scripture criticize their theology and way of life. This is exactly what happened to the teachers of the law in their conflict with Jesus.

Their ultimate value was to study Scripture and teach it, guaranteeing that they would deify the Bible and glorify the mind. Jesus confirmed this in his evaluation of them:

> "And the Father who sent me has himself testified concerning me. You have never heard his voice nor seen his form, nor does his word dwell in you, for you do not believe in the one he sent. You study the Scriptures diligently because you think that in them you have eternal life. These are the very Scriptures that testify about me, yet you refuse to come to me to have life.
>
> "I do not accept glory from human beings, but I know you. I know that you do not have the love of God in your hearts. I have come in my Father's name, and you do not accept me; but if someone else comes in his own name,

---

2. *TDNT* 2:142.
3. See ibid.

you will accept him. How can you believe since you accept glory from one another but do not seek the glory that comes from the only God?"

John 5:37–44

Jesus said that the Bible teachers of the Jews, instead of hearing from God, nullified the commands of God in order to observe their own traditions and that their teaching was nothing but human rules (Matthew 15:3–9; Mark 7:6–13). The teachers of the law became the biggest enemies of God (Matthew 23:2–36). That is what always happens when religious people worship the Bible and their interpretations of the Bible.

The teachers of the law defiled not only themselves but also all those who listened to them. Jesus said, "Woe to you experts in the law, because you have taken away the key to knowledge. You yourselves have not entered, and you have hindered those who were entering" (Luke 11:52). Jesus had a completely different way of teaching.

THE TEACHING OF JESUS AND THE APOSTLES WAS EMPOWERED BY THE HOLY SPIRIT

Jesus used the Bible, but he did not receive his knowledge of the Bible independently of his Father. He claimed that all his teaching came by revelation from his Father (John 7:16; 8:28; 12:49–50; 14:24).[4] Jesus promised the apostles that God would also reveal

---

4. I came of age in a theological tradition that thought the spiritual gift of teaching was the ability to explain the Scripture. If you look up every reference to "teaching"

to them what they were to teach. He said, "But the Advocate, the Holy Spirit, whom the Father will send in my name, will teach you all things and will remind you of everything I have said to you" (John 14:26). I used to think this promise only applied to the apostles to help them write Scripture. But only three of the original twelve wrote Scripture. If the Son of God needed the revelation of his Father for his teaching, how much more did the apostles need the revelation of the Holy Spirit for their teaching? It follows, then, that all of us who are teachers need the revelatory ministry of the Holy Spirit to guide us into truth.

Jesus was dependent on the Spirit not only to see truth but also to deliver that truth with power. After Jesus was tempted in the wilderness, he "returned to Galilee in the power of the Spirit" (Luke 4:14). When Jesus spoke in the synagogue at Nazareth, he claimed to be speaking by the power of the Holy Spirit. He said, "The Spirit of the Lord is on me, because he has anointed me to proclaim good news to the poor" (Luke 4:18). When Jesus finished the Sermon on the Mount, "the crowds were amazed at his teaching, because he taught as one who had authority, and not as their teachers of the law" (Matthew 7:28–29).

The same was true of the apostles. Peter was filled with the Holy Spirit to preach the first sermon of the new church on the day of Pentecost. The Holy Spirit used his words to pierce the hearts of three thousand people that day (Acts 2:37).

(*didasko*, used about 95 times), it rarely refers to anyone teaching the Scriptures. Even the phrase "the word of God" does not normally refer to the Scriptures. It is used most often in the OT sense of a particular message, as in 1 Chronicles 17:3, "the word of God came to Nathan." In the NT it usually refers to the teaching of Jesus (Luke 5:1) or to the message about Jesus (Luke 3:2; Acts 4:31; 6:2, 7; 8:14; 11:1; 13:5, 7, 46; 17:13; 18:11; 2 Corinthians 2:17; 4:2; Philippians 1:4; Colossians 1:25; 1 Thessalonians 2:13; Titus 2:5; Hebrews 6:5; 13:7; Revelation 1:2, 9; 6:9; 20:4).

Even the enemies of the apostle Paul recognized that he was one of the smartest people on the planet (Acts 26:24). But when it came to his teaching and preaching, he was totally dependent on the Holy Spirit. First Corinthians 2 is a tribute to the Spirit's power in Paul's ministry. The Holy Spirit empowered Paul's words to produce faith in his hearers. "My message and my preaching were not with wise and persuasive words, but with a demonstration of the Spirit's power, so that your faith might not rest on human wisdom, but on God's power" (2:4–5). The Holy Spirit revealed the content of Paul's teaching. Paul and the other apostles taught a secret wisdom that "God has revealed to us by his Spirit" (2:10). "What we have received is not the spirit of the world, but the Spirit who is from God, so that we may understand what God has freely given us. This is what we speak, not in words taught us by human wisdom but in words taught by the Spirit, explaining spiritual realities with Spirit-taught words" (2:12–13).

In the New Testament, the spiritual gift of teaching is supernatural from beginning to end. For the teacher is dependent on the Holy Spirit to reveal the content of the teaching, as well as on the power of the Spirit to give that teaching a home in the hearts of the hearers.

NEW TESTAMENT TEACHERS REVEAL THE EXCELLENCIES OF THE TRINITY AND OF THE KINGDOM OF GOD

Unlike the teachers of the law, Jesus' goal was never to simply teach Scripture by drawing out rules for people to follow. The main subjects of Jesus' teaching were his Father, himself, the Holy Spirit, the gospel, and the kingdom of God. He used the Scriptures, but he also used parables, his miracles, his wisdom, and prophecy to reveal the beauty of God and of his kingdom. His miracles revealed the power and compassion of the Father and showed that the kingdom had come in the person of Christ.

In the Gospels, Jesus never commanded his disciples to teach Scripture. He commanded them to "go and make disciples of all nations, baptizing them in the name of the Father and of the Son and of the Holy Spirit, and teaching them to obey everything I have commanded you" (Matthew 28:19–20). His main command was that they love God and one another.

In Acts, the apostles preach and teach about Jesus, the gospel, and the kingdom. This is not an academic point. It tells us that the goal of their teaching was not to explain the Scriptures, but to reveal the excellencies of the Lord Jesus Christ by the power of the Holy Spirit. Jesus sent the Spirit of truth to the apostles to testify about the Son of God so they could testify about him with power (John 15:26–27). To testify about Jesus is to tell the story of our experience of Jesus.

The book of Acts ends with Paul under house arrest in Rome doing what he was created to do: "He proclaimed the kingdom of God and taught about the Lord Jesus Christ—with all boldness and without hindrance!" (Acts 28:31). It was a brilliant ending. Luke was saying to all the teachers in the church who would come after him, "If you want to have a church like the church I just described, devote yourselves to preaching the kingdom of God and teaching about the Lord Jesus."

SEEING THE GLORY OF GOD LEADS US
INTO A DEEPER FRIENDSHIP WITH GOD

The night before the cross, Jesus said to his apostles, "I no longer call you servants, because a servant does not know his master's business. Instead, I have called you friends, for everything that I learned from my Father I have made known to you" (John 15:15). The essence of friendship is not service, but pleasure. Jesus wanted his disciples to enjoy him like a best friend, and he wanted the apostles to feel his pleasure in them. This is what characterizes our best friendships.

Jesus revealed the beauty of the Father to the apostles so they might love the Son of God like the Father loves him (John 17:26). Jesus sent the Holy Spirit to the apostles to show them the glory of the Son of God so they might love him with all their hearts. Seeing God not only causes us to love God more but also transforms us to be more like him. John described the ultimate experience of seeing Jesus at the end of time: "Dear friends, now we are children of God, and what we will be has not yet been made known. But we know that when Christ appears, we shall be like him, for we shall see him as he is" (1 John 3:2).

THE KEY TO THE KNOWLEDGE OF
GOD IS PRAYER AND LOVE

The gospel writers never show Jesus studying the Bible, but they do show him getting up in the dark to pray in a solitary place (Mark 1:35) and spending the whole night in prayer before he chose the Twelve (Luke 6:12). Jesus is still praying for us

(Romans 8:34; Hebrews 7:25), and so is the Holy Spirit (Romans 8:26–27). Every good thing begins with prayer. Jesus taught that we should always pray and not give up (Luke 18:1). Paul said that we should "pray continually" (1 Thessalonians 5:17).

Coming to Christ and loving him are the keys that unlock the meaning of Scripture. Jesus said, "'Love the Lord your God with all your heart and with all your soul and with all your mind.' This is the first and greatest commandment. And the second is like it: 'Love your neighbor as yourself.' All the Law and the Prophets hang on these two commandments" (Matthew 22:37–40).

It is the lovers of God who hear his voice and understand Scripture. Our first prayer is to love God.

Paul wrote, "The aim of our charge is love that issues from a pure heart and a good conscience and a sincere faith" (1 Timothy 1:5 ESV). To the Galatians he wrote, "The only thing that counts is faith expressing itself through love" (5:6). Jesus told his enemies that the ability to understand his teaching rested on one's willingness to do God's will (John 7:17). And his will is that we love him and love one another.

Paul wrote, "Christ is the culmination of the law so that there may be righteousness for everyone who believes" (Romans 10:4). All of Scripture is about Christ and is meant to lead us to Christ and to the righteousness that comes through faith.[5]

---

5. "Law" in Romans 10:4 does not mean the Mosaic law. It means all of Scripture. For more on this, see *nomos* 3b in Walter Bauer, *A Greek-English Lexicon of the New Testament and Other Early Christian Literature*, ed. Frederick W. Danker, 3rd ed. (Chicago: University of Chicago Press, 2000), 678 (see also Romans 3:19; 1 Corinthians 14:21). C. E. B. Cranfield has a masterful discussion of the meaning of Romans 10:4. The three most common interpretations of Christ being the end of the law are that he is the (1) fulfillment, (2) goal, or (3) termination. All of these are true, but Cranfield argues that in the context of Romans 10:4, Paul is thinking of Christ as being the goal of Scripture (*Romans* [New York: T&T Clark, 1979], 2:515–20).

To summarize, the goal of our teaching is to lead our hearers to experience God's love for them with their whole hearts and to love one another. We put God at the center of every message rather than our obligations to God. Prayer empowers the whole process.

Before I knew that Jesus wanted to be friends with me, I stood on my Sunday morning stage and proclaimed principles that I had dug out of the Hebrew or Greek text. I told my audience to follow these principles so they could have a better life. My preaching was more about a better life than it was about Jesus. So much of the teaching and preaching I hear in the church today is not about God; it is about our obligations to God. Most people come to church knowing they don't pray enough, witness enough, study the Bible enough, or do any of the spiritual disciplines enough. Then they hear a sermon about praying more, witnessing more, and studying the Bible more. And they leave church feeling worse than when they came in. Eventually they learn how to tune out the principle-spouting preacher. Thirty minutes after the sermon, they can't tell you more than 5 percent of what they heard.

Preachers preach like this because their teachers have taught them to relate to God primarily as an obligation, not as a Person who delights in them. They may not even know that God. It's easy to preach obligations. Guilt is not difficult to produce. But to make someone's heart beat fast with the hope that God wants them to feel his pleasure in them can only be done through the power of the Holy Spirit.

When I was a young professor, I hurled Hebrew and Greek words at my church. I sent them a dual message: Look how great God is, and look how smart I am. After a few years of dazzling my friends with my facility in ancient languages, a man said to me after a service, "I'm not going to read the Bible anymore. I could never learn Greek or Hebrew. I get so much more out of your sermons than I do when I read the Bible. I'm just going to listen to your sermons and get all your tapes from now on." Since then, it has been rare for me to mention the original languages in a sermon. If I can't make the point from an English translation, the point probably doesn't need to be made.

People ask me all the time which translation of the Bible I recommend. I always say, "Get the one that says to love your enemies." I try to keep my focus on the main and the plain. We don't fail because we can't defend our view of the millennium; we fail because we want some things more than we want a friendship with God.

Many teachers should forget about Greek and Hebrew and stick with the main and the plain in the English translations. Many teachers will benefit more from a good English dictionary than a Greek lexicon.

Seventy-five percent of the preachers I hear say "the Greek means this . . ." or "the Hebrew means this . . ." are wrong; the other 25 percent aren't helpful. They're just spouting off English synonyms. When I was a young Hebrew professor, a famous preacher spoke in our chapel. He made a big point about the meaning of the Hebrew word for "behold." He was dead wrong. Immediately after chapel, the lesson in my first-year Hebrew grammar class was on "behold" (*hinneh* in Hebrew). The Hebrew grammar I used back then was written by Thomas O. Lambdin, a Harvard professor. I opened the grammar to page 168, paragraph 135, and dreaded what was to come. Within fifteen minutes, hands shot up. "This is the opposite of what Dr. Chapel Speaker said," complained the class chorus. There was no way I was going to lord it over the royalty of my seminary. "Well," I said, "he took Hebrew here a long time ago. The grammar they used back then was misleading on the use of *hinneh*." That speaker was a good teacher and a bestselling author.

Here are my priorities in preaching and teaching.

The older I grow, the more I love the Bible, and the more I realize how little I really know it. I read the Bible every day. I read it with pleasure and awe. I love the Bible. I love God more. God has given me the great honor of standing on stages around the world and telling his family the story of my experience of his excellencies. My first obligation in standing before his people is not to be articulate but to have a spiritual life that my hearers want. Paul told his hearers, "Follow my example, as I follow the example of Christ" (1 Corinthians 11:1).[6]

I use the Bible when I speak for God, but I no longer trust my exegetical skills or theological knowledge to understand the Bible. I follow the writer of the greatest psalm ever written on the beauty and power of Scripture. This psalmist wanted more from Scripture than his natural abilities could perceive. He prayed, "Open thou mine eyes, that I may behold wondrous things out of thy law" (Psalm 119:18 KJV). When I open my Bible, I lay my hand on the page I am about to read, and I pray for God to open my eyes. I have more confidence in Jesus' desire to teach me about himself both from my daily experience and from Scripture than I do in my skills to dig truth out of the Bible.[7]

Before I ever stand on a stage, I pray each day for the big

---

6. This is a major theme in Paul's letters (see 1 Corinthians 4:16; Philippians 3:17; 4:9; 1 Thessalonians 1:6; 2 Thessalonians 3:7, 9).

7. The writer of Psalm 119 prays throughout the psalm for God to teach him and give him understanding of the Scriptures (119:12, 26, 33, 64, 108, 124, 135).

things. I ask God to dazzle me with his beauty (Psalm 27:4). I ask the Father to grant me a work of the Holy Spirit to love his Son like he loves his Son. The Son is still revealing the Father to his followers for this purpose (John 17:26). I ask Jesus to grant me grace to be one of his friends (John 15:15). I ask him to let me be one of his best friends like Mary or John (Luke 10:42; John 19:26–27). And I try to ask for these things throughout the day. I want to enjoy God, not endure him.

I meditate on Scripture. I pray every day to be the man in Psalm 1, the one "whose delight is in the law of the LORD, and who meditates on his law day and night" (Psalm 1:2). God continues to answer this prayer for me. My goal is not simply to pray and read the Bible; it is to enjoy being with a Person. When I pray and read Scripture, I feel God's delight in me. When I stand on a stage, I take that joy with me, and before I say a word, I remind myself that the audience that counts most is not the audience in front of me, but the audience above me. I want to honor the Trinity first and then to help the people of God.

I've been a Christian for more than fifty years. I've heard and read all the Christian clichés, and I try to banish them from my teaching. I ponder the biblical passage, looking for what it is teaching about God and his affection for us. How does the passage help me in my pursuit of God? I try to keep the Lord at the very center of my thinking about the passage and the message. Often, I won't tell people to pray, read the Bible, memorize Scripture, or witness to unbelieving friends. I will tell them stories about the joy I've had when I've done these things. And I always set the commands of Scripture in the context of a friendship with Jesus. Before I give my hearers a command to follow, I give them a Person to enjoy.

Every time I hear a teacher say "you . . ." to an audience, I wince. They are setting themselves above their hearers. I say "we . . ." I communicate much better, especially the hard things, when I stay on the same level as my audience. One of the temptations we teachers face is to make ourselves look more spiritual than we are. When we do that, we present a version of the Christian life that doesn't exist. This makes our hearers think that their Christian experience is not authentic. Instead of confessing their sins so they can be prayed for and healed (James 5:16), they go underground with their sins, and sins flourish in the dark.

I share my failures as much as my successes these days. Frequently, people are more encouraged by my failures than by my successes. God tells the truth about the failures of his favorite people—Abraham, Moses, David, and the apostles. Those failures don't diminish his affection for them. Sometimes when I'm revealing one of my sins to an audience, I sense God's pleasure in me, and I feel his strength; if I didn't, I wouldn't be able to reveal my failings (2 Corinthians 12:8–10).

Sometimes I watch preachers throw multiple verses and principles at their audience. This kind of preaching bores people, and nobody remembers it. People remember good stories, and they are moved by them, which is one reason that the Bible is mostly stories of God and his people. Great teachers are great storytellers. I have studied the art of telling stories and have read the classics and many of the great modern storytellers.[8] I save the best story for the conclusion of the message.

---

8. Among the traditional Christian authors are Dante (I reread the *Divine Comedy* every year), Shakespeare, C. S. Lewis, and J. R. R. Tolkien. On the secular side, I love the Pulitzer Prize winners Rick Bragg (*All Over but the Shoutin'*) and J. R. Moehringer (*The Tender Bar* and *Open*). Anne Lamott and Mary Karr are great writers who have

But great preaching is not primarily about telling stories. It is about getting stories that are worth telling. If we want to be great teachers, teaching has to take on a secondary role in our lives. When teaching becomes more important to me than my friendship with Jesus, my teaching loses power.

I listen to preachers quote a passage that teaches God loves us. Then they say to their audience, "You just have to believe this. Preach it to yourself over and over until you believe it." But love does not work this way. It's useless to throw theological principles at emotions and tell people to act as though those principles are true. This is brainwashing, not faith. When I was a Young Life leader, many high school boys said to me, "I know my father loves me." They stared at the ground when they said it, and they were sad. They had a theoretical belief in their father's love, but little actual experience of that love. That's where so many of us are in the church today—we have a theoretical belief in God's love, but not much experience of it.

I feel loved by God today. For years, feeling the love of God has been a daily goal for me. I pray the great apostolic prayers like Ephesians 3:16–19:

> I pray that out of his glorious riches he may strengthen you with power through his Spirit in your inner being, so that Christ may dwell in your hearts through faith. And I pray that you, being rooted and established in love, may have power, together with all the Lord's holy people, to grasp how wide and long and high and deep is the love of

---

written excellent books on writing and have great conversion stories. Every time a classic memoir comes out like Jeanette Walls's *The Glass Castle*, I read it.

Christ, and to know this love that surpasses knowledge—
that you may be filled to the measure of all the fullness
of God.

I stand on a stage and explain this great prayer to people,
and then I tell stories about my experience of God's love. At the
same moment, I tell stories about my present-tense sins. I want
people to get the message that we don't have to clean up our
lives in order to feel the affection of God. It is our experience
of God's love that gives us power to give up sin. When I teach
like this, I see hope through the Holy Spirit come into the eyes
of my hearers.

People don't become like Jesus by mainly listening to sermons on Sunday. People become like Jesus in deep, redemptive
friendships. Jesus said, "As I have loved you, so you must love one
another" (John 13:34). For those of us who are leaders, whether
we lead a home group or a church, one of our primary responsi-
bilities is to create an atmosphere that is conducive to the forming
of deep friendships.

twenty-four

CULTIVATING THE SPIRITUAL GIFTS

At the end of the church service, there were forty of us on the healing team laying our hands on people and asking God to heal their physical maladies. My newest disciple—a beaming, gung-ho young man in his twenties who had converted to Christ just two months earlier—prayed with me for a single woman in her early twenties. We prayed earnestly; the young woman cried softly; and nothing happened. Then the young man whispered to me, "Ask her if she thinks God won't heal her because of the abortion she had when she was eighteen." My first thought was, *You ask her.* Although he was a brand-new Christian, he had demonstrated an accurate prophetic gift.

I sighed. "Forgive me if this question is too invasive," I said to the young woman, "but we think that God may be telling us that you think he won't heal you because of an abortion you had when you were eighteen." She cried. It was true.

This kind of story became normal for me because in my new

church we no longer went to church only to sing and hear a sermon. We trained everyone to come to church with a gift to give away (1 Corinthians 14:26). We were trying to follow the priorities that Peter set for the church of the last days (1 Peter 4:7–11). Because "the end of all things is near," Christians are to focus on three things:

- prayer
- love
- spiritual gifts

Pray so we can find the power to love. Use our spiritual gifts so we can love more effectively.

SPIRITUAL GIFTS ARE THE TOOLS OF EMPOWERED LOVE

On the morning of December 6, 2016, I spoke to the ministry school of Living Waters Church in Tainan, Taiwan. I stood on the eighth floor of a building in front of seventy young people and spoke on 1 Peter 4:7–10. The interpreter and the students read the passage aloud in Mandarin. When they finished, I repeated the first sentence in a loud voice, "The end of all things is near!" Before I finished the sentence, an earthquake shook the building. The students screamed, "Earthquake!" and then clapped and cheered. It was a 3.8 earthquake, one that was only felt in Tainan. That was the third time God punctuated an end-time passage with an earthquake while I was reading it.

Everyone got the message. The gifts of the Spirit are not

an afterthought to spice up our meetings. They are the tools for building the Lord's house. We could build a house without tools, but it would be more like a shelter. Both Paul and Peter stress the fact that every Christian receives at least one spiritual gift.[1] Spiritual gifts are not human talents energized by the Holy Spirit. A person may be an outstanding leader of a business but not have the spiritual gift of leading in the church. Peter said the spiritual gifts are endowments of grace empowered by the Spirit and given to each Christian so we may serve the body of Christ (1 Peter 4:10).

The NIV's translation of 1 Corinthians 12:11 obscures the supernatural character of the spiritual gifts: "All these are the work of one and the same Spirit, and he distributes them to each one, just as he determines."

The ESV is the accurate translation: "All these are *empowered* by one and the same Spirit, who apportions to each one individually as he wills" (emphasis added).

The verb translated as "empowered" (*energeo*) is used of the power to work miracles (Matthew 14:2; Ephesians 1:20; Galatians 3:5). Just before Paul lists the spiritual gifts, he writes, "There are varieties of activities, but it is the same God who empowers (*energeo*) them all in everyone" (1 Corinthians 12:6 ESV). Spiritual gifts are supernatural empowerments of grace that enable Christians to glorify God by serving others and bringing them into deeper friendship with God when we use our gifts under the guidance of the Holy Spirit (1 Corinthians 12:7; 14:12, 26; 1 Peter 4:10). The Holy Spirit doesn't just give the gifts; he empowers their use.

---

1. See 1 Corinthians 7:7; 12:7, 11; 1 Peter 4:10. The Greek word for "spiritual gift" is *charisma*. It is derived from "grace" (*charis*).

All of the spiritual gifts are supernatural, and the Holy Spirit guides our use of the gifts.

Cessationists since John Calvin have divided the spiritual gifts into "ordinary" gifts (teaching, encouragement, helps) and "extraordinary" gifts (healing, miracles, prophecy), but Scripture does not honor this division. In the previous chapter, I listed multiple texts that showed that both the content of teaching and the delivery of the message are empowered by the Holy Spirit. This is true of all the spiritual gifts, for they are all gifts of grace (1 Peter 4:10). Though all spiritual gifts are supernatural, they vary in power according to the grace given us and the measure of our faith (Romans 12:6). Our spiritual gifts also grow in strength through constant use. As we grow closer to the Lord, we also grow wiser in the use of our gifts.

We cannot use our spiritual gifts at will. We are dependent on the Spirit to guide us. Paul had one of the greatest gifts of evangelism in the first-century church, but the Holy Spirit would not allow him to use that gift on a missionary journey through Asia (Acts 16:7–9). Paul had an amazing healing gift, but the Lord would not allow him to use it to heal three of his closest friends.[2]

SPIRITUAL GIFTS ARE GIVEN IN FOUR WAYS

No Christian has all the spiritual gifts (1 Corinthians 12:27–31). Any believer may experience any of the gifts. Someone may be given a gift of evangelism to lead an unbeliever to the Lord

---

2. See chapter 8, p. 65.

without being an evangelist. Usually one or two gifts are dominant in each believer. Spiritual gifts are not awarded for merit. It is possible to have a powerful gift and poor character. Samson had supernatural strength, but he did not cultivate the character to bear that strength with grace (Judges 16). The believers at Corinth had all the spiritual gifts functioning in their church (1 Corinthians 1:7), but they behaved like baby Christians (1 Corinthians 3:1–4).

The spiritual gifts are given in four ways. First, the Holy Spirit gives us spiritual gifts just "as he wills" (1 Corinthians 12:11 ESV), probably at the instant we are born again. This is the most common way we receive gifts. The Holy Spirit never asked my permission or explained what he had done; he simply gave me a gift of teaching. Within a few months of my new birth, I taught a Bible study at 5:30 in the morning to a group of five guys. I didn't even know what a spiritual gift was.

A second way gifts are given is through apostolic impartation. When Paul laid his hands on Timothy and prayed for him, God gave Timothy a spiritual gift (2 Timothy 1:6). Paul wrote to the church in Rome, "I long to see you so that I may impart to you some spiritual gift to make you strong" (Romans 1:11). God gives some people authority to do the same thing today. My father in the gifts of the Spirit, John Wimber, did not believe he was an apostle, but I watched him impart gifts to people frequently.

A third way gifts are given is through prophetic impartation. Paul told Timothy, "Do not neglect your gift [*charisma*], which was given you through prophecy when the body of elders laid their hands on you" (1 Timothy 4:14).

And a fourth way is through personal prayer. Paul told the Corinthians who spoke in tongues that they should pray for the

spiritual gift of interpretation (1 Corinthians 14:13). If anyone
has the energy to labor in prayer for a particular gift of the Spirit,
it is likely that God will give them that gift. I prayed for the word
of knowledge for nine months before I experienced my first word
of knowledge.

WE DISCOVER OUR SPIRITUAL GIFTS THROUGH TRIAL AND ERROR UNDER THE GUIDANCE OF A MENTOR

It is essential that we discover our spiritual gifts and learn how to use
them effectively. For each of us was put on earth to fulfill a divine
purpose. Our gift is given to help us fulfill that purpose. A spiritual
gift is one of the weapons we have been given to help us fight the
good fight. There is also a special realm of joy I enter when I'm
flowing in my spiritual gift that I don't experience at any other time.

I have not found "spiritual gift inventories" to be effective
in helping us discover our spiritual gift. They are testing for
abilities or talents rather than spiritual gifts. And we don't discover our spiritual gifts by taking a test. We discover our gifts
with hands-on trial and error under the supervision of one who
equips and trains the church to function in spiritual gifts. No one
becomes good at golf by reading a book about golf. They get a
coach. The same is true with spiritual gifts.

David wrote, "Delight yourself in the LORD; and He will
give you the desires of your heart" (Psalm 37:4 NASB). If the
Lord is our principal source of joy, then we can trust the desires
of our heart to help us find our gift. But the most effective help
is to find a mentor and a safe place to try our gifts.

In Ephesians 4:7–13, Paul outlined God's plan to help us find our gifts and ministry. When Jesus ascended to heaven, he gave gifts to his body (4:7–10). Then Jesus gave trainers to show his body how to use their spiritual gifts:

> And he gave the apostles, the prophets, the evangelists, the shepherds and teachers, to equip the saints for the work of ministry, for building up the body of Christ, until we all attain to the unity of the faith and of the knowledge of the Son of God, to mature manhood, to the measure of the stature of the fullness of Christ.
>
> *Ephesians 4:11–13 ESV*

The primary task of the leaders of the church is not to do "the work of ministry," but to train church members to do "the work of ministry." Surveys show that 50 percent of the pastors in America would quit if they could support their families by doing something else. They complain about being burned out. They are not burned out because they work too hard, but because they have labored for years to do what they have not been gifted to do. They are crushed by the bulk of the ministry of the church, a ministry that the members are supposed to be doing.

In the army, leaders equip and train soldiers for war. They give a soldier a rifle and show him how to use it, and then they lead their soldiers into battle. God's plan has always been for his leaders to help Christians discover their spiritual gifts, train them in the use of those gifts, and then give them a place in the church to serve with their gifts. But most churches don't equip and train people to use their gifts.

WARNING: THE CHURCH THAT PRACTICES THE SPIRITUAL GIFTS IS NOT SUPERIOR TO THE CHURCH THAT DOESN'T

The typical church service has two parts: singing and sermon. There may be a time when leaders stand at the front and invite anybody who wants prayer to come forward after the sermon. Offering prayer after the service has become common. I went to a singing and sermon church for years, only no one stood at the front to pray after the sermon. And it was wonderful. I was a brand-new, shiny, seventeen-year-old convert from a traumatized family. In my first church, I saw stable families. Husbands kissed their wives in front of me. Men bragged on me and loved me. I saw people won to Christ. My second church was a singing and sermon church. I was one of the pastors of some of the finest people I have ever known. I miss them to this day.

It's always open season on the church. People outside the church say that the church is full of hypocrites and that the church just wants people's money. People inside the church criticize other churches because they do ministry differently. I've been in a larger variety of churches than most people, and I've had one consistent experience in every church: I've been loved. When we collapsed into our dark night of the soul, it was the church that picked us up. In spite of all our faults, I do not know another place in the world where a person could go and be loved like they would be loved in the church of the Lord Jesus Christ.

I am passionate in my belief that the church should equip and train in the spiritual gifts. But I don't think the church that practices the gifts of the Spirit is superior to the church that doesn't. The only one who is capable of judging the ministry of the church is the Lord of the church. And he is also the one who guides the ministry of each church. Once I was sure that God no longer gave most of the gifts of the Spirit to the modern church. What changed? Jesus came to me and guided me through a series of events and brought people to me who introduced me to the gifts of the Spirit. No one changes unless Jesus enables the change. Nobody wrote more about the diversity of Christ's body than Paul, and here was his conclusion: "The only thing that counts is faith expressing itself through love" (Galatians 5:6).

The Sunday Morning Service Is Not the Place to Practice Learning the Gifts of the Spirit

There is no one right way of using the gifts of the Spirit in the church. Every church is free to experiment and find out what works for them. The gifts must always be used under the authority of the leaders of the church. However, I do not think it is wise to let people try out their gift in the Sunday morning worship service in front of the whole church. That is the time for the mature expression of the spiritual gifts. One way to teach people to despise prophecy is to allow anyone who feels moved to come up to the microphone and give a "prophetic word" to the whole church. In my opinion, this was one of the few mistakes that the Anaheim Vineyard made in its Sunday service. After worship, there was a five-minute programmed pause in which anyone could shout out a prophetic word to the thousands of people attending. People endured it because it only lasted five minutes.

We would not come to church on Sunday morning and say, "Who would like to give the sermon this morning?" We demand an exceptional level of maturity and expertise for a teacher to address the whole church on Sunday morning. If we want the gift of prophecy to disclose the secrets of hearts and cause people to fall on their faces and declare, "God is really among you!" (1 Corinthians 14:25), we have to demand the same level of expertise and maturity we expect of the Sunday morning teacher before we let a prophetic person address the whole body on Sunday morning.

Home Group Meetings Are Effective and Safe Places to Discover Our Gifts

The purpose of home groups is to give people an intimate setting where they can form close friendships and care for one another. In a home group of fifteen to twenty people, members share their successes and stresses of the week. They can ask questions and request prayer. The leader should be both a facilitator of discussion and a trainer in the spiritual gifts.

I frequently use the first twenty minutes to ask the Lord to speak to us about people in the group he wants to heal or give a message to. I tell them to discard what they know about each other. Then we wait in silence with our eyes closed for an impression or a picture that seems to come out of nowhere. Not everyone receives an impression or a picture, but some do. Then we tell the group what we heard. Some impressions are accurate, and some are silly, probably made up by the person trying to make something happen. Then we pray for the people who were singled out by accurate impressions.

At some point everyone fails, for no one can learn anything without making mistakes. I try to create an atmosphere where we can laugh at our failures. We keep doing this week after week, and everyone improves. After a few months of being with the same people each week, I can discern people's spiritual gifts.

Then we give them an opportunity to serve on one of the ministry teams for healing, caring for prisoners, shepherding the homeless, teaching kids, leading home groups, cultivating the gift of prophecy, doing administration, and being involved in other forms of service.

A Large Weekly Meeting Gives People Greater Opportunities to Discover and Use Their Gifts

I also lead an ongoing meeting on a weeknight to help people find and use their spiritual gifts. This meeting will have hundreds of people in it, and people will come from other churches to learn how to hear God and discover their spiritual gift. From the stage, a team and I demonstrate words of knowledge, prophecy, healing, and other gifts to those who want to discover their gift.

In every gathering, there will be depression, loneliness, insomnia, and back pain. Sometimes God will lead me to pray for one of these conditions en masse. But in training times, we don't call out general words. We ask God to show us specific conditions and specific individuals he wants to heal or speak to. Most of us on the team have been doing this for years, and it's normal for us to hear from God specifically and accurately. We feel no pressure to make anything happen. We simply wait for that impression or picture to come out of nowhere.

If we're praying for healing, one of us may look at a person and ask, "Do you have tinnitus in your right ear?" Most of the time, that specific impression will have been true. Then we pray for the person, and usually the tinnitus goes away. Each time we do something like this, the Holy Spirit increases hunger for his supernatural ministry in the people we're training. They also grow in hope that God will speak to them in specific ways.

Christians are hungry for supernatural experience. They want to know that there's more to the Christian life than just their discipline. I speak about hearing God's voice to crowds from different denominations every month. Frequently, after only one session, people have their first supernatural experience of hearing God's voice. All they needed was someone to show them how to hear the Spirit of God.

Ministry Teams Give People a Place to Grow in Their Spiritual Gifts and to Build Up the Church

Out of the home groups and our larger weekly training sessions, we place people on different ministry teams. Churches can form ministry teams that specialize in prophecy, healing, evangelism, care for the homeless and prisoners, care for the elderly in the church, and many other forms of ministry. I'll give one example of how a ministry team—the prophetic team—worked in my last church.

Prophecy is the gift that allows someone to predict the future. The prophet Agabus "predicted that a severe famine would spread over the entire Roman world" (Acts 11:28). Or a prophet can tell a person God's present priorities for their life. There were prophets and teachers in the church at Antioch. Through the prophets, the Holy Spirit said, "Set apart for me Barnabas and Saul for the work to which I have called them" (Acts 13:2). That's how Paul's first missionary journey began.

We formed teams with three prophetic people on each team. Before the service, people signed up for a team to prophesy over them after the service. The team, knowing only the first name of the person, prayed silently for a couple of minutes and then digitally recorded their words over the person so each one could have a copy of what was prophesied. We had four teams that took three appointments of ten minutes each after the Sunday service. It was one of the most meaningful and popular ministries in the church.

If a prophetic team member had an impression about someone attending our worship service, they were free to give a word to that person privately before or after the service if they felt like the Lord had given them permission to do so.

A woman named Jean, who lived sixty miles north of us, planned to come with her friend to our prophetic conference on Saturday morning. On Friday night, her husband told her that he had never loved her and was leaving her. Even though her world was wrecked, her friend persuaded her to go to our prophetic conference. Before the first session began, one of the young women on our prophetic team saw Jean and received a message for her. She went up to Jean and said, "This may sound weird to you, but when I first saw you, I think the Lord told me something about you. Would it be okay if I shared with you what I heard?"

"Yes," said Jean.

"The Lord wants you to know that he really loves you. You are walking through the valley of the shadow of death right now, but the Lord said that it is not your fault. He is right beside you and won't leave you. He will make sure you come out on the other side," said the young woman.

The reason I know about this is that Jean sent me an email the next day in which she told me the story. She wrote in the email, "That young woman's word turned the worst day of my life into one of the most special days I've ever had. And you know, I didn't even get the young woman's name. But I guess it doesn't make a difference because it was the Lord Jesus who was speaking to me all along."

A skeptic may argue that you could apply those words about "the valley of the shadow of death" to a lot of people. That may be true, but in this case, they were applied with perfect timing. And one of the ways we judge if a ministry is from the Lord is by the fruit it produces (Matthew 7:15–20). In this case, the word gave comfort and produced hope in a woman who had just received one of the worst blows the devil could deliver. And then there is the context for this word. It wasn't just a onetime lucky hit. The word was given in my church, where we trained prophetic teams and where this kind of accuracy was normal and happened often.

Young People Excel at Supernatural Ministry

Young people excel at healing and hearing God's voice. They will take risks that older people won't take. The older we get, the more we have to protect. I've taken twenty-year-olds around the world with me. I've put them beside me on a stage in front of thousands of people and watched them amaze people with accurate, life-changing prophetic words.

During one of our weekly meetings, some two hundred people were trying to hear God speak about someone he wanted to heal. A nine-year-old boy named Josiah raised his hand to give a word of knowledge for healing. I didn't think he would be accurate, but I thought it was cute that he was trying, so I called on him. He named a specific disease he thought God would heal. I don't remember the disease, but someone with the disease raised their hand, and we prayed for them. Over the next few weeks, Josiah did this again and again, sometimes calling out rare diseases and never missing it. His family did not go to our church. They only came on Wednesday nights. I said to his father, "You know that Josiah is special, right? God has marked him out for supernatural ministry."

The father said, "That's why we come here on Wednesdays. Our church does not train in the gifts of the Spirit."

One of the exercises we did regularly was to ask everyone to find a partner, someone they did not know well. We told them to ask God to show them something about their partner by revelation that would be encouraging. We gave them a few minutes to pray silently, and then they took turns telling their partner what they heard.

At the beginning of one of these exercises, I saw Josiah wandering around at the front of the church.

"Hey, Josiah, can't you find a partner?" I asked.

"No, everyone is taken," he said.

"Come here. I'll be your partner," I said.

After a minute of silent prayer, Josiah asked, "You want me to go first?"

"Sure," I said.

"Well, the Lord shows me that you are bored with his Word. You are not reading it much anymore. But he doesn't want you to worry about it. It's just a phase you're going through, and he's going to bring you back," said Josiah.

It was true. The big Bible guy was bored with the Bible. But I hadn't told anyone. So no one was praying for me. I felt like a hypocrite. Now God came down from heaven to tell me that it was just a phase, that I didn't need to worry about it, that he would bring me back because he loved and missed me. That's what I took away from this nine-year-old boy's prophetic word.

When the church of Jesus began, the Holy Spirit promised us, "Your sons and daughters will prophesy" (Acts 2:17). God has kept that promise, and a generation of young people are waiting to be trained to use God's gifts.

twenty-five

ETERNAL REWARDS

In the first months of my new life, I crashed into 2 Corinthians 5:10:

> For we must all appear before the judgment seat of Christ, that each of us may receive what is due us for the things done while in the body, whether good or bad.

I asked Scott Manley, the Young Life leader whom God had sent to disciple me—to love me and to teach me to love what Jesus loved—what this mysterious verse meant. He said that the most important appointment of my life would come after my earthly life was over. I will stand all by myself before Jesus, who sits on a special throne from which he will hand down the verdict on the way I used the grace and gifts he had given me. All believers go to heaven, and all believers will be happy in heaven. But not all believers will experience heaven in the same way. Some believers will be called "least in the kingdom of heaven," and some will be called "great" (Matthew 5:19). Scott said that theologians refer to this as the doctrine of rewards, for Jesus wants to reward those who have lived faithfully for his honor.

All Christians are unconditionally accepted by Jesus the moment they trust in him to forgive them and give them new life. At that moment he gives us eternal life—a gift we can never lose or give back (John 5:24; 10:28). We can never be loved more, because at the moment he comes into our hearts, we are infinitely loved forever and ever. Rewards are not about being accepted by Jesus, but about being approved by him.

Most Christians don't know about divine rewards, and preachers seldom preach about them, which is amazing given how much Jesus taught about them.[1] So what exactly is the judgment seat of Christ?

The Greek word for "judgment seat" is *bema*. The Roman governor sat on the *bema* in a public court and announced his decisions for all to hear. In AD 52, Jews from the synagogue in Corinth brought Paul before the *bema* of Gallio, the governor of Achaia, who dismissed the charge against Paul that he had broken Roman law (Acts 18:12–17).[2]

The word translated "appear" in 2 Corinthians 5:10 means "to appear in a way that reveals our true character." Whatever has been hidden in darkness will be brought out into the light, even the motives of our hearts (1 Corinthians 4:5). When we appear before the judgment seat of Christ, we will have an audience. God the Father and all the angels will watch as Jesus

---

1. There are about forty separate references to rewards in the teaching of Jesus: Matthew 5:5, 12, 19; 6:4, 6, 18, 20; 10:41–42; 16:27; 18:4; 19:21, 28, 30; 23:12; 25:21, 23; Mark 9:41; Luke 6:35; 12:8, 33; 19:17, 19; 22:30; Revelation 2:7, 10–11, 26–27; 3:4–5, 11–12, 18, 21; 19:7–8; 20:4, 6; 22:5, 12.

2. Archaeologists have found the *bema* in Corinth before which Paul stood. It is on the south side of the marketplace; see Murray J. Harris, *The Second Epistle to the Corinthians* (Eerdmans: Grand Rapids, 2005), 406.

hands down the verdict on our lives (Luke 12:8; Revelation 3:5).

The nature of heavenly rewards is revealed in the way the Father rewarded his Son. Jesus has the highest reward of anyone in heaven:

> But about the Son he says,
>
> "Your throne, O God, will last for ever and ever;
> > a scepter of justice will be the scepter of your
> > > kingdom.
> You have loved righteousness and hated wickedness;
> > therefore God, your God, has set you above your
> > > companions
> > by anointing you with the oil of joy . . .
> Sit at my right hand
> > until I make your enemies
> > a footstool for your feet."
>
> *Hebrews 1:8–9, 13*

Jesus' reward was to share his father's throne (Revelation 3:21), and he is the only person who has been granted the honor of sitting in his Father's presence. The Father poured out joy on Jesus so that he is the happiest person in heaven. The essence of the heavenly reward for living faithfully is the approval of God, which is expressed in the gifts of God to share his rule, joy, and honor and to be close to him in heaven.

Jesus is surrounded by his companions in heaven. Their position next to him is the reward for being his best and most faithful friends. They too receive his approval and share his rule, joy, and honor.

Jesus uses rewards to show his faithful followers how he feels about the way they have loved him. It is his way of praising the ones who endured the long race, suffered for his name, and grew in their love for him. The greatest words anyone will ever hear spoken over them, the greatest honor in the universe, come from a person who can't be bribed or fooled, a perfect judge who sees our whole life—all the good and all the bad, from beginning to end—and then in the presence of his Father and all the angels says, "Well done, good and faithful servant! You have been faithful with a few things; I will put you in charge of many things. Come and share your master's happiness!" (Matthew 25:21).

The glory of earthly royalty, of movers and shakers, of movie stars, of sports heroes, and of geniuses is all straw burned up at the end of the earth, forever forgotten. But the word of the Lord—"Well done, good and faithful servant"—will be worn as an eternal crown. For the word of the Lord stands forever (Isaiah 40:8). And that crown will grow forever larger because heaven is an unending revelation of the greatness of the Lord and therefore also an unending revelation of the greatness of his reward.

The reward is all out of proportion with the effort expended to receive it. A person who was faithful in a few things will be put in charge of many things. A person who was faithful for a few years on earth will wear the crown forever in heaven. Some great believers have given their bodies to be burned for the Lord Jesus. But most of us won't be called to that sacrifice. We are called to pray so that we can find the grace to do small acts of love habitually. The ones who continually find pleasure in giving cups of cold water see the face of Christ in every poor person and in every prisoner they serve (Matthew 25:37–40; Ephesians 6:7–8).

What does it mean to be put "in charge of many things"? No one knows.[3] It is one of the surprises that "God has prepared for those who love him" (1 Corinthians 2:9). That promise of future rule teaches us that this life is only a time of training for a greater life to come.

Sometimes the reward of ruling is expressed by God giving his faithful children crowns. There is a "crown of life" (James 1:12) given to those who preserve under trials. There is the "crown of righteousness" given to those who long for the return of the Lord (2 Timothy 4:8). These are the believers who pray every day for the Lord's name to be hallowed and for his kingdom to come. And then there is the "crown of glory" that the Lord gives to those who have loved and shepherded his flock (1 Peter 5:4). The crowns not only reflect reward of ruling, but they are also symbolic of the honor and beauty that God confers on his faithful ones.

The teaching of rewards scares some people. One person said to me, "I thought when I was born again, I didn't have to worry about God judging me anymore." But the judgment seat of Jesus is not about Jesus excluding believers from heaven. That can never happen. All believers, regardless of the quality of their lives, go to heaven.

Some teach that if a person is truly born again, there will be

---

3. The book of Revelation teaches that faithful believers will reign as royal priests on the earth during the kingdom that Jesus will establish when he returns to the earth. This kingdom will last for one thousand years. Resurrected, faithful saints will reign over those who have survived the great tribulation. This is when Jesus will answer the prayer, "Your kingdom come, your will be done, on earth as it is in heaven" (Matthew 6:9; see Revelation 5:9–10; 20:1–15). Those who interpret Revelation in this way are called "premillennialists." Those who believe John was speaking metaphorically or symbolically and that there will be no intervening kingdom on earth before the eternal state are called "amillennialists." Regardless of which position anyone takes, the faithful believers will rule in the eternal state, and no one knows what that will look like.

fruit in that person's life. But that is not true. Paul teaches that some born-again people will waste their lives on earthly pleasures and have nothing to offer Jesus when their life is over:

> By the grace God has given me, I laid a foundation as a wise builder, and someone else is building on it. But each one should build with care. For no one can lay any foundation other than the one already laid, which is Jesus Christ. If anyone builds on this foundation using gold, silver, costly stones, wood, hay or straw, their work will be shown for what it is, because the Day will bring it to light. It will be revealed with fire, and the fire will test the quality of each person's work. If what has been built survives, the builder will receive a reward. If it is burned up, the builder will suffer loss but yet will be saved—even though only as one escaping through the flames.
>
> *1 Corinthians 3:10–15*

The judgment seat of Christ is a place of the revelation of the love of Christ, not the anger of Christ.

I believe that no one, not even the apostle Paul or the apostle John will stand before the judgment seat of Christ and not feel some measure of sorrow.[4] When we see for the first time with our spiritual eyes the perfect beauty of the Lord Jesus—the beauty we could never come close to seeing in our natural bodies—we will all be undone. We will all feel or say something like, "My Lord and my God, I never knew. I never imagined . . . If only I'd known, I wouldn't have wasted so much of my time."

---

4. When Jesus appeared to John in his heavenly glory, John fell at the feet of Jesus like a dead man (Revelation 1:12–17).

Those of us who receive rewards will be overcome with wonder—"How could you give me so much when I gave you so little?" For those of us who have wasted our lives on the world, we will also be overcome with wonder. The fire we go through won't be due to his anger, for the great fathers aren't ruled by anger for their disobedient children; they are ruled by love. Those of us who have wasted our lives will also see the perfect beauty of the Son of God, but instead of seeing joy in his face, we will see pain. For we will have denied him the pleasure he longed for, the pleasure of commending us for a life well lived. All great fathers and mothers long to praise their children. Even if we've wasted our lives and have nothing to offer Jesus, we will also be overwhelmed by his love and mercy, for he will welcome us into heaven, where we will live forever forgiven and forever happy.

Jesus taught us about rewards, not to intimidate us, but to help us yearn to please him. As long as there is breath in us, there is still time to please him, still enough time left to live in a way that allows him to say, "Well done, good and faithful servant!" Think of the thief on the cross. He not only came to Jesus in the last few minutes of a wasted life, but he became the supreme example of salvation by grace. And I imagine we will see him in a place of honor.

Some have complained that the doctrine of rewards means that those who do not receive rewards will be "second-class citizens" of heaven. But the pain for wasting one's life and losing rewards is only momentary. Jesus will lift up the unfaithful believer and dry his tears. The one who wasted his life will enter the glory of heaven and be eternally happy. He won't be jealous of those who are honored by the Lord. He won't even be sad that he is called "least" in heaven. For he will be a perfected saint, completely righteous, rejoicing in the mercy of God that brought him to heaven in spite of his unfaithfulness and celebrating the grace of the Lord that gave some the honor of being called "great" in heaven.

Some complain that the desire for rewards introduces an impure motive for serving Jesus. A person said to me, "We should serve Jesus out of gratitude. I don't need a crown. I don't want to rule over anyone. Just being with Jesus is enough for me." This complaint is based on misunderstanding the symbolic nature of rewards and the essence of rewards.

We are going to heaven to be united with an eternal, infinite Person. Heaven is a transtemporal and transfinite "place." It can only be described in earthly symbols to people limited by earthly life. John saw a sea of glass before the throne of God (Revelation 4:6; 15:2). He saw the new Jerusalem made of pure gold and its wall decorated with precious stones (Revelation 21:18–21). These are symbols meant to teach that heaven is a place of beauty and value beyond human calculation. The crowns and white robes promised to faithful believers are symbols. The fire of judgment that will test the works of all Christians (1 Corinthians 3:13–15) is a symbol. Even the promise to be with Christ is to some extent symbolical. C. S. Lewis argued:

> For though it may escape our notice at first glance, yet it is true that any conception of being with Christ which most of us can now form will be not very much less symbolical than the other promises; for it will smuggle in ideas of proximity in space and loving conversation as we now understand conversation, and it will probably concentrate on the humanity of Christ to the exclusion of His deity. And, in fact, we find that those Christians who attend

solely to this first promise always do fill it up with very earthly imagery indeed.[5]

These symbols represent the honor Jesus will give to his faithful friends. At the very heart of the reward is the approval of Jesus for the way his friends have followed him. To want the approval of Jesus for the sake of the approval alone is one of the purest and most mature forms of love for God.

In my early Christian experience, I thought mostly about God the Father, not so much about Jesus. I related to God more as a Judge than as a Father. I was determined to be good so God would be good to me. I often felt like he was irritated with me and that the only reason he was withholding judgment was because he thought I might change. My self-esteem rose and fell on the quality of my performance. When I think about my first twenty years with God, I can't remember feeling God's love apart from my performance.

But from the very beginning, I have always carried the hope that Jesus would speak those magnificent words over me: "Well done, good and faithful servant! You have been faithful with a few things; I will put you in charge of many things. Come and share your master's happiness!" (Matthew 25:21).

At first, I wanted to hear those words because they meant I would be a winner and not a loser in the Christian life. But now, at the end of my life, I want to hear those words because Jesus has become my hero. I enjoy Jesus and often feel his pleasure in me. I don't care about becoming a ruler over a city in the next life. To have the approval of the Savior I love, to make a perfect Person happy, would be the greatest reward in the world.

---

5. C. S. Lewis, *The Weight of Glory* (Grand Rapids: Eerdmans, 1965), 7–8.

twenty-six

HEARING THE VOICE OF GOD

Believing in the gifts of the Spirit has become an immeasurable blessing in my pursuit of the approval of Jesus for the sake of the approval alone.

For the first twenty years of my walk with Jesus, I counted on my discipline and knowledge of Scripture to earn rewards at the judgment seat of Jesus. When someone said they wanted "more," I feared for their emotional stability. I tried to talk them off the ledge of irrationality. I said, "We have God's inerrant Word. Jesus died for us. We have the promise of eternal life. What more do you need than that?" But my logic never saved anyone from that insidious longing for more.

I did not understand then that for a long time, the body of Christ has been divided into two camps that are critical of each other and blind to their own faults. One group emphasizes the truth of God; the other emphasizes the experience of God. The highest value of my group was to believe correct doctrine;

the highest value of the group I opposed was to experience God's supernatural power.

Each group claims to have the support of Scripture. But the truth is that most people don't believe what they believe because they made a careful study of Scripture. Someone they trusted told them what to believe. Later they learned to support that belief with a little Scripture. The other truth is that our personalities influence our choice of groups in the same way that our personalities influence our choice of a spouse. Having been raised by a raging mother, I found it impossible to ever marry an angry woman. The boy battered by the emotional chaos of his youth found security in the cool rationality of the doctrinal group.

By the time I reached my late thirties, I was an esteemed member of the doctrinal group. I thought I had more knowledge of Scripture, better exegetical skills, and better speaking skills than most people in my theological world. I had never heard a sermon on humility, so I did not know that feeling superior to almost everyone was a sin. I did not know that "though the LORD is on high, he looks upon the lowly, but the proud he knows from afar" (Psalm 138:6 NIV, 1984 ed.). I didn't even know that verse was in the Bible, though I taught the Psalms in Hebrew. My real problem was that I was a born-again Christian who knew plenty of Scripture and theology but did not know God as well as I knew the Scripture.

The number one complaint against me was that I was harsh, which is a common characteristic of unhealed boys raised in traumatic homes. And I didn't believe in healing, especially not the healing of emotions. Strong people didn't need healing. They simply got over their trauma by believing Scripture and doing what was right. And I didn't believe I was harsh. I simply told the truth to some people who were too sensitive to handle the truth.

Just before my heart completely hardened and turned me into one of those teachers of the law who opposed everything the Holy Spirit was doing, Jesus saved me with the very thing I had hated. He saved me with the gift of healing. After one conversation and four months of exhaustive scriptural study, I believed in healing. I thought the Lord had led me into a healing ministry because he needed a good exegete to lead conservative evangelicals to pray for the sick. It turned out that he brought me into the world of healing so that he could heal me and give a shot at becoming one of his friends. I didn't know the Lord wanted friends; I thought he wanted students.

When I came into the world of healing, I came into a world where God was accessible outside the pages of the Bible. The Bible became a book of supernatural possibilities, not just a book of doctrines. The book of Acts became a manual for ministry, not a record of things God no longer did. In Acts, everyone was dependent on the voice of God to guide them in their ministries. It was visions, trances, angels, and the voice of God that brought Cornelius and Peter together (Acts 10). The Holy Spirit spoke through the prophets at Antioch to launch Paul and Barnabas on their first missionary journey (Acts 13:1–3). The Holy Spirit showed Paul where he could and could not preach on his second missionary journey (Acts 16:6–10). If the apostle Paul needed the revelation of the Holy Spirit to fulfill the highest purposes of God in his ministry, how much more did someone like me need the revelation of the Holy Spirit?

When praying for people to be healed became a part of my daily life, the Holy Spirit frequently showed me people I should pray for and revealed specific things about those people. Then gradually, God began to speak to me about my friendship with him.

One sunny fall morning in 1990, I lurched along the State Route 91 freeway in Orange County, California, on the way to my church office. I was singing at the top of my voice in the car. People don't sing on the 91 freeway; they curse. But I was cheerful on the 91 that morning. I pondered my happiness. I had no exotic ministry trips to look forward to, no new toys to enjoy, and no recent compliments to savor. *Why am I so happy?*

I took a spiritual inventory of my life. I read the Bible more than ever for my own pleasure in addition to preparing for sermons. I prayed more than I had ever prayed. I left my office for an hour each day and found a dark corner in the huge warehouse we used for our church—the Vineyard Christian Fellowship of Anaheim. I prayed for that whole hour. I did not just pray; I enjoyed praying, and often I could feel the presence of the Lord, and sometimes that hour flew by, and sometimes I felt so loved that I cried. And for the first time in my Christian life, I fasted regularly. I hated fasting. I always found reasons not to fast. But now I looked forward to my fasting day. I thought, *This is why you are so happy. You are more spiritual than you have ever been.*

Then that voice out of nowhere interrupted my self-congratulatory reverie. It said, *Don't rejoice in your commitment to Jesus; rejoice in Jesus. If you rejoice in your commitment to Jesus, it will lead you into self-righteousness.* The voice was not audible, but it was as clear as any audible voice I've ever heard.

I said, "Lord, this is so great. It's got to be in Scripture. Where is it?"

He did not answer me. Instead, he gave me a vision. I saw

myself joyfully climbing up a beautiful mountain while staring at its peak. Then I looked around and delighted in the heights I had scaled. I gazed down and smiled at how much higher I had come than the people below me. And instantly I was cast out into a desert all alone.

The voice and vision showed me the trap I had fallen into all my Christian life. I did a spiritual activity because I loved it. Then I loved my skill in the activity more than the activity and felt superior to those not as skillful as me. Then I lost my joy in that spiritual discipline as it turned into another dry obligation in the Christian faith.

A few days later, the exact reference for the Lord's words on the 91 freeway came to me. It was Luke 18:9–14, the parable of the Pharisee and the tax collector. The spiritually superior Pharisee rejoiced in his commitment to God, but the tax collector implored God for mercy. God rejected the Pharisee, but he went home with the tax collector.

I had preached sermons on the self-righteousness of the Pharisee in the parable of Luke 18:9–14, but I never saw myself rejoicing in *my* righteousness. The Bible tells me that self-righteousness is a sin, but it can never tell me that I am self-righteous. Only the Holy Spirit can do that. Our worst sins are spiritual, and we never see them by our discipline and knowledge of Scripture because they lie camouflaged in caverns of deceit at the bottom of our hearts. We can only see them by the special, supernatural revelation of God. That's why the great saints always pray for God to show them their sin (Psalm 139:23–24).

With the command to "rejoice in Jesus," the Lord invited me into a deeper friendship with him. Best friends rejoice in one another. They delight in talking to each other. They share secrets. Their friendship is not about serving one another, although they will do that gladly if their friend needs help. The chief characteristics of our best friendships are love, pleasure, and gratitude. I don't just *know* my best friends love me; I feel their love because they habitually demonstrate their love for me in spontaneous and creative ways. Once I learned the different ways God speaks and how to recognize his voice, I had regular, spontaneous encounters with him in which I felt his love.

A few years ago, I drove home from Dallas and planned to take a shotgun to the Bass Pro gun shop to be repaired. I had an impression to take the gun to a small gun shop twenty minutes farther away. I ignored the impression because I didn't have the extra twenty minutes, but the impression wouldn't go away. When I have an impression that comes out of nowhere and is contrary to what I think, that impression is usually from the Lord. God told Isaiah, "For my thoughts are not your thoughts, neither are your ways my ways" (Isaiah 55:8). I thought of this passage and decided to go to the small gun shop.

I laid the shotgun on the counter and said to the young man waiting on me, "I need this gun back by Friday. I'm a pastor, and we are taking our men on a skeet-shooting retreat this weekend. One of the men will need to use this shotgun."

"You're a pastor?" he asked.

"Yes."

"Could I talk to you?" he asked in a lower voice.

"Yes."

He motioned for us to go outside. We stood in the parking lot.

"Do you know anything about drugs?" he asked.

"I know a lot about drugs, rehabs, and getting clean," I said.

He was a meth addict, and that night he planned to tell his

parents and was scared to death about how they might react. I introduced him to some young men in our church, and we were able to help him for a time.

That afternoon, God had come down into my car and directed me to a boy oppressed by the same demon that killed my boy. Ever since that Montana morning when I held Scott's shattered head in my hands and asked God to bring him back, God has been redeeming my pain. I felt so honored and loved that God would invite me into this young man's pain. Hearing God's voice like this has become a normal experience for me.

I can't imagine how I could ever be close friends with Jesus without hearing his voice regularly. Everyone who keeps the main thing the main thing—who loves God, loves others, and teaches others to love what God loves—has learned how to hear the voice of God. I no longer only "know" that God loves me; I *feel* his love often. Fulfilling the Great Commandment (Matthew 22:36–40) and the Great Commission (Matthew 28:18–20) begin with feeling the love of our great God.[1]

---

1. The Holy Spirit–inspired prayer for feeling God's love is Ephesians 3:16–19: "I pray that out of his glorious riches he may strengthen you with power through his Spirit in your inner being, so that Christ may dwell in your hearts through faith. And I pray that you, being rooted and established in love, may have power together with all the Lord's holy people, to grasp how wide and long and high and deep is the love of Christ, and to know this love that surpasses knowledge—that you may be filled to the measure of all the fullness of God."

appendix one

THE INDIVIDUAL GIFTS OF THE SPIRIT

"MESSAGE [LIT. WORD] OF WISDOM"
1 Corinthians 12:8

Paul doesn't define or illustrate this gift, and this is the only mention of it in the Bible. In the Old Testament, "wisdom" (*hochma*) refers to skill at living life. The book of Proverbs is a collection of the proverbs of Solomon and other wise men. Their sayings offer readers skill in the practical matters of life: raising children, enjoying marriage, walking in sexual purity, prospering in the use of money, taming the tongue, having redemptive friendships, and avoiding the traps that sabotage our lives. I understand a word of wisdom to be a solution given by the Holy Spirit to a practical difficulty in our life. All counselors would benefit greatly from this gift.

"MESSAGE [LIT. WORD] OF KNOWLEDGE"
1 Corinthians 12:8

A word of knowledge is frequently taken to be a beneficial supernatural insight into someone's life. The most common example is Jesus' encounter with the Samaritan woman at the well:

> He told her, "Go, call your husband and come back."
> "I have no husband," she replied.
> Jesus said to her, "You are right when you say you have no husband. The fact is, you have had five husbands, and the man you now have is not your husband. What you have just said is quite true."
> "Sir," the woman said, "I can see that you are a prophet."
>
> *John 4:16–19*

This kind of revelatory insight happened all the time for Jesus and the apostles. I don't know if that experience is what Paul was talking about in this list of spiritual gifts. But I do know that the experience is true and beneficial. I pray for it daily. And it happens to me all the time, whether I'm standing onstage at a conference or church service or sitting in a home group. I "know" things about people that turn out to be beneficial. These "knowings" frequently help a person to have faith for healing, but they don't guarantee healing.

"FAITH"
1 Corinthians 12:9

Sometimes people cite Matthew 17:20 and 1 Corinthians 13:2 to explain that the gift of faith can move mountains. But that would be the same thing as the gift of miracles. The gift of faith enables a person to labor in prayer for something that is not promised in Scripture, and to receive it.

D. A. Carson suggests that George Müller is a good example of a person with the gift of faith.[1] Muller and his wife took care of thousands of orphans. He never solicited funds or even made his needs known. He prayed and received one remarkable answer after another. In an often repeated story, George gave thanks for breakfast one morning as three hundred children sat at the table, even though there was nothing to eat in the house. As they finished praying, the baker knocked on the door with sufficient fresh bread to feed everyone, and the milkman gave them plenty of fresh milk because his cart had broken down in front of the orphanage.[2]

"GIFTS OF HEALINGS"
1 Corinthians 12:9, 28

There is no physical problem mentioned in the New Testament that was not healed. But all the specific examples of healings come from the signs and wonders ministry attributed to Jesus, Peter, Philip, and Paul. Jesus sent out the Twelve with the authority to preach the gospel, heal the sick, raise the dead, cleanse those with leprosy, and drive out demons (Matthew 10:1, 7–8), but neither Matthew nor Luke tells us the specific results of their mission. Jesus sent out the seventy-two out to preach and heal the sick. The only result mentioned when they came back is, "Lord, even the demons submit to us in your name" (Luke 10:17). Signs and wonders summaries are offered for the Twelve (Acts

---

1. D. A. Carson, *Showing the Spirit: A Theological Exposition of 1 Corinthians* (Grand Rapids: Baker, 1987), 39.

2. See "George Müller's Life of Prayer," www.georgemuller.org/uploads/4/8/6/5/48652749/george_muller_life_of_prayer.pdf.

2:43; 5:12), Stephen (Acts 6:8), and Paul and Barnabas (Acts 14:3) without mentioning specific examples. Many people who were demonized, paralyzed, and lame were healed in Samaria by Philip (Acts 8:7). These specific examples are attributed not to Philip's spiritual gift of healing but to the ministry of "great signs and miracles" that the Holy Spirit poured out in revival (Acts 8:13).

We don't have a specific example of what the gift of healing looks like in a first-century church member.[3] Actually, we don't have specific examples for most of the spiritual gifts in the first-century church. This is by design, for the New Testament is the story of progress of the gospel under the leadership of Jesus and the apostles. They are to be our models in godliness and in power, just as Paul wrote, "For the kingdom of God is not a matter of talk but of power" (1 Corinthians 4:20).

When it comes to the spiritual gift of healing, Paul never refers to it in the singular. He says that God has given "gifts of healings" to the church (1 Corinthians 12:9, 28, 30). I've been in the healing community of the church for more than thirty years, and I've observed that some people are gifted to heal specific things. Some are great at praying for bone and joint problems. Blindness is one of the most intimidating things to pray for, but John Wimber saw a lot of blind people healed. Some people are more successful at praying for the healing of emotional trauma. Maybe this is what the plural "gifts of healings" reflects. It may also reflect the fact that healing gifts vary in their strength.

Sometimes the biblical writer classifies driving out demons as a healing (Matthew 15:21–28; probably Acts 8:7) and sometimes as a miracle (Mark 9:38–39).

---

3. Ananias healed Paul's blindness (Acts 9:17–18), but this is attributed not to a gift of healing Ananias possessed but to a special commission of the Lord.

"Workings of Miracles"
1 Corinthians 12:10, 28 (ESV)

The Greek word translated "miracles" in the ESV is *dynamis*, which means "power." It is used about 119 times in the New Testament. Like *gifts* in "gifts of healings," Paul puts "workings of miracles" in the plural, suggesting that God gives grace to do certain kinds of miracles to different believers, or that some believers have faith for certain kinds of miracles but not for other miracles.

A miracle is a specific display of God's power. Wayne Grudem defines a miracle as "a less common kind of God's activity in which he arouses people's awe and wonder and bears witness to himself."[4]

Another common word for miracle is *semeion* (occurring about 77 times), which is typically translated "miraculous sign." This is John's favorite word for Jesus' miracles. The following are some examples of what John calls "signs":

1. Jesus turned water into wine (John 2:11).
2. A dying boy was healed by the word of Jesus without Jesus even going to the boy. He simply pronounced him healed (John 4:43–54; see Psalm 107:20).
3. Jesus fed five thousand from five barley loaves and two small fish (John 6:14).
4. Jesus gave sight to a man born blind (John 9:16).
5. Jesus raised Lazarus from the dead (John 12:7).

---

4. Wayne Grudem, *Systematic Theology: An Introduction to Biblical Doctrine* (Zondervan: Grand Rapids, 1994), 355 (see pp. 355–58 for this definition and a criticism of other definitions). This is the finest one-volume systematic theology available. It belongs in the library of everyone who loves to study Scripture. I have cited Grudem's discussion of the definition of miracle in footnote 5 of chapter 8.

Though not called miracles by the gospel writers, Jesus' acts of walking on water (John 6:16–21) and instantly calming the storm on the Sea of Galilee with a single rebuke (Mark 4:35–41) should be included. Where there was a concentrated outpouring of supernatural power, Luke deemed it miraculous with regard to Stephen (Acts 6:8), Philip (Acts 8:6–7, 13), and Paul and Barnabas (Acts 14:3; 15:12).

I would also include the outpourings of power from Jesus as examples of the miraculous. At Gennesaret, the sick mobbed Jesus as they tried to simply touch the edge of his cloak, "and all who touched it were healed" (Matthew 14:36). My favorite scene is just before the Sermon on the Plain when so much power was coming off Jesus that every sick and demonized person who touched Jesus was healed. That was the introduction to the sermon. Luke said that people came from all over "to hear him and to be healed of their diseases" (Luke 6:18). Those are still two pretty good reasons for going to church.

Some miracles are more amazing than others and can be called "great" (Acts 8:13) or "extraordinary" (Acts 19:11).

It takes great character to bear the power to work miracles and not be corrupted by that power. Paul tells us he did not have the character to bear the power that God had given him, so God assigned a demon ("thorn in my flesh") to torment Paul to keep him walking in humility (2 Corinthians 12:7–10).

Miracles have three origins.

1. First, there are the believers who do miracles to honor God and bring his compassion to the hurting. Before praying for the gift of miracles, it may be wise to remember that great miracle workers tend to become martyrs.

2. Second, God will allow unbelievers to traffic in his power and do miracles in the name of Jesus. These are real miracles that can be a blessing to Christians and to people who don't know the Lord. Jesus said there would be many people like this, but they would never enter the kingdom of heaven (Matthew 7:21–23). It's important to know this, because even though the miracles of these unbelievers can be a blessing, their overall impact will be defiling. I once knew a man who I think fell into this category. His healing and prophetic power and his skill at concealing his double life blinded people to his cruelty and self-worship.

3. Third, the devil can empower his servants to do counterfeit miracles (2 Thessalonians 2:9). Satan's purpose in doing miracles is to deceive those who are perishing and keep them in his camp.

"PROPHECY"
1 Corinthians 12:10, 28, 29; 14:26;
Romans 12:6; Ephesians 4:11

The Holy Spirit reveals the future to those who have the gift of prophecy. The prophet Agabus "predicted that a severe famine would spread over the entire Roman world" (Acts 11:28). This happened during the reign of Claudius.

The Holy Spirit also reveals the present priorities of God for a person or a group. Paul was stoned and left for dead in Lystra (Acts 14:19). When a similar opposition began in Corinth, the wise thing would have been to leave town. But the Lord revealed a different set of priorities: "One night the Lord spoke to Paul in a vision: 'Do not be afraid; keep on speaking, do not be silent. For I am with you, and no one is going to attack and harm you, because

I have many people in this city.' So Paul stayed in Corinth for a year and a half, teaching them the word of God" (Acts 18:9–11).

Another example of the Holy Spirit revealing the present priorities of God comes from the church at Antioch, which had prophets and teachers. Through the prophets the Holy Spirit said, "Set apart for me Barnabas and Saul for the work to which I have called them" (Acts 13:2).

Sometimes people try to distinguish prophecy from teaching by claiming that prophetic words come spontaneously and directly from God, in contrast to the content of teaching, which comes from meditation on Scripture. But when you read the great prophets like Isaiah, Jeremiah, and Ezekiel, it is obvious they spent a great deal of time meditating on Scripture and took great pains to put their revelation into writing. According to Jesus, teaching is also revelatory (John 7:16; 8:28; 12:49–50; 14:24).

Often when I'm teaching, a spontaneous insight comes to me in the middle of a message. So it is not the manner in which the revelation comes that distinguishes prophecy from teaching. Both are revelatory gifts. It is the *content* that distinguishes them. Prophecy predicts the future and reveals the present priorities of God for specific individuals. The gift of teaching is the supernatural empowerment to reveal the excellencies of the Trinity and the kingdom of God in a way that leads all people into a deeper friendship with God.

In the New Testament with writers like John and Paul, who are both great teachers and great prophets, there can be a seamless transition between the two, as in John's telling of the story of Jesus turning water into wine (John 2:1–11). Isaiah's prediction of the anonymous suffering servant is some of the greatest writing in the Old Testament and is both teaching and prophecy (Isaiah 42:1–9; 49:1–9; 50:4–11; 52:13–53:12).

Based on Acts 2 and 1 Corinthians 14:1, next to service and helps, prophecy is probably the most widely given gift in the body. The least given gift is teaching (James 3:1).

Mature prophets consistently reveal the secrets of hearts, causing people to worship God (1 Corinthians 14:25). Where do you find prophets like that? You don't find them; you raise them up. Somewhere in the first two or three hundred years of the church, bureaucratic leaders kicked prophets out of the church. The only gift they honored was teaching. They paid lip service to evangelism. We've been a one-gifted church for a long time. But that's changing now. We're beginning to train for all the gifts of the Spirit. One of the greatest pleasures of my life has been training young people to prophesy and watching them train others to prophesy. I'm now a proud spiritual father, watching my grown-up gifted kids traveling around our country and the world as they do healing and prophetic ministry.

I have written two books explaining how to do this kind of ministry and how to introduce prophetic ministry into the church without splitting it.[5]

"DISCERNING OF SPIRITS"
1 Corinthians 12:10 (KJV)

In contrast to the discussions in the commentaries, I think this is one of the simplest gifts to understand. I use it all the time. Behind everything that happens, there is a spiritual power. It could be the Spirit of God, an evil spirit, a human spirit, or a mixture of these. The gift of discernment allows us to see the

---

5. Jack Deere, *Surprised by the Voice of God* (Grand Rapids: Zondervan, 1996); Jack Deere, *Prophetic Power* [previously titled *The Beginner's Guide to the Gift of Prophecy*] (Grand Rapids: Baker, 2001).

nature of the spiritual power or the mixture of powers behind the activity.

John and Carol Wimber had this gift. Sometimes just by looking at someone, they could see an evil spirit tormenting that person. I love counselors. I'm grateful for antidepressants and antianxiety drugs. But you can't counsel or medicate a demon out of a person. They have to be driven out. This gift also allows us to evaluate prophecies.

The highest level of this gift is found in John's description of "the Spirit of truth." In John 14:17, Jesus promises to give the Spirit of truth to the disciples. Immediately after the promise, Jesus takes up the theme of loving him. The Spirit of truth showed the apostles what promoted the love of Jesus and brought all of the Lord's teaching back to their minds. In John 15:26, Jesus promises that the Spirit of truth will testify about Jesus to the disciples. The Spirit of truth specializes in showing us what activity promotes the testimony of Jesus. In John 16:13–14, Jesus promises that the Spirit of truth will bring glory to Jesus by guiding the disciples into all truth.

So the Spirit of truth helps evaluate ministries or activities by showing us whether they promote the love, testimony, and glory of Jesus.

"SPEAKING IN TONGUES"
1 Corinthians 12:10, 28, 30; 14:2, 4, 5, 6,
13, 14; Acts 2:4; 8:17–18; 10:46; 19:6

Paul taught that there were "different kinds of tongues" (1 Corinthians 12:10). In Acts 2:4, speaking in tongues is the power to speak in a language that the speaker has not learned in order to declare the wonders of God (Acts 2:11). Speaking in tongues is described differently in 1 Corinthians 14:2: "For anyone who speaks in a tongue does not speak to people but to God. Indeed, no one understands them; they utter mysteries by the Spirit." Here it is a spiritually empowered form of prayer in a heavenly language that no one but God understands.[6]

"INTERPRETATION OF TONGUES"
1 Corinthians 12:10, 30

The Spirit empowers those who have this gift to understand what is being spoken, whether it's in a human language that they haven't learned or in a heavenly language that no one can understand.

"APOSTLES"
1 Corinthians 12:28; Ephesians 4:11

The original twelve apostles were appointed by the Lord (Mark 3:13–19). Matthias was chosen by the Lord to replace Judas (Acts 1:21–26). The requirement for membership in the original group of twelve was to have been with Jesus since the baptism of John and to have been an eyewitness of his resurrection (Acts 1:21–22). This group of twelve men was unique and could not be expanded. The names of these twelve are inscribed on the twelve foundation stones of the wall of the new Jerusalem (Revelation 21:14).

---

6. Everything I've just written about tongues is hotly debated. This is probably the most controversial of all gifts. I planned to write a whole chapter on it. But while I was writing this book, Sam Storms sent me a prepublication form of his book *The Language of Heaven: Crucial Questions about Speaking in Tongues* (Lake Mary, FL: Charisma House, 2019). I planned to skim it and write a good endorsement for it. Every book Sam writes is helpful and true to Scripture. By the third chapter, the book had taken me prisoner. It is the best book I have ever read on speaking in tongues, and it is a great book on the spiritual life. Check out Sam's book. I endorse what he wrote and cannot improve on it.

Why did Jesus choose the Twelve? "He appointed twelve (whom he also named apostles) so that they might be with him and he might send them out to preach and have authority to cast out demons" (Mark 3:14–15 ESV).

The key to apostleship is found in three words, "be with him." The Twelve gave up their day jobs to be with Jesus. Their whole lives were organized around Jesus. They were his best friends (John 15:15). Their ministry flowed out of their friendship with Jesus. It gave Jesus pleasure to love them and to teach them to love what he loved. They were to lead the church of Jesus by loving Jesus, loving the church, and teaching the church to love what Jesus loved. When the church of Jesus expanded beyond Jerusalem, they had authority over those churches.

In addition to the Twelve, Paul and Barnabas were apostles (Acts 14:4, 14). James, the Lord's brother, was an apostle (Galatians 1:19, 31; see 1 Corinthians 15:7). James also appears, along with Peter, as one of the major leaders of the church at Jerusalem during the council at Jerusalem (Acts 15:13–21).[7]

There are slightly different requirements for those who became apostles after the Twelve. The most important requirement is the specific commission from the Lord Jesus Christ (Romans 1:1, 5; 1 Corinthians 1:1; 2 Corinthians 1:1; Galatians 1:1). The other two requirements are set forth in 1 Corinthians 9:1–2: "Am I not free? Am I not an apostle? Have I not seen Jesus our Lord?

---

7. It is possible that Paul also refers to Silas as an apostle (1 Thessalonians 2:7). Romans 16:7 may indicate that Andronicus and Junia were apostles, but there are a number of interpretive difficulties with this passage. Some suggest Epaphroditus (Philippians 2:25) and Titus (2 Corinthians 8:23). Finally, the phrase "all the apostles" in 1 Corinthians 15:7 may refer to an unspecified number of apostles in addition to the twelve already mentioned in 15:5. Most commentators argue that for all of the foregoing (with the possible exception of Silas), the word *apostle* was used in its nontechnical sense of "messenger."

Are you not the result of my work in the Lord? Even though I may not be an apostle to others, surely I am to you! For you are the seal of my apostleship in the Lord."

The second requirement as noted by Paul is that an apostle must have "seen Jesus our Lord." In Paul's case, this requirement was met on the Damascus road when he saw the risen Christ (Acts 9:1–9). The third requirement is perhaps not a requirement but a characteristic or proof of apostleship. Paul is appealing to his effectiveness in ministry when he claims that the Corinthians are the "seal" of his apostleship.

Paul repeatedly stresses five things that are characteristics of an apostle. First is the *suffering* that an apostle will face. The most important texts here are 1 Corinthians 4:9–13; 2 Corinthians 6:3–10; 11:23–33; and Galatians 6:17. A beautiful passage explains the purpose of apostolic suffering.

> But we have this treasure in jars of clay to show that this all-surpassing power is from God and not from us. We are hard pressed on every side, but not crushed; perplexed, but not in despair; persecuted, but not abandoned; struck down, but not destroyed. We always carry around in our body the death of Jesus, so that the life of Jesus may be revealed in our body. For we who are alive are always being given over to death for Jesus' sake, so that his life may also be revealed in our mortal body. So then, death is at work in us, but life is at work in you.
>
> *2 Corinthians 4:7–12*

The suffering of the apostles was divinely intended. God publicly displayed their weakness by allowing them to suffer and be persecuted. He allowed them to be misunderstood and to appear as unprotected (they go hungry, cold, and naked) so that no one would put their confidence in the "jars of clay" but in the power of God to use those earthen vessels. Suffering for Christ is a privilege and an honor that lays up for the apostles and for us "an eternal weight of glory" (2 Corinthians 4:17 ESV). Suffering for God also releases power. The greatest suffering in the world, the cross of Jesus, is also responsible for the greatest release of power. Suffering for God keeps the apostles dependent on Jesus and keeps them from being corrupted by the great power that flows through them.

A second characteristic of apostolic ministry is the presence of signs and wonders as they proclaim the Lord Jesus. Jesus promised the apostles that they would be clothed with power from on high (Luke 24:49; Acts 1:8). This was fulfilled in the Twelve (Acts 2:43; 5:12) and in the ministry of the apostles who came after the Twelve (note the miracles done through Barnabas and Paul in Acts 14:3 and 15:12 and through Paul alone in Romans 15:19 and 2 Corinthians 12:12). This characteristic of apostolic ministry is not uniquely apostolic, because Stephen and Philip did signs and wonders also, and probably the seventy-two did as well (Luke 10:1–17).

A third characteristic is special insight into the divine mysteries of Christ (Ephesians 3:1–6), of godliness (1 Timothy 3:16), and of Israel's conversion (Romans 11:25–32). Paul had seen visions and heard revelations that he was not permitted to speak on earth (2 Corinthians 12:1–4, 7).

A fourth characteristic is the blameless integrity of the apostles (1 Corinthians 1:12; 2:17; 4:2; 7:2).

The fifth characteristic is apostolic authority. The apostles were given authority to build up the church (2 Corinthians 10:8; 13:10; Ephesians 2:20)

Writing Scripture was not a characteristic of the apostles. Only three of the original twelve apostles wrote Scripture— Matthew, John, and Peter. Paul and James the Just, the Lord's brother, also wrote Scripture. But 40 percent of Scripture was written by those who were not apostles.

Apostleship is not called a spiritual gift in the New Testament. Most commentators prefer to think of apostleship as an office, though *office* is never used in reference to the apostles. I prefer to think of apostleship as a "ministry" assigned by the Lord, as in 1 Corinthians 12:5.

The fact that there were false apostles (2 Corinthians 11:13) indicates that the number of apostles could not have been fixed in New Testament times, or else there would be no possibility for these men to masquerade as apostles.[8] But the number of the apostles named in the New Testament is small in relation to the size of the body of Christ.

There is no scriptural text that unequivocally teaches that God stopped giving apostles.[9]

In one of my first lunches with John Wimber, I asked him, "Do you think you are an apostle?"

---

8. This observation was made long ago by Archibald Robertson and Alfred Plummer, *First Epistle of St. Paul to the Corinthians*, 2nd ed. (Edinburgh: T&T Clark, 1914), 279.

9. The fact that the apostles had a foundational role in the establishing of the church (Ephesians 2:20) does not mean that the Lord could not or would not give more apostles. Someone had to found the church. The founding director of a company or corporation will always be unique in the sense that he or she was the founder, but that does not mean the company would not have future directors or presidents. Ephesians 4:11–13 may indicate that God intended apostles to continue until the return of Jesus.

"No," he said.

"You have influence in the church around the world, and people call you an apostle," I said.

"That's true, but the Lord has never called me an apostle. Jack, one day I'm going to stand before him, and I don't want to hear him say, 'So you're my apostle?'"

Too many people are calling themselves apostles today. I know some wonderful teachers and leaders to whom God has given translocal authority over a number of churches, but I don't know of anyone who has the five characteristics of apostles that I mentioned above. However, I only know an infinitesimally small part of the body of Christ in the world today. I read and hear things about heroes in the persecuted church in other parts of the world that sound apostolic.

Before the Lord comes back, he will raise up leaders with apostolic power. Jesus' name and the Father's name are written on the foreheads of the 144,000 who follow the Lamb wherever he goes, symbolizing that they have taken every thought captive to the obedience of Christ. They sing a song of worship before the throne of God that no one else can learn. They are not angels, for they have been redeemed from the earth. They are pure. No lie is found in their mouths. They are blameless (Revelation 14:1–5; see 7:1–8). John presents them as though they are apostles in the last days.

"TEACHERS"
1 Corinthians 12:28, 29; 14:26 [word of instruction, **didache***]; Romans 12:7; Ephesians 4:11*

See chapter 23 for an extended discussion of the gift of teaching.

"HELPING"

1 Corinthians 12:28

Although the noun *antilempsis* occurs only here in the New Testament, its meaning is not in doubt. It has been translated as "helpful deeds; helps; helping." Paul used the verbal form of the noun in his farewell to the Ephesian elders at Miletus: "In everything I did, I showed you that by this kind of hard work we must help the weak, remembering the words the Lord Jesus himself said: 'It is more blessed to give than to receive'" (Acts 20:35).

We don't have a specific example of how the early church benefited from this gift. But in all the churches I have been in, I have always noticed people who thrive on helping others. They provide rides, deliver meals, run errands, take care of the sick, and do many other things. They are the first to volunteer to help. It's just like the Lord said—they are happier giving than receiving.[10]

"ADMINISTRATION"

1 Corinthians 12:28

This word *kubernesis*, an abstract noun, only occurs here. The NIV translates it "administration." The word occurs three times in the Greek translation of Proverbs, where it means "guidance" (1:5; 11:14; 24:6). The cognate personal form, *kubernetes*, is used of the "pilot" of a ship (Acts 27:11; Revelation 18:17 ["sea captain"]). What is probably in view here is someone who is gifted to guide ministries of the church, making sure they fulfill their

---

10. This saying of the Lord is not found in the Gospels. It was part of an oral or written tradition of the Lord's sayings that was still in circulation in the first century. Luke said that "many" had composed orderly narratives of the life of Jesus (Luke 1:1). He sifted through many sources to write his gospel and Acts.

goal. This person could organize all the people with the gift of "helping" into teams, making them more effective in helping those in need. They could perform the same function for the healing, evangelistic, and prophetic teams. The "administrator" or "guide" would serve in this way under each leader of the various ministry teams of the church.

"SERVING"
Romans 12:7

The Greek word *diakonia* is translated "serving." This word is used for so many different kinds of service, both in the New Testament and in secular Greek, that it is difficult to pin down what Paul means. He offers no examples here. Professor Doug Moo writes, "Words from the [Greek] root *diak-* were originally used to denote 'waiting at table,' a connotation that was preserved into the NT period (see Luke 17:8)."[11]

In the early days of the church, the Greek-speaking Christians complained to the apostles, against the Hebrew-speaking Christians, that the Grecian widows were being neglected in the daily distribution of food. The apostles said, "It would not be right for us to neglect the ministry of the word of God in order to wait on [*diakoneo*] tables. Brothers and sisters, choose seven men from among you who are known to be full of the Spirit and wisdom. We will turn this responsibility over to them and will give our attention to prayer and the ministry [*diakonia*] of the word" (Acts 6:2–4). Here are the two primary contrasting forms of service. The seven men are "proto-deacons" who serve the material needs of the church. The apostles serve the gospel

---

11. Douglas J. Moo, *The Epistle to the Romans* (Grand Rapids: Eerdmans, 1996), 766.

message to the church and to unbelievers. Most commentators end up seeing the gift of service as relating to the deacons who look after the material needs of the church.

"To Encourage"
Romans 12:8

Paul used both the verb *parakaleo* and the noun *paraklesis* to denote this gift. The spiritual gift of encouragement is not throwing out random compliments. To encourage someone is to give them hope. It is a revelatory gift. People who have this gift are able to fill people with hope by the power of the Holy Spirit. The best prayer for hope is Romans 15:13: "May the God of hope fill you with all joy and peace as you trust in him, so that you may overflow with hope by the power of the Holy Spirit." Every day I ask God to grant me hope and the grace to lead others into this experience of hope.

Hope is the second member of Paul's triad of holy power: "And now these three remain: faith, hope and love. But the greatest of these is love" (1 Corinthians 13:13). Faith is confidence in God to do what he said he would do. It looks to the present. Hope looks to the future. It is confidence in God that my future will be good, regardless of my present circumstances, because God alone holds my future.

All of the spiritual gifts are endowments of the Spirit's power to produce faith, hope, and love in those we serve. No one can serve God effectively without hope. Prophets frequently have the gift of encouraging (Acts 15:32; 1 Corinthians 14:3, 31). This gift was a regular feature of Paul's ministry (Acts 14:22; 16:40; 20:1–2; Colossians 2:1–2; 1 Thessalonians 2:11–12). He wanted his spiritual sons Timothy and Titus to thrive in the use of this gift (2 Thessalonians 3:2; 2 Timothy 4:2; Titus 2:15). Paul required elders of the church to be able to use sound doctrine to encourage believers (Titus 1:9). The writer of Hebrews commands believers to encourage one another (Hebrews 3:13; 10:25).

Hurling obligations at people and threatening them with judgments for not measuring up often discourages those who listen to us. There is a place for warning people of the consequences of sin, but we preachers should do it gently and include ourselves in that warning. My freshman year in college, my dormmates described porn films they had seen over the weekend. I wanted to watch porn, but when I was seventeen, C. S. Lewis had warned me away from porn with a single sentence defining addiction: "An ever increasing craving for an ever diminishing pleasure is the formula."[12]

Now that's the way to warn someone away from sin—by showing the ugliness of the sin, not the ugliness of the sinner. But I had something greater than Lewis's warning to keep me away from porn. I had the hope that God would give me a beautiful girl whom I would love with all my heart. Why fill my mind with pictures of other girls that could diminish my gratitude for her beauty? Warnings are fine, as long as we major in the encouragement that gives us hope by the Holy Spirit.

"GIVING"
Romans 12:8

All Christians are supposed to give, but Jesus doesn't consider giving money one of the more important commandments (Matthew 23:23). It's so much easier for me to give money to God than to forgive someone who has devastated me. Jesus considered

---

12. C. S. Lewis, *The Screwtape Letters* (New York: Macmillan,1961), 42.

money the least of all our assets, but how we handle money is the first test we must pass before God will entrust us with "true riches" (Luke 16:10). The apostles left everything to follow Jesus. Look at what he gave them in return (Luke 18:28–30). All Christians are supposed to give cheerfully, not grudgingly like paying a traffic ticket (2 Corinthians 9:7–15).

The spiritual gift of giving enables a person to go beyond normal giving. They give generously and simply, with no other motive than meeting the needs of others and pleasing God.[13] My friends who have this gift take great joy in supporting all kinds of mission work, paying hospital bills for people, paying college tuition for kids whose parents can't afford college, supporting the poor, and engaging in ministries to the poor.

Leesa has the gift of giving. For our entire married life, she has urged me to give away more than I've wanted to. Not to the church, for the church has always come first in our giving. Her entreaties come after we've given to the church. She wants to give to people she cares about and who have less than we do. Sometimes I give in; sometimes I resist her; sometimes I say, "Let's pray about this and see if the Lord will give us a specific dollar amount." And more often than not, God separately gives both of us the same amount.

In September 2012, Leesa's mother died. Some months later, Leesa received her share of the inheritance. It wasn't a huge inheritance as inheritances go, but it was substantial for us. She wanted

---

13. *Aplotes*, the word translated "generously" in Romans 12:8, occurs seven times in the New Testament. Three times it denotes generosity (2 Corinthians 8:2; 9:11, 13). Three times it is used of the "simplicity" or "sincerity" of devotion to a master, as in "the simplicity . . . of devotion to Christ" (2 Corinthians 11:3 NASB), or of slaves to their earthly masters (Ephesians 6:5; Colossians 3:22). In verses describing giving, it probably means both generosity and simplicity, as in "give liberally, with no ulterior motives."

to give a gift to the church. "Sure," I said. I thought it might be prudent to invest the rest. The year 2013 looked like it could be a difficult one for us. But she nixed the investment idea. She wanted to give to people she loved and who had gone through a hard year. Her generosity provoked a discussion that lasted a few days.

First of all, I weighed this fact: it was *her* inheritance; my side of the family does not leave inheritances.

When Leesa told me how much she wanted to give, I tried to restrain her "reckless" giving. But she said, "When I think about giving those gifts, I get such joy." I could not argue with the light in her eyes. I sighed and gave in.

Within a few days of her inheritance check clearing the bank, she had given away half of her inheritance, and I hadn't seen her this happy since the birth of our children—the best gifts God has ever given us.

Well, what did Leesa buy with her cheerful giving?

She didn't buy prosperity, at least not in the sense in which some preachers and investment bankers talk about prosperity.

She surely didn't buy health.

A few months after her giving spree, she ended up in an ICU bed with her spirit barely tethered to her body. At the time, no one really knew where her spirit was. And the physicians did not expect her to wake up.

Her cheerful giving did not buy one of those great "Get up! Pick up your mat and walk" miracles.

And her cheerful giving has not bought a complete recovery.

The only thing I can say for sure that Leesa bought with her cheerful giving was the pleasure of Jesus. She made God a little happy, maybe like another woman who broke an alabaster jar of perfume and "wasted" her inheritance on Jesus.

And that is the purpose of the gift of giving—to love people and to make the Giver of life smile when he looks our way.

"TO LEAD"
Romans 12:8

The verb Paul chose to express the spiritual gift of leading is *proistemi*—the same verb he used for elders leading the church: "Let the elders who rule [*proistemi*] well be considered worthy of double honor, especially those who labor in preaching and teaching" (1 Timothy 5:17 ESV). All elders lead, but not all leaders are elders. If Paul had wanted to confine the gift of leading to elders, he would have used the word *elder* with the gift of leading in Romans 12:8. All elders lead, but not all elders are preachers or teachers.

Four different words are used to describe the ministry of those who direct the affairs of local churches:

- They are called *elders*—a word that emphasizes the wisdom and fatherly heart that come from walking with Jesus over a long period of time.
- They are called *shepherds*. The best description of what the shepherds of God's people do comes from Ezekiel 34:4: they strengthen the weak, heal the sick, bind up the injured, bring back the strays, and search for the lost. This word emphasizes their protecting and compassionate caregiving role.
- They are called *overseers* (1 Timothy 3:2) and *leaders* (Hebrews 13:17)—words that emphasize their authority to make decisions that affect the direction of all the ministries of the church.

These words—elders, shepherds/pastors, and overseers/ leaders—are all used interchangeably in the New Testament (Acts 20:28; Hebrews 13:7, 17; 1 Peter 5:1–4). Later the word *overseer* (*episkopos*) was rendered as "bishop" in English and elevated to have authority over several churches.

All elders must be Christlike in character (1 Timothy 3:2–7; Titus 1:6–8) and have an unshakable understanding of the gospel message so they can encourage the church "by sound doctrine and refute those who oppose it" (Titus 1:9). Elders have authority to lead the entire ministry of the church, but not authority to direct the personal lives of church members.

Those who have the spiritual gift of leading but are not elders may lead various ministries within the church. All of the ministry teams in the church need leaders and administrators to guide them. I'm thinking of the worship teams, the mercy teams that serve in the prisons and care for the poor and homeless, the healing teams that pray for physical and emotional healing, the deacon teams, the teaching teams for small children all the way up to adults, the evangelistic teams, the prophetic teams, and the teams that are responsible for equipping and training the church in the gifts of the Spirit.

"TO SHOW MERCY"
Romans 12:8

To show mercy is to show kindness to those who have no claim on that kindness. The people who regularly have joy in showing mercy are those with the spiritual gift of mercy. They have joy in feeding the poor, in clothing the homeless, and in visiting prisoners, and they have a great inheritance reserved for them in heaven (Matthew 25:34–40). People who have the gift of serving or helping often have the gift of mercy as well. The leaders of the church should take special care in facilitating the ministry of those who have the gift of showing mercy, for this gift may reflect the heart of Jesus to those outside the church more than any other spiritual gift.

"EVANGELIST"
Ephesians 4:11

Every believer should pray for their unbelieving friends to come to the Lord. Every believer can share the good news of the gospel. The ones who regularly lead people to the Lord have the gift of evangelism. Jesus said, "The harvest is plentiful but the workers are few. Ask the Lord of the harvest, therefore, to send out workers into his harvest field" (Matthew 9:37–38). This is still true in our day. It would be so helpful if every church had an evangelist whose full-time job was to recruit, equip, train, and deploy evangelists for the harvest.

"PASTOR"
Ephesians 4:11

The dominant view of "the pastors and teachers" of Ephesians 4:11 is that these two gifts are always given together. Every pastor is a teacher, and every teacher is a pastor. This view is based on a misunderstanding of Greek grammar,[14] as well as on

---

14. The dominant view appeals to the Granville Sharp rule, which states that under certain conditions when a single definite article governs two personal nouns connected by the conjunction *and* (*kai*), the nouns always refer to the same person. One of the conditions for this to be true is that both nouns have to be singular. In Ephesians 4:11, they are both plural, so the Granville Sharp rule does not apply. For a lucid discussion of the Granville Sharp rule and its application to Ephesians 4:11, see Daniel B. Wallace, *Greek Grammar beyond the Basics: An Exegetical Syntax of the New Testament* (Grand Rapids: Zondervan, 1996), 284.

a misunderstanding of the nature of these gifts. I know a number of people who have the spiritual gift of pastoring but not the gift of teaching. In a perfect world, the leader of a church may be both a pastor and a teacher, but in our world, even if a person has both gifts, one of the two tends to dominate.

Another factor that makes it unlikely that all pastors are teachers is that teaching is one of the rarer spiritual gifts. James said, "Not many of you should become teachers, my fellow believers, because you know that we who teach will be judged more strictly" (James 3:1). Pastors strengthen the weak, heal the sick, bind up the injured, bring back the strays, and search for the lost (Ezekiel 34:4). Pastors are the healers and counselors of the church. It's impossible for one person to pastor the whole church. The healthiest churches I've seen have vibrant home groups led by those with the spiritual gift of pastoring.

A CELIBATE LIFESTYLE
1 Corinthians 7:1–7

This is the rarest of all the spiritual gifts. The person who has this gift will have a more fulfilling life by staying single.

appendix two

MORE REASONS WHY GOD HEALS AND WORKS MIRACLES

The following examples confirm the fact that miracles and healing were meant to continue throughout the history of the church.

God heals to remove hindrances to ministry. Jesus found Peter's mother-in-law lying sick with a fever. He "took her hand and helped her up. The fever left her" (Mark 1:31). As soon as she was healed, Mark says that "she began to wait on them." In this case, her sickness was a hindrance to her service to the Lord Jesus, so the Lord healed her. Yet sometimes the Lord does not choose to remove a hindrance to ministry by healing but gives grace to bear the hindrance while still engaging in service (see 2 Corinthians 12:7; 1 Timothy 5:23).

God does miracles in order to teach us. Theologians call this the "pedagogical purpose" of miracles (from the Greek *paideuo*, "to bring up, educate"). John had this in mind when he called the miracles of Jesus "signs." A sign is something that points beyond itself to something greater.

All of Jesus' miracles teach us something about his nature, ministry, and kingdom. When Jesus turned the water into wine, for example, he was not just demonstrating his power over nature; he was showing us a common characteristic of his kingdom. In his kingdom, the ordinary will be turned into the extraordinary. The fact that the master of the banquet comments specifically that the best wine was saved for last may also tell us something about the way in which the kingdom will culminate.

Jesus drew lessons from his miracles. When he cursed the fig tree so that it withered, his disciples asked him about the meaning of this. He used that miracle to demonstrate the power of faith (Matthew 21:18–22). If we took the time to meditate on his present-day works and to ask him for the illumination of the Holy Spirit, his miracles, healings, and special answers to prayer would teach us something beyond the miracles themselves.

God does miracles to bring people to salvation. Theologians refer to this as God's "soteriological purpose" (from Greek *soteria*, "salvation"). God's soteriological purposes can be divided into three categories: (1) God does miracles to lead people to repentance; (2) he does miracles to open doors for evangelism; and (3) he does miracles to authenticate his Son and the gospel message.

Miracles can lead people to repentance. When Jesus led Peter, James, and John to a miraculous catch of fish, Peter "fell at Jesus' knees and said, 'Go away from me, Lord; I am a sinful man!'" (Luke 5:8). Jesus said this is what should have occurred in the cities where he had done most of his miracles (Matthew 11:20–24). He made a similar claim about the religious leaders:

"If I had not done among them the works no one else did, they would not be guilty of sin. As it is, they have seen, and yet they have hated both me and my Father" (John 15:24).

Miracles open doors for evangelism and can produce faith in Jesus. The Gospels record that the report of miracles went out through the land, causing people to want to hear Jesus for themselves (Matthew 9:26, 31; Mark 5:20; Luke 5:15; John 4:30, 42; 6:2; 12:9–11, 17–19). Luke writes, "When the crowds heard Philip and saw the signs he performed, they all paid close attention to what he said" (Acts 8:6). Peter healed the paralytic Aeneas, and "all those who lived in Lydda and Sharon saw him and turned to the Lord" (Acts 9:35). When Peter raised Dorcas from the dead, "this became known all over Joppa, and many people believed in the Lord" (Acts 9:42).

Although miracles always draw a crowd, they do not guarantee faith. After the raising of Lazarus, John records, "Therefore many of the Jews who had come to visit Mary, and had seen what Jesus did, believed in him" (John 11:45; see 12:11). But the raising of Lazarus made the hardened religious leaders determined to kill Jesus (John 11:45–53).

Miracles manifest the kingdom of God. In the messianic kingdom, the Holy Spirit was poured out on all people, without distinction in regard to age, sex, or economic position (Joel 2:28–29). According to Joel's prophecy, the outpouring of the Spirit would result in an abundance of dreams, visions, and prophecies. Unlike the Old Testament period in which only a few prophesied or worked miracles in any one generation, these miraculous phenomena would be distributed widely across the people of God in the messianic kingdom.

These miraculous phenomena were not simply signs of the

kingdom of God; they were an essential part of it. The kingdom of God is the rule of God. When Jesus came, the kingdom of God came. God exercised his rule in a new and more decisive fashion.

Jesus brought an authority over demons that had never been seen or heard of before (see Mark 1:27). Jesus said, "But if it is by the Spirit of God that I drive out demons, then the kingdom of God has come upon you" (Matthew 12:28). The power to drive out demons is not simply a sign that the kingdom is here, but an essential part of the rule of God. For Jesus came "to destroy the devil's work" (1 John 3:8).

Miracles and the kingdom of God are inseparably linked. Wherever the kingdom was preached in the New Testament, miracles were performed.

God heals for his sovereign purposes. There are a number of healings in the New Testament for which no explanation is given. The writer does not mention faith on the part of those being healed or on the part of those bringing them. There is no mention of the glory of the Lord or the compassion of the Lord. Jesus healed simply because he wanted to. This is true of a group of miracles that take place on the Sabbath day (Matthew 12:9–13; Mark 3:1–5; Luke 6:6–10; 14:1–4; John 5:1–9). And there is also the healing of Malchus's ear (Luke 22:50–51), where Jesus refuses to accept the consequences of Peter's rash act.

Today there are times when the Lord heals someone we never would have expected him to heal, or he does it in a way we would not expect, and he gives no reason for it. Conversely, there are times when we would expect him to heal and he doesn't, and again he gives no reason for it, for God is sovereign.

THE UNIVERSAL DISTRIBUTION OF SPIRITUAL GIFTS

Those who follow B. B. Warfield argue that only the apostles and two of their "deputies"—Stephen and Philip—healed in the book of Acts. This argument is flawed methodologically and factually.

Even if it were true that we could only find a few people in the book of Acts who actually displayed supernatural gifts, it wouldn't mean that only a few people in the New Testament received supernatural gifts. The narrative literature of the Bible only tells the story of the few. The book of Acts, for example, has Peter as its main character in the first twelve chapters, with a small role played by John and somewhat larger roles played by Stephen and Philip. From chapter 13 to the end of the book, Paul is the dominant character.

The narrative literature of the Bible is *the story of special people*—people who play significant roles in God's redemptive history. The overwhelming majority of biblical examples of both godly ministry and passionate devotion are drawn from the lives of the few and exceptional characters who became prominent in salvation history. It is impossible, therefore, to justify logically or biblically a hermeneutical principle that (1) is primarily based on the observation that only a few in the Bible possess or do certain things and (2) functions to justify the cessation of these things.

For instance, Paul is the only truly significant church planter in the New Testament, and most of the apostles seem to stay in Jerusalem rather than go out to plant churches. Does that mean only the few were intended to plant churches, and that when Paul died, church planting also died? Even though the observation is correct, the conclusion is false, because it contradicts New Testament commands to evangelize and disciple the world (see Matthew 28:18–20; Luke 24:47; Acts 1:8). The fact that only a few possess or do certain things, therefore, is irrelevant *in itself* to determine whether such things were meant to be temporary or permanent in the life of the church.

If God only healed to show that the apostles were trustworthy teachers of doctrine, why didn't he just say that? Why did he let anyone else heal and do miracles? There is not a single unambiguous text teaching that miracles authenticated the apostles.

In Luke 10:9, Jesus grants authority to the *seventy-two* to heal the sick in their preaching mission. In verse 17, they return full of joy, saying, "Lord, even the demons submit to us in your name." This is a tremendous exception to the theory that only a few received miraculous gifts, and then only for the purpose of authenticating the apostles. Why did Jesus give the seventy-two authority to heal the sick and drive out demons if he intended only a few to do miracles and only for the purpose of authenticating the apostles?

There was also the anonymous man who was the subject of the interchange between John and Jesus in Mark 9:38–39: "'Teacher,' said John, 'we saw someone driving out demons in your name and we told him to stop, because he was not one of us.' 'Do not stop him,' Jesus said. 'For no one who does a miracle in my name can in the next moment say anything bad about me.'"

Here we have an anonymous man in the Gospels who was doing something that only Jesus and the apostles thus far had been empowered to do—namely, driving out demons. Yet neither Jesus nor the apostles had laid hands on this man. If Mark believed that only the Twelve could do miracles, he never would have included this story. The story proved that Jesus had followers outside the apostolic circle who could do miracles, and it served as a warning against a haughty spirit of exclusivity.

The fact that God was so liberal in his distribution of other supernatural gifts in Acts disproves the theory that only the apostles and those they laid their hands on did miracles:

- There were 120 people who were filled with the Spirit and spoke in tongues (Acts 2). According to cessationist theory, only the apostles should have spoken in tongues.
- Many were filled with the Spirit and spoke the message about Jesus boldly in the prayer meeting in Acts 4:23–31. This is one of the most important prayers in Acts. The leaders of the church prayed for signs and wonders, not to authenticate the ministry of the apostles, but to save hostile unbelievers through bold preaching. For cessationists, this prayer is obsolete today.

- There are also a number of people mentioned in Acts who had received the gift of prophecy:
  - the prophet Agabus in Acts 11:28; 21:10–11
  - the individuals in Acts 13:1
  - the prophets Judas and Silas in Acts 15:32
  - the disciples at Tyre who "through the Spirit . . . urged Paul not to go on to Jerusalem" in Acts 21:4
  - Philip's four unmarried daughters who prophesied in Acts 21:9
  - Ananias in Acts 9:10–18
- When Stephen and Philip are added to the list, we see an impressive variety of people outside the circle of the apostles receiving and exercising miraculous *charismata* in a book that is almost exclusively devoted to the ministries of Peter and Paul.

Now add to all the evidence from Acts the widespread distribution of miraculous gifts in the first-century churches. All the spiritual gifts are found in the Corinthian church (1 Corinthians 1:7; 12:8–10). Prophecy is found in the churches in Thessalonica (1 Thessalonians 5:20), Rome (Romans 12:6), and Ephesus (Ephesians 4:11), and miracles were being done in the churches of Galatia (Galatians 3:5).[1]

---

1. According to Peter Masters, Paul is not referring to miracles that God was doing through members of the Galatian churches, but to miracles that he did in his recent visit to the Galatian churches (*The Healing Epidemic* [London: Wakeman Trust, 1988], 134). If this view were true, Paul would not have used the present tense of the participle to describe this experience in Galatia. If Paul were referring to miracles that he did while he was in Galatia, he would have said, "Does the one who gave you his Spirit and *worked* miracles among you do so because you observe the law, or because you believe what you heard?" But Paul does not use a past tense. He uses the present tense of a participle, which indicates that this activity is going on at the time of his writing; that is, God is presently working miracles among the Galatian churches in Paul's absence. Some may

The New Testament shows a wide distribution of the miraculous gifts of the Spirit throughout the churches. Supernatural ministry was not limited to the apostles and their close associates.

---

allege that Paul says here that God works miracles, not that people gifted by God work miracles. In the New Testament, however, God is always the ultimate subject where miracles are concerned. For example, just prior to listing the *charismata*, Paul writes that it is the same God "who works [*energon*] all things in all persons" (1 Corinthians 12:6 NASB). At the time Paul wrote Galatians, it would have been much more normal according to New Testament practice to imagine that Galatians 3:5 refers to the gift of miracles in operation. Ernest DeWitt Burton argues that Paul's language "implies that the apostle has in mind chiefly the charismatic manifestation of the Spirit" (*The Epistle to the Galatians* [Edinburgh: T&T Clark, 1921], 151). J. B. Lightfoot draws attention to the similarity of the participle *energon* in Galatians 3:5 with the *energemata* used to describe the gift of working miracles in 1 Corinthians 12:10 and concludes that "as in the Epistle to the Corinthians, St. Paul assumes the possession of these extraordinary powers by his converts as an acknowledged fact" (*The Epistle of St. Paul to the Galatians* [1870; repr., Grand Rapids: Zondervan, 1957], 136).

appendix four

WERE THERE ONLY
THREE PERIODS
OF MIRACLES?

John MacArthur is a modern-day proponent of the view that there are only three periods of miracles in the biblical record. He formulates the argument in the following way:

> Most biblical miracles happened in three relatively brief periods of Bible history: in the days of Moses and Joshua, during the ministries of Elijah and Elisha, and in the time of Christ and the apostles . . .
>
> Aside from those three intervals, the only supernatural events recorded in Scripture were isolated incidents. In the days of Isaiah, for example, the Lord supernaturally defeated Sennacherib's army (2 Kings 19:35–36), then healed Hezekiah and turned the sun's shadows back (20:1–11). In the days of Daniel, God preserved Shadrach,

Meshach and Abednego in the furnace (Daniel 3:20–26). For the most part, however, supernatural events like those did not characterize God's dealings with his people . . .

Miracles introduced new eras of revelation. All three periods of miracles were times when God gave his written revelation—Scripture—in substantial quantities. Those doing the miracles were essentially the same ones heralding an era of revelation. Moses wrote the first five books of Scripture. Elijah and Elisha introduced the prophetic age. The apostles wrote nearly all of the New Testament.[1]

There are a number of difficulties with this argument, and it seems that most cessationists no longer use it. The first difficulty is with the alleged purpose of three periods of miracles. The reason for each period of miracles, according to the theory, is that they authenticate the written revelation that God was giving at the time. In the case of Moses and Joshua, and Christ and the apostles, there was written revelation being given. But in the case of Elijah and Elisha, there was no written revelation being given. The first written prophetic revelation does not come until the time of Isaiah, Micah, and Amos, almost a hundred years after the death of Elijah and fifty years or more after the death of Elisha.

The idea that miracles were common only at the time of Moses to Joshua and Elijah to Elisha is also contradicted by a specific statement of Scripture. Jeremiah claimed, "You performed

---

1. John MacArthur, *Charismatic Chaos* (Grand Rapids: Zondervan, 1992), 134–36, italics original. It was B. B. Warfield who popularized this argument. He was, however, more careful than MacArthur in stating the argument. He maintained that there were four periods of revelation, not three. He included the time of Daniel as the fourth period (see B. B. Warfield, "Miracles," in *A Dictionary of the Bible*, J. D. Davis, ed., 4th ed. [Grand Rapids: Baker, 1954], 505).

signs and wonders in Egypt and have continued them to this day, in Israel and among all mankind, and have gained the renown that is still yours" (Jeremiah 32:20).

If Jeremiah's statement is to be taken literally, he sees signs and wonders occurring in his own time (his ministry began in 626 BC and ended sometime after 586 BC) both in Israel and in other nations.[2]

---

2. MacArthur heard a tape of a message in which I made this point. He took issue with my interpretation in the following way: "Deere is so determined to find biblical support for an ongoing ministry of signs and wonders that he misreads Jeremiah 32:20 . . . Deere believes Jeremiah was saying that signs and wonders continued in Egypt and Israel after the Exodus and that Jeremiah was acknowledging their existence even in his day. What Jeremiah actually wrote, of course, was that God had made a name for himself through the signs and wonders he performed in Egypt, and that his name was known 'even to this day' both in Israel and among the Gentiles. Anyone familiar with Old Testament history knows that the miracles of the Exodus were unique, and the Israelites always recalled them as evidence of their God's greatness" (*Charismatic Chaos*, endnote 19, pp. 373–74).

MacArthur criticized my interpretation of Jeremiah 32:20 by simply asserting that virtually everyone knows that Jeremiah was referring to signs and wonders of the past rather than to signs and wonders of his day. He thought that this assertion was sufficient both as an explanation of Jeremiah 32:20 and as a refutation of my use of it. He did not refer to the Hebrew text underlying the expression "even to this day" to see if it could bear the meaning he had assigned to it. Nor did he explore any contextual reasons that may have led him back to a more literal interpretation of what Jeremiah actually wrote. Nor did he cite any scholarly studies or any other support that could justify his rejection of the literal meaning of Jeremiah 32:20.

Although in MacArthur's opinion I may not qualify as "anyone familiar with Old Testament history," I still want to suggest that Jeremiah's statement should be taken literally. The reasons for doing so are as follows. *First, this is exactly what a literal interpretation of the Hebrew text means.* The phrase translated "even to this day," when used of customs or other activities, refers to the continuation of that activity at least up to the time of the speaker or writer (see Joshua 9:27; 13:13; 15:63; 16:10; 23:8–9; see also F. Brown, S. Driver, and C. Briggs, *The Brown-Driver-Briggs Hebrew and English Lexicon* [1906; repr., Peabody, MA: Hendrickson, 2004], 401, for many other examples). The NIV has translated the Hebrew text in its normal sense when it says of signs and wonders that God has "continued them to this day." *Second, contextually the spirit of prophecy is still in the land at the time of Jeremiah's writing.* Prophecy is both a sign and a wonder, according to the Bible. Consider Isaiah's statement: "Behold, I and the children whom the LORD has given me are for signs and wonders in Israel from the LORD of hosts, who dwells on Mount Zion" (Isaiah 8:18 NASB). In light of the prophetic tradition, Jeremiah's own presence and ministry in the land is a sufficient condition for a literal understanding of "even to this day." *Third, there is the ministry of Daniel (605–537 BC), chronologically*

There is another inconsistency in this theory. MacArthur claims that Elijah and Elisha introduced the prophetic age. This is not true. It is Samuel who introduced the prophetic age. He was the prophet of whom it was said, "The LORD was with Samuel as he grew up, and he let none of Samuel's words fall to the ground" (1 Samuel 3:19). Furthermore, at the time of Samuel there were already groups of prophets prophesying (1 Samuel 10:5). If MacArthur's theory was accurate, we would expect the period of Samuel to be introduced with an outbreak of miracles.

Finally, I do not dispute that the New Testament age was clearly an age of new revelation, but MacArthur is certainly in error when he claims that "the apostles wrote nearly all of the New Testament." Mark, Luke, and Jude were not apostles, and Hebrews is anonymous. These books comprise approximately 40 percent of the New Testament.

Another fault with the theory is that there are simply too many supernatural events occurring outside of these three periods for the theory to be meaningful. A quick survey of the Old Testament will reveal how commonly miraculous events occurred. We won't look at the books of Exodus through Joshua, because these books deal with the period of Moses and Joshua, nor will we consider any supernatural occurrences from 1 Kings 17 through 2 Kings 13 (nor 2 Chronicles 17–24), because these books deal with the period of Elijah and Elisha.

---

close to Jeremiah (626 BC to after 586 BC), which is filled with signs and wonders. Daniel's ministry would justify, if not demand, a literal interpretation of "even to this day." MacArthur does not interact with these reasons or any other linguistic, contextual, or historical reasons for understanding Jeremiah's words in their normal meaning. Instead, motivated by a theological prejudice that already predetermined what Jeremiah can or cannot mean, he simply paraphrases Jeremiah's words into a vague theological axiom that only halfway resembles the words of the original text.

Scripture	Description
Genesis	
1–3	The creation of the earth and the fall of mankind
5:24	The rapture of Enoch
6:2–8	The sons of God (demonic beings) married the daughters of humans
6:9–8:19	The Noahic flood
11:1–9	The confusing of human language at the Tower of Babel
12:1–3	The supernatural call of Abraham
12:17	The plague on Pharaoh's house
15:12–21	Abraham's trance, the smoking firepot, and the blazing torch
16:7	The angel of the Lord appears to Hagar
17:1–27	The Lord appears to Abraham
18:1–15	The Lord and angels appear to Abraham and eat a meal with him
19:11	Angels blind the men of Sodom
19:23–25	The Lord destroys Sodom and Gomorrah
19:26	Lot's wife is turned into a pillar of salt
20:3–18	God warns Abimelech in a dream not to touch Sarah
21:1–8	Sarah miraculously conceives Isaac
21:8–21	God supernaturally saves the life of Hagar and Ishmael
22:11	The angel of the Lord prevents Abraham from sacrificing Isaac
24:12ff.	Abraham's servant is supernaturally led to Rebekah
25:21	Rebekah supernaturally conceives twins
25:23	The Lord speaks to Rebekah concerning the destiny of the twins in her womb
26:2	The Lord appears to Isaac

Scripture	Description
26:24	The Lord appears to Isaac again
28:12–15	The Lord appears to Jacob
31:3	The Lord speaks to Jacob, commanding him to return to Canaan
32:1	Angels of God meet Jacob
32:24–32	Jacob wrestles with the angel of the Lord all night
35:9	God appears to Jacob and blesses him
37:5–11	Joseph's dreams
38:7–10	The Lord kills Er and Onan
40:1–23	Joseph interprets the dreams of the cupbearer and the baker
41:1–40	Joseph interprets Pharaoh's dream
Judges	
2:1–5	The angel of the Lord appears to all Israel
3:9–11	The Spirit of the Lord empowers Othniel to deliver Israel
3:31	Shamgar kills six hundred Philistines with an oxgoad
4:4–10	Deborah prophesies to Barak
6:11	The angel of the Lord appears to Gideon
6:36	The miracle of Gideon's fleece
7:1–25	The Lord sends divine panic against Midian so that Gideon can defeat them with only three hundred men
11:29–33	The Spirit of the Lord comes on Jephthah to deliver Israel from the Ammonites
13:3–5	The angel of the Lord appears to Manoah and his wife
14–16	Samson's supernatural feats
1 Samuel	
1:19–20	Hannah supernaturally conceives Samuel

Scripture	Description
3:1–18	The Lord appears to Samuel the first time
3:19–21	The Lord lets none of Samuel's words fall to the ground
5:1–5	The destruction of the idol Dagon
5:6–8	The Lord strikes the Philistines with tumors
6:19–20	The Lord kills some of the men of Beth Shemesh
9–10	Samuel's prophetic ministry to Saul
10:20–25	Saul is chosen by lot to be king over Israel
11:6–11	The Spirit of the Lord empowers Saul to deliver Israel from the Ammonites
16:1–12	Samuel's prophetic ministry to David
16:13	The Spirit of the Lord comes upon David
16:14	The Spirit of the Lord leaves Saul, and an evil spirit from the Lord terrorizes him
18:10–11	An evil spirit causes Saul to try to kill David
19:9–10	Again an evil spirit causes Saul to attempt to kill David
19:20–21	Three times the Spirit of the Lord comes on Saul's messengers and they prophesy
19:23	The Spirit of the Lord comes on Saul and he prophesies
23:4, 10–12; 30:8	The Lord repeatedly gives supernatural guidance to David
28:12–19	Samuel appears from the dead to Saul
2 Samuel	
2:1; 5:19, 23–24	The Lord gives supernatural guidance to David
6:7	The Lord kills Uzzah
7:5–17	Nathan prophesies to David
12:1–14	Nathan exposes David's sin

Scripture	Description
12:15–17	The Lord kills David's child
12:25	Nathan prophesies concerning Solomon
21:1	The Lord explains the cause of the famine to David
24:11	The Lord speaks to David through Gad and kills seventy thousand Israelites
1 Kings	
3:4–15	The Lord appears to Solomon and grants him great wisdom
8:10–13	The glory of the Lord fills the temple
9:2–9	The Lord appears a second time to Solomon
11:11–13	The Lord tells Solomon that he will take the kingdom from him
11:29–39	The prophet Ahijah tells Jeroboam that the Lord has given him the tribes of Israel
13:1–6	A man of God prophesies the birth of Josiah; the Lord splits the altar at Bethel; and the Lord withers Jeroboam's hand and then heals it
13:20–30	An old prophet prophesies the death of the man of God, and the Lord kills the man of God with a lion
14:5	The Lord prevents Jeroboam's wife from deceiving the prophet Ahijah, and he prophesies judgment on Jeroboam's house
16:1–4	Jehu prophesies judgment against Baasha
2 Kings	
15:5	The Lord strikes Azariah with leprosy
19:20–34	Isaiah prophesies to Hezekiah concerning Sennacherib
19:35	The angel of the Lord kills 185,000 Assyrians
20:5–6	Isaiah prophesies to Hezekiah that the Lord will add fifteen years to his life

Scripture	Description
20:10–11	The Lord causes the sunlight to go back ten steps on the stairway of Ahaz
20:16–18	Isaiah prophesies judgment to Hezekiah
21:9–11	The Lord prophesies judgment on Judah through his prophets
22:14–20	The prophet Huldah prophesies judgment on Judah but blessing on Josiah
1 Chronicles	
12:18	The Holy Spirit prompts Amasai to prophesy to David
21:1	Satan incites David to take a census of Israel
21:16	David sees the angel of the Lord
21:20	Araunah sees the same angel
21:26	The Lord sends fire from heaven to David's altar
2 Chronicles	
7:1	Fire comes down from heaven and consumes Solomon's offerings
11:2	Shemaiah prophesies to King Rehoboam not to fight against Israel
12:5	Shemaiah prophesies against Rehoboam
12:7	Shemaiah prophesies again to Rehoboam that God will have a measure of mercy on him
13:15–18	God supernaturally delivers Judah
13:20	The Lord kills Jeroboam
14:12–15	The Lord supernaturally delivers Judah from the Cushites
15:1–7	Azariah prophesies to King Asa
16:7–9	Hanani the seer prophesies judgment on King Asa
25:7–9	A man of God prophesies to Amaziah not to take the army of Israel into battle with him

Scripture	Description
25:15–16	A prophet prophesies judgment on Amaziah for his idolatry
28:9–11	Oded prophesies judgment against the Israelite army if they refuse to release their captives from Judah
Ezra	
5:1	Haggai and Zechariah prophesy to the Jews who are in Judah
Job	
1–2	Supernatural satanic persecution of Job by God's permission
38–42	God's conversation with Job and the restoration of Job's fortune
Daniel	
2:1–45	God supernaturally reveals Nebuchadnezzar's dream and its interpretation to Daniel
3:1–27	Daniel's three friends walk in the fiery furnace with the preincarnate Christ and are preserved
4:19–27	Daniel interprets a second dream of Nebuchadnezzar
4:28–33	God afflicts Nebuchadnezzar with insanity
5:5–12	A hand supernaturally appears and writes Belshazzar's judgment on the wall
5:17–28	Daniel interprets the writing
6:1–23	Daniel is supernaturally preserved in the den of lions
7–12	Supernatural visions of the last days and angelic visitations are given to Daniel

According to MacArthur, all we should find are a few "isolated incidents" of supernatural events. You be the judge of how accurate this theory is as you consider the events from the following table.

Just a casual glance at the table will demonstrate that neither MacArthur nor anyone else can purge the abundance of supernatural events from the Old Testament by trying to cram them all into two brief time periods. Supernatural events are consistently spread over the entire Old Testament.

What kind of supernatural events are we talking about here? The table can be summarized in the following way:

- many appearances of the Lord to individuals
- many appearances of angels to individuals and even to groups of people
- supernatural rescues of individuals
- supernatural deliverances of groups and even the whole nation
- supernatural empowerment for:
  - superhuman strength
  - prophetic understanding and prophetic words for people who are not prophets
  - supernatural guidance and direction in a variety of ways
- supernatural judgments:
  - the destruction of individuals
  - the destruction of armies
  - the destruction of cities
  - other supernatural judgments such as illness, blindness, insanity, and plagues
- supernatural dreams, trances, and visions
- supernaturally given interpretation of the above
- miraculous conceptions
- miraculous healings

- supernatural satanic and demonic interaction with man
- cosmic signs, such as the sunlight falling back ten steps, fire falling from heaven, and so on
- consistent prophetic ministry from the time of Samuel until the end of the Old Testament canon

These are the kinds of things that occur throughout the Old Testament period. Nor is this all that occurs during the Old Testament period. With the exception of Daniel, I have not even surveyed any of the other prophetic books. For example, I have omitted things like the vision Isaiah had in the year that king Uzziah died, when Isaiah was caught up into heaven and commissioned for his prophetic ministry (Isaiah 6:1–13). Nor did I discuss the strange visions and happenings that Ezekiel experienced about 140 years later. We must remember that canonical prophets were in Israel through the time of Malachi (approximately 450–400 BC). So at least from the time of Samuel through Malachi, there is consistent prophetic ministry to Israel. Prophetic ministry is, of course, supernatural ministry.

The book of Daniel is devastating to John MacArthur's theory that the supernatural is basically confined to the periods of Moses and Joshua, and Elijah and Elisha. Daniel ministered from 605 to at least 539 BC, well beyond the time of Elijah and Elisha. Yet proportionately Daniel's book contains more supernatural events than the books of Exodus through Joshua (the books dealing with the ministries of Moses and Joshua) and 1 Kings through 2 Kings 13 (the books dealing with the ministries of Elijah and Elisha). Every chapter in the book of Daniel has supernatural occurrences.

With the exception of the book of Daniel, and possibly the

book of Genesis, the periods of Moses and Joshua, and Elijah and Elisha, do show the greatest concentration of miracles in the Old Testament period. As the table shows, however, you cannot find any period in Israel's history when supernatural events were not common among the people of God.

MacArthur would dispute the significance of this table. He is able to do this by a semantic sleight of hand. He defines a miracle as "an extraordinary event wrought by God through human agency, an event that cannot be explained by natural forces."[3] He offers no scriptural support for this definition; instead, he appeals to A. H. Strong's *Systematic Theology* for support. My point is that he does not and cannot define miracles in this way by using Scripture. The miraculous vocabulary of the Old and New Testaments simply will not permit it.

By defining a miracle as something that must occur through "human agency," he is able to rule out such things as angelic visitations, divine cataclysmic judgments, and cosmic signs as miracles. This would prohibit us from calling Peter's deliverance from prison by an angel in Acts 12 a miracle, nor could we call the earthquake in Acts 16 a miracle, nor could we call the tearing of the veil in the temple at Jesus' crucifixion a miracle (Matthew 27:51). When Jesus was crucified, God raised many saints from their graves (Matthew 27:52), but since no "human agency" was involved there, MacArthur would not allow us to call this a miracle in the same way that he calls other New Testament raisings from the dead miracles. But most ludicrous of all, on MacArthur's view, we could not call the resurrection of Jesus Christ a miracle.

---

3. MacArthur, *Charismatic Chaos*, 127–28.

What are we to call these things then? What are we to call the other phenomena in Scripture that are supernatural but not occasioned by direct human agency? MacArthur does not tell us what the Scriptures call these events. He does say, however, that "miracles in Scripture are also called 'signs and wonders.'"[4]

It is true that the phrase "signs and wonders" refers to miracles done through human agency, but it is also true that "signs and wonders" or just the word "signs" can refer to miracles done apart from human agency. Peter, for example, refers to Jesus as "a man accredited by God to you by miracles, wonders and signs, which God did among you through him" (Acts 2:22). But three verses before this, Peter also quotes the Joel prophecy in which God says, "I will show *wonders* in the heavens above and *signs* on the earth below, blood and fire and billows of smoke. The sun will be turned to darkness and the moon to blood before the coming of the great and glorious day of the Lord" (Acts 2:19–20, emphasis mine). Here *signs* and *wonders* refer to supernatural, cataclysmic judgments on the earth done apart from human agency.

God also did many miraculous things apart from human agency during the forty-year sojourn of Israel in the wilderness. For instance, he led them by a pillar of fire by night and a cloud during the day; he fed them with manna; he sent plagues on them to discipline them; and so on. Stephen refers to all of these things as God's "wonders and signs" (Acts 7:36). When Daniel was thrown into the lions' den, God sent an angel to deliver Daniel (Daniel 6:22). Afterward, King Darius praises God for this deliverance and refers to it as one of God's "signs and

---

4. MacArthur, *Charismatic Chaos*, 128.

wonders" (Daniel 6:27).[5] MacArthur's definition of miracles, therefore, simply cannot stand in light of Scripture.

MacArthur does not want to accept as normative any of the supernatural events described in the table. From the book of Samuel on, for example, there is a constant stream of prophetic words of guidance, judgment, blessing, warning, and promise. There are regular visions, dreams, angelic appearances, theophanies, divine afflictions and disease, divinely caused panic among Israel's enemies, the splitting of altars, supernatural strength given to the judges, and on and on. The Scriptures teach that these supernatural events are a *normal* part of life in the Old Testament. This is not to say they are everyday events, but they occur with some regularity in virtually every generation of believers in the Old Testament.

This leads us to another point.

When supernatural phenomena do not occur, what is the attitude of the writers of Scripture toward their absence? When there is an absence of the supernatural in the Old Testament, the Scripture writers do not take that as normative for the people of God; they take it as a sign of judgment.

Psalm 74 begins like this: "O God, why have you rejected us forever? Why does your anger smolder against the sheep of your pasture?" (74:1). Then after describing the judgment under which Israel has fallen, the psalmist laments, "We are given no signs from God; no prophets are left, and none of us knows how long this will be" (74:9). The psalmist takes the absence of signs and prophets as the judgment of the Lord.

There is a similar lament in Psalm 77:7–10. The psalmist

---

5. Jesus also refers to cataclysmic judgments done apart from human agency as "signs" (Luke 21:11, 25).

refuses to accept the absence of the Lord's supernatural deeds as normal living conditions for the people of God. His answer to this dilemma is to remember the supernatural works of the past (77:11). The word *remember* very likely means to cause to remember or to extol these deeds.[6] He then refers to the Lord as "the God who performs miracles" (77:14). He does not say "the God who *performed* miracles," but "the God who *performs* miracles." He uses a present tense participle for the expression *performs miracles*. He means that God is still doing miracles. The fact that Israel was not experiencing these miracles was a sign of judgment, not a sign that God was no longer doing them.

The prophets speak the same way. One of the worst judgments that God could pronounce on Jerusalem was recorded by Isaiah: "The LORD has brought over you a deep sleep: He has sealed your eyes (the prophets); he has covered your heads (the seers)" (Isaiah 29:10). Not to have the benefit of the ministry of the prophets and seers was regarded as a disastrous judgment from the Lord in the Old Testament.

Even if it could be proved that all supernatural occurrences in the Bible were confined to these three periods in the Scripture—the periods of Moses and Joshua, Elijah and Elisha, and Christ and the apostles—it still wouldn't mean the Scriptures teach that miracles ended with Christ and the apostles. It would still have to be proved that Scripture actually teaches that miracles would end with this third period.

The Scriptures end with the introduction of the kingdom

---

6. The *kethib* of the Masoretic Text has *zakar* in the *Hiphil* stem. In the *Hiphil*, *zakar* means "to bring to mind" or "to mention" and can be used even in the sense of praising or extolling the Lord and his works (see Brown, Driver, and Briggs, *Hebrew and English Lexicon*, 270–71).

of Christ, an introduction that is accompanied by miracles and supernatural phenomena. The only divinely inspired record we have of church life is one in which miracles and supernatural guidance are relatively common. Even if there had only been two periods of miracles in the Old Testament, that would not prove that the kingdom of Christ would only have a brief period of miracles. All things have changed with the coming of Christ and his kingdom. Now *all things* are possible to the one who believes.

Healing gifts are given to the whole church, and the elders of the church are to have a regular healing ministry (James 5:14–16). Whether there were one, four, or five periods of miracles in the Old Testament is irrelevant in determining whether the kingdom of Christ is meant to have miracles as a normative part of church life. This must be determined on the basis of specific statements in the New Testament.

appendix five

NEW TESTAMENT TEACHING ABOUT DEMONS

I. The New Testament has various names for demons, revealing their nature and function.

  A. There are different kinds of evil spirits and different degrees of evil among the spirits.

    1. Mark 9:29 KJV: "**This kind** can come forth by nothing, but by prayer and fasting."

    2. Matthew 12:45: "Then it goes and takes with it seven other spirits **more wicked than itself**, and they go in and live there. And the final condition of that person is worse than the first."

    3. Mark 5:9: "Then Jesus asked him, 'What is your name?' 'My name is **Legion**,' he replied, 'for we are many.'" This text demonstrates that evil spirits have names relating to their character or function.

B. Demon: In secular Greek, this term could refer to gods (Acts 17:18). In the New Testament, with the exception of Acts 17:18, it refers to purely evil spiritual beings—fallen angels who follow Satan (Matthew 25:41; Jude 6).

C. A spirit (Luke 9:39; 13:11).

D. Impure spirit (Matthew 12:43; Mark 5:2; Luke 8:29; 9:42). The word *impure* is used of sexual impurity.

E. The impure spirit of a demon (Luke 4:33; see Revelation 16:13–14).

F. Evil spirits (Luke 8:2).

G. A spirit of sickness (Luke 13:11).

H. A spirit of divination (Acts 16:16).

I. Snakes and scorpions (Luke 10:19).

J. The enemy (Luke 10:19).

II. The New Testament uses various expressions to denote coming under the influence of a demon.

A. *Daimonizomai* occurs thirteen times in the New Testament.

   1. The first occurrence is Matthew 4:24 and is translated variously:

      a. KJV: "possessed with devils"

      b. NASB: "demoniacs"

      c. NIV: "the demon-possessed"

      d. NKJV: "those who were demon-possessed"

      e. NRSV: "demoniacs"

   2. The literal translation of *daimonizomai* is "demonized," which means that a demon has gained regular access to a person to hurt or hinder them in some way.

B. "He has a demon" (Matthew 11:18; Luke 7:33).

C. "A spirit seizes him" (Luke 9:39).

D. Impure spirits "go in and live there" (Matthew 12:45).

E. "Whom Satan has kept bound" (Luke 13:16).

III. The New Testament uses the following words for freeing people of demonic influence.

A. They are said to be healed.

1. *therapeuo* (Matthew 4:24; 12:22; 17:18; Luke 8:2)

2. *iaomai* (Matthew 15:28; Luke 9:42)

B. Driven out (Matthew 7:22; 8:16; 9:32; 10:8).

C. Rebuked (Matthew 17:18; Luke 4:35; 9:42).

D. Luke said that the Gerasene demoniac had been "saved [*sozo*]" (Luke 8:36). In this case, "saved" means that his sins were forgiven and that he had been healed of demonic torment. The NIV translates "saved" as "cured," and the ESV as "healed."

IV. The New Testament teaches that demons have some supernatural knowledge.

A. They knew who Jesus was before the people knew who Jesus was (Matthew 8:29; Mark 1:34; 5:7; Luke 4:34, 41; 8:28; see James 2:19).

B. Demons have an ability to foretell the future to a limited degree (the spirit of divination in Acts 16:16).

C. Demons know that a time has been fixed for their torment (Matthew 8:29).

V. The New Testament describes the various ways that demons torment people.

A. Demons "trouble" people (Luke 6:18).

B. The devil "oppresses" people (Acts 10:38 ESV). The verb can also mean "dominate" or "exploit."

C. Impure spirits "afflict" (ESV) or "torment" (NIV) people (Acts 5:16).

D. There are degrees of demonic torment. Some people can be said to be "cruelly" (NASB), "severely" (ESV), or "terribly" (NIV) demonized (Matthew 15:22).

E. They can cause muteness (Matthew 9:32; 12:22; Luke 11:14).

F. They can cause blindness (Matthew 12:22).

G. Demons can produce supernatural strength in a person (Mark 5:3–4; Acts 19:16).

H. They may cause epilepsy or seizures (Matthew 4:24; 17:15).

I. They may cause self-destruction (Matthew 17:15).

J. They may cause mental illness (Luke 8:26–39, especially verse 35). This was a common belief among the people (John 7:20; 8:52; 10:20).

K. They may tear or convulse a person (Luke 9:39, 42).

L. They may visit and then leave a person (Luke 9:39).

M. They may bruise, break, shatter, crush, or maul a person (Luke 9:39).

N. They may throw a person to the ground (Luke 9:42).

O. They have a teaching ministry; that is, there are doctrines of demons that are used to seduce believers (1 Timothy 4:1–5).

P. They may also produce supernatural miracles as false signs (2 Thessalonians 2:9; Revelation 16:13–14).

Q. There are a number of cases in the New Testament of more than one demon inhabiting a person (Mark 5:9; Luke 8:2).

R. They cause various sicknesses and deformities (Luke 13:11)

S. The demonized man from the region of the Gerasenes not only had supernatural strength but also was characterized by:

1. Self-mutilation (Mark 5:5). The modern phenomenon of young children cutting themselves may come from demonization.
2. Constant crying out (Mark 5:5).
3. Lewdness and nudity (Luke 8:27).
4. Shunning people and living among tombs (Luke 8:27).
5. Mental illness (Luke 8:35).

Caution: Do not be intimidated by or fearful of the evil power that Satan and his demons wield. The power that God gives us is far greater. God tells us about the devil's power and tactics "in order that Satan might not outwit us. For we are not unaware of his schemes" (2 Corinthians 2:11). Anyone who is called into the healing ministry of the Holy Spirit and prays for the hurting regularly will see the handiwork of demons. The Spirit has given us this promise: "Submit yourselves, then, to God. Resist the devil, and he will flee from you" (James 4:7).

Even in Our Darkness

A Story of Beauty in a Broken Life

Jack Deere

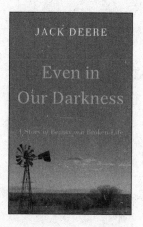

"*Filled with the raw pain, beauty, mystery, and grace that our hearts were meant for.*"
Matt Chandler

Prepare yourself for an unvarnished look at the Christian life, told now for the first time. A powerful memoir of finding beauty and friendship through the pain of loss, tragedy, and brokenness, *Even in Our Darkness* explores what it means to know God and be known by him.

Jack Deere tells the true story of his life growing up near Fort Worth, Texas, in the 1950s and the disintegration of his family following his father's suicide. In his mid-twenties, Jack would rise to fame and success as a leading scholar, popular speaker, and bestselling author.

But despite being rescued and exalted, Jack would ultimately be crushed in the years that followed. He would lose his son to suicide and his wife to alcoholism. Only then would Jack wrestle with his own addictions, surrender control, and experience true healing.

An authentic story of the Christian life, *Even in Our Darkness* will serve as your own guide in overcoming life's disappointments and learning to hear God speak in unbelievable ways.

Available in stores and online!

ZONDERVAN®
.com

Surprised by the Voice of God

How God Speaks Today Through Prophecies, Dreams, and Visions

Jack Deere

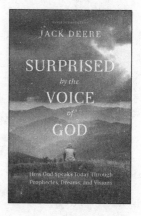

Surprised by the Voice of God takes you to the Bible to discover the variety of creative, deeply personal ways God still communicates with us today. You'll learn how God speaks with people apart from the Bible, though never in contradiction to it. Jack Deere first describes the ways God revealed his thoughts to first-century Christians. Then he tells why God continues to speak to us using the same methods. Finally Deere tells how accurately God speaks through prophecies, dreams, visions, and other forms of divine communication.

With candor, sensitivity, and a profound understanding of Scripture, Deere identifies our hindrances to hearing the Holy Spirit and calls us beyond them to a more intimate relationship with God. Filled with fascinating stories and personal accounts, *Surprised by the Voice of God* is for all who want to walk in the dynamic scope of Christianity.

Available in stores and online!

ZONDERVAN®
.com